OTHER BOOKS BY HAL BORLAND

An American Year

Beyond Your Doorstep

Sundial of the Seasons

The Enduring Pattern

Countryman: A Summary of Belief

Hill Country Harvest

Homeland: A Report from the Country

This Hill, This Valley

Seasons

High, Wide and Lonesome

Country Editor's Boy

The Dog Who Came to Stay

Penny

The Seventh Winter

The Amulet

When the Legends Die

King of Squaw Mountain

Rocky Mountain Tipi Tales

The Youngest Shepherd

This World of Wonder

America Is Americans

Our Natural World (EDITOR)

Hal Borland's

BOOK OF DAYS

Hal Borland's
BOOK OF DAYS

New York
ALFRED A. KNOPF
1976

THIS IS A BORZOI BOOK
PUBLISHED BY ALFRED A. KNOPF, INC.

Some passages of this book were published in a different form in *The Enduring Pattern* (New York: Simon & Schuster, 1959).

Library of Congress Cataloging in Publication Data
Borland, Hal Glen, [date]
Hal Borland's Book of days.
1. Natural history—Addresses, essays, lectures.
I. Title: Book of days.
QH81.B742   500.9   76–13688
ISBN 0–394–40187–5

Manufactured in the United States of America

FIRST EDITION

FOR BARBARA:

At turn of year, when winter's past
and spring's at hand, I think at last
I understand. Then comes the night
when peepers shrill and geese in flight
gabble the moon. And then I say
that all I know can be stowed away
in an acorn cup. But this is plain:
That snow is snow and rain is rain,
that wind is change, that water ran
before earth felt the foot of man;
that flesh and blood of me are kinned
with grass and bush and tree and wind;
that love is sweet and salt are tears;
that days become the turning years;
that I am new and time is old;
that love is warm and hate is cold.
What more is there to understand
when winter's past and spring's at hand?

Foreword

This book is intended neither as a calendar nor as an almanac. It is a daybook simply because it records my day-to-day thinking about this world around me and my fellow creatures here. In it, too, are reports about what is happening here and now, with observations on a snowflake, a spring rain, a wood thrush singing in the dusk, an apple tree in bloom, the last shrill notes of a katydid before November's hard frost. But through it all is the persistence of three questions: *Who am I? Where am I? What time is it?*

Those three questions have haunted me a long time. There are easy answers, of course: I am a man, a member of the human race. I live in a particular valley on this planet, Earth. The time is late in the twentieth century A.D. But all such answers are plainly superficial. What is a man, and what is his relationship to other forms of life? Just what is the Earth, and where did it come from? How did it become this Earth we know? And as for time, this twentieth century is only one era of one phase of human life. How old is life? Where do I stand on the scale of life? How long is the big time span, and what time is it by that clock?

As a writer, I have spent much of my life dealing with one or another phase of the questions Who? Where? When? But seldom in this context. So a year ago I began writing this journal of my own search among the sand and stones and fragments of bone and bits of charcoal that make up so much of our knowledge of the past. I have been, since then, picking over a midden heap of my own mind and experience, looking for scraps of truth.

I find no alternative to belief in life. Man is a unique form of that life, but certainly not unrelated to other forms. That is why I have also written here about ants and frogs and foxes and salamanders and trees and grass. It is reassuring, somehow, to write about those who share this earth, for, despite the massive telescopes that bring millions of stars and thousands of galaxies somewhat like our own into view, the Earth is a lonely place. Mars, our celestial neighbor just down the road, is 50-odd million miles away. Beyond Mars is Jupiter, close to 400 million miles away. And beyond Jupiter, fading into remote, incomprehensible distance, are four other known planets in our fairly minor solar system.

But man lives right here, on Earth, not in the dark recesses of space. Man must find his answers here, if he is ever to find them. And I must find them in my own valley. That is what this book is about, my search. It is a personal book, a book of personal opinion and speculation; and for that I would apologize if I were not better acquainted with my own thoughts than those of anyone else. I have now my full share of years. I have known the bite of winter ice many times, and the burn of summer sun. Some of the things I have learned have been set down here.

That is the kind of book this is.

H. B.

Salisbury,
Connecticut

JANUARY

JANUARY 1

A clear, cold morning, one of those icy-brittle mornings when sounds carry far. It is as good a way as I can imagine to start a year, if one follows the Gregorian calendar, which came from the Augustan and Julian calendars, both memorials of human vanity and of scientific fallibility. The year, being merely that segment of time the earth requires to make one complete orbit of the sun, can begin anywhere. For a long time man began his calendar year with the vernal equinox, the beginning of spring. That at least made sense. But when emperors began tinkering with calendars they were more interested in having their names remembered than in being logical. Somehow, in all the maneuvering, the year's beginning was pushed back toward the winter solstice, which would have been another logical place to begin. But it never quite made connections—the first day of January misses the solstice by ten days, and apparently they never did coincide.

So here we are, at the start of an arbitrary year, with 365 days ahead before we say the year has ended. Or, if we would be fully accurate, 365 days, 5 hours, 48 minutes, 46.9 seconds. Those five hours-plus are responsible for the extra days in leap years.

And let's be through with that at this point. Let's accept the calendar as it stands. Illogical as it may be, it is a convenience.

This is a clear, cold morning, then, and the year is on its way. The old saying still holds: "The day lengthens, the cold strengthens." True of January a hundred years ago, true now, true a hundred years hence. Here where I live we have already gained five minutes from the shortest day of the year, less than two weeks ago. For a time now we will continue to gain about one minute a day. Then, about mid-month, we will begin gaining an average of two minutes a day, and by the month's end the gain will be almost three minutes a day, the year's maximum daily gain. By May it will drop back to two minutes a day, then to one, till the summer solstice in June. After that the days will begin to shorten again.

3

As for temperature, look at your own thermometer. Mine showed just two degrees above zero at six this morning. It probably will be colder at January's end than it is now. It usually is. Cold feeds upon itself in the country. In the city all those warm buildings warm the air, and city temperatures average about ten degrees above country temperatures. Here in my rural area the only really warm objects are farmhouses, barns full of cattle, cows themselves, and people. People aren't very warm this morning unless they stay inside those warm houses.

JANUARY 2

Watching the sun this morning, and I was looking out a window that faces almost due south, I thought how logical it was that the ancients had such deep doubts about that sun. From September till ten days ago it kept sliding off there toward the south, farther and farther from the zenith each day. If I didn't have a background of belief and some knowledge of the working of the solar system, I too would have done my full share of worrying.

Now, of course, the sun has stopped going away from us, as it seemed to do, and apparently is moving up the sky again toward the zenith. The change is so slight I have to measure shadows to prove it, and the shift thus far is little more than a finger's breadth, but enough to prove there has been change. Actually, of course, it is the motion of the earth rather than the sun that makes this happen. The earth revolves on a tilted axis. Hence we see the sun from a different angle at different times of the year.

The earth actually is closer to the sun right now than it will be next summer. The distance now is 91,406,000 miles, and next summer it will be 93,500,000 miles. We get our coldest weather now, to greatly simplify a complex matter, because the tilt of the earth's axis makes the sunlight bounce off our northern hemisphere instead of striking directly and warming things up.

It is so cold today that the blue jays are fluffed big as ruffed grouse.

JANUARY 3

I look out across these snow-covered hills, these old upthrusts that mark my countryside, and think of time, of the earth's age. Estimates of that age are largely guesswork, but most informed guessers say our particular planet came into being about five billion years ago, give or take a billion. How it came into being is a matter for theorists, but it is now believed to have been whirling around the sun for at least three billion years before any kind of life appeared upon it. How and whence that life came are also matters of theory and speculation. Those who try to pin down its source, I have noticed, sometimes end up in myth or fable, sometimes try to credit omnipotence, and sometimes honestly say, "We don't know—yet."

The first life, according to good evidence now available, appeared on earth about one and a half billion years ago. As far as we know, that life consisted of very small one-celled entities—they may have been neither plant nor animal, but as yet undetermined in form. At first those bits of life lived in the warm waters of the earth, which presumably at that time were not saline as are the oceans of today.

From the earliest forms of life evolved, more or less in succession, seaweed, sponges, small worms, shellfish, primitive fish with backbones, and the early amphibians and insects. From the amphibians came the first reptiles, and after them came the giants of their tribe, dinosaurs and their kind. The lizards persisted for about 150 million years. By the end of their age, birds and early mammals had appeared, forerunners of most of the animals we know today. Finally, perhaps a million years ago, perhaps two million, the earliest men appeared.

Not only is the earth's age a matter of analytical guesswork, based on the best information available, but so are the approximate dates for the geological and biological eras, periods, and epochs. For a long time, for example, it was believed that the earth's age could be stated in thousands, not millions or billions, of years. Until recently the geologists and geophysicists based their estimates on sedimentation and erosion rates as revealed in the earth's rocks and on the probable rate of salting in the oceans from leaching of the land. Now the atomic physicists have provided a check on those estimates in the radioactive component tests, which indicate how long the elements in the rocks have been radioactively "decaying." These tests have already revised a good many geological dates. For example, the last Ice Age was supposed to have ended about 25,000 years ago by geological evidence, but radioactivity tests appear to make the date 11,000 years ago instead.

I suppose the age of the mountain behind my house could be determined radioactively, but nobody ever bothered. All I know is that it is a remnant of one of the older mountain upthrusts on this continent.

JANUARY 4

Few authorities have ever insisted that the geological dates generally accepted were absolute, but there has been general agreement that they were relatively correct. That is to say, the eras, periods, and epochs did occur in the same order and in the same approximate relationships as those indicated in the dates suggested. It is that order and those relationships that are important, and there seems little doubt that the terms used, even in any revision of actual dates, will still remain in the millions and even the billions of years. It is in those terms that any broad view of the time span and the whole picture of life must be considered. It is the relative picture that is important, not the actual number of millions or hundreds of thousands of years that eventually may be accepted as absolute dates. I have difficulty comprehending these enormous time spans in themselves. My life is bounded by hours, days, weeks, months, and a million or a billion years have little meaning. But I can perhaps begin to grasp their relative significance if I compress them into terms of my daily experience.

Suppose we say arbitrarily that the earth is now forty-eight hours old, that it is now high noon and the earth was created at noon the day before yesterday. On that basis, the first sign of life did not appear until late yesterday. It was nine o'clock last night before the first primitive sponges appeared. The first fish with a backbone, the earliest vertebrate, did not evolve until four o'clock this morning. It was eight thirty this morning, only three and a half hours ago, when the earliest form of plant life began to grow on land. At nine this morning the first amphibians appeared, and by nine fifteen the insects were here and growing swiftly in numbers. At ten the dinosaurs and other giant lizards were here and thriving; they were still dominant when the first mammals appeared at ten thirty, and they persisted until almost eleven, only an hour ago. Then the mammals we know today began to dominate the scene. And finally, only one minute ago, at a few seconds after eleven fifty-nine, man came into being and began to develop.

When I first broke down the big time spans this way, I was suspicious of my own figures. But geologists and paleontologists are broadly agreed on the basic dates, and my figures are in agreement with their timetables. The Quaternary and Tertiary periods of geologic time, the past 60-odd million years, represent less than 2 percent of the total life of the earth. In my compressed example they are represented by about fifty-eight minutes, less than one hour.

So, whether we deal in incomprehensible billions of years or figuratively compress those years into a matter of hours, man is a newcomer on this earth. In a sense, he is still a stranger here, trying to fit himself into his environment—or to fit his environment to him—and learning, slowly, to live with his own kind and all the other forms of life around him. His tenure here is unpredictable. Even while he is here his life depends on a thousand variable conditions, most of which really are beyond his control.

This should leave little room for human arrogance.

JANUARY 5

The wind rose in the night and continues to blow today. It is cold. The temperature is in the twenties, according to the thermometer, and last night's low was two above zero. It is hard to keep the house warm and it is cruel outdoors. I had to go out and close a door at the old barn that was flapping in the wind, and I thought I was going to freeze my nose and maybe my fingers before I got back indoors. That wind is to blame. Cold can maim, but wind is the killer. Even with the temperature where it is today, near twenty degrees, a twenty-mile wind created the equivalent of ten degrees *below* zero. If the temperature drops to ten degrees above zero and that twenty-mile wind continues, the effect will be equivalent to twenty-five degrees below zero. And the harder the wind blows, the more severe is the effect. Zero temperature and a forty-mile wind create the equivalent of fifty-three degrees below zero.

That is why those Midwestern blizzards are so dangerous to all life. A true blizzard is a snow-driving wind of forty miles an hour or more, usually from some quarter of the north, accompanied by zero cold. Properly dressed, anyone can endure twenty or twenty-five degrees below zero safely. But temperatures, or temperature equivalents caused by wind, below that point are dangerous.

I obviously wasn't properly dressed when I went out to shut that barn door. Either that, or I haven't yet hardened into winter shape.

JANUARY 6

Frost flowers fascinate me. They are related to frost ferns, those intricate patterns that formed on windowpanes before we slept in heated bedrooms. Frost ferns were indoor plants, created by the humidity in the room. Frost flowers are wildlings, outdoor growths created by humidity in the starlight. I find them on new black ice on the river, but they also form on ponds and lakes. Pure ice crystal, dazzling white, they look like tufts of snowy feathers. There may be only a few in a clump, or there may be a tussock of them two or three inches high. They stand upright on the ice. They are a form of frost rather closely related to the hoar frost that bedazzles me on all the weed stems and bushes here along the river from time to time. The frost flowers, like hoar frost, are fragile. A strong gust of wind can shatter them. A few degrees of warmth from the morning's sunlight can melt them. But in really cold weather, down to ten degrees above zero, they will persist all day.

JANUARY 7

Many animals of the past were bigger, stronger, better armed or armored than relatively puny man. Why did they vanish and man survive? Because, I suspect, man had more brain capacity than those big creatures that preceded him, and he had the urge to use that power. Man invented speech, probably the most important invention of all time, and it became the means of shaping ideas and communicating them. When he began to talk and think about matters beyond his own rather limited self, he began to outrank the other forms of life around him. Thus man became a creature with a dual nature—he was an animal that still needed food and shelter, but he was also a thinking, rational, emotional being with the urge to know and understand the conditions and limitations of the life of which he was a part. He began to examine the world around him and reach beyond the range of instinct into the realm of reason and imagination.

Biologically I am an animal. I need food and water to sustain me, and I can tolerate only a relatively narrow range of ·temperature and humidity. Because I am a weakling among animals, I need clothing and shelter against the extremes of heat and cold. I am capable of procreation. My life span is relatively limited, since I am subject to disease and injury and because I, like all living creatures, am going to wear out as an organism. I am a mobile creature; I can move from place to place. I am omnivorous, eating either plants or animals. But like all other animals, I can subsist only on other living things or their products. Only plants can live on inorganic, nonliving substances. Yet my blood, in terms of chemistry, contains hemoglobin, not greatly different from the chlorophyll in green leaves, which enables plants to create food from air, moisture, and sunlight. Hemoglobin enables me to take oxygen from the air, which is essential for my life processes. And the substance of my flesh and bones and vital organs is, chemically, almost pure mineral.

But somewhere in that complexity of material of which I am composed is the element of life, which governed my beginnings and my growth from the time I first appeared as a fertilized ovum only a quarter of a millimeter in diameter. That life force created me and it sustains me, as an animate creature.

Somewhere along the road of evolution from whatever ancient creature was the human ancestor, the node of nerves that enable the body to perform its simple acts of living began to grow and change. It grew phenomenally, in anthropological terms. Out of that elemental nerve center eventually evolved a complex brain, which has reached its present degree of high development only in man. That brain is the primary difference between me and all the other animals.

JANUARY 8

What happens in my brain is only dimly understood. Orders go out from there to the muscles and other elements of my body, apparently by rhythmic impulses along the network of nerves. I do not understand this, although I am using that power to discuss it. We say that thought consists of ideas and their interrelation. But how explain an idea? The power of thought apparently is related to rhythmic impulses and, in one way or another, to all the senses.

When I reach that point, I think how completely my life processes, and those of all living things, are governed by rhythms. My breathing, my pulse, my unconscious processes of digestion, my hearing, my eye-sight, my sense of touch, my speech and my thoughts—all are matters of rhythm. The female animal has rhythmic periods of fertility. The sex act of fertilization is rhythmic. Birth is accomplished in rhythmic labor. And all these rhythmic processes are essential to growth, maturity, and the continuation of life. When they cease, a unit of life has come to its physical end.

Until man evolved, with his power of thought, imagination, speech, and communication, and until he had the means of exchanging and accumulating knowledge and ideas, one generation to the next, life was primarily a matter of survival and change was limited to accident and evolution. Man has altered that somewhat, particularly with relation to his own kind and to those forms of life on which he is dependent or which immediately endanger him. But mostly man has changed himself as he advanced from the trees to the caves, from the caves to the river valleys, from the valleys onto the open plains, thence out across the whole of the land, until every habitable part of the world has come to know him.

JANUARY 9

Man has done remarkable things, but he has never escaped his link with the basic rhythms of life. He never will. What he has accomplished has been within the framework of those natural laws, and his primary achievements have been in the study and use of those laws. (Actually, they are not laws at all. They are merely statements of what happens under certain conditions. It is no law that water must run downhill; it is simply a fact, a demonstration of the working of gravity.)

And man must still live in the environment to which he was born, or a close approximation of it. That is to say, on this planet, Earth; or, if he goes to the moon, in an artificial environment that provides air to breathe, water to drink, food to eat, warmth to sustain the body heat. And all his means of reaching the moon or other planets are limited by the conditions of the solar system, and those are the conditions man has learned to live with here on earth—gravity, light, sound, time, atomic motion. And all such plans are limited by that mysterious rhythmic capacity in us, the power of thought.

The disquieting thought in all this is man's tendency to drift or stray from the basic elements of his own environment, the fundamental rhythms of life. As he evolves complexities of living which he calls civilization, he loses perspective on himself and his cosmos. He sometimes thinks he can ignore or repeal the most enduring fundamental of all, cause and effect. And he tends to minimize the importance of life itself —not his own life, perhaps, but that great stream of life of which he is only a part.

JANUARY 10

I saw a robin yesterday. Half a dozen robins, in fact. They were hiding from a bitter wind in a clump of brush at the edge of a small bog down the road. Winter robins. We have them every year. They are not new, of course. There must have been winter robins here fifty and maybe a hundred years ago. They were so seldom seen that they were considered most unusual. There weren't many birdwatchers fifty years ago.

Not all the common beliefs about migratory birds can stand close scrutiny. I keep hearing that evening grosbeaks are relative newcomers to the East. Actually, they were recorded in considerable numbers in New York City in 1911. And in 1916 a large flock of them spent several winter weeks in Portland, Maine.

JANUARY 11

The January wind has a hundred voices. It can scream, it can bellow, it can whisper, it can sing a lullaby. It can roar through the leafless maples and shout down the mountainside, and it can murmur through the white pines below the ledges where the lichens make strange hieroglyphics. It can whistle down a chimney and set the hearth fire to dancing. In the cold of a lonely night it can rattle the sash and stay there muttering of ice and snowbanks and deep-frozen ponds.

Sometimes it comes from the farthest star in outer darkness, so remote and impersonal is its voice. And sometimes, when it comes in the half-light that trembles between day and night, it is a wind that merely quivers the trees, its force sensed but not seen, a force that could hold back the day if it were so directed.

It was thus this morning. Then the brightness in the east began to glow and the wind began to relax. The stars, that wind's source, dimmed. Daylight came and the day began with barely a whisper of air stirring.

JANUARY 12

I have no quarrel with the ornithologists, but I do wonder where they got the name "junco," and I can't understand why they stopped calling one of my favorite birds the snowbird. The scientific name is *Junco hyemalis,* and depending on where you look, the "junco" comes either from the Spanish word meaning "reed" or "rush" or from the Latin word meaning "seed." True, the bird is a seed-eater, but so are a great many others. It has no connection that I know of with reeds.

Anyway, here are the snowbirds—or juncos, if you would rather— like a wind-blown cloud. Their coats are gray and their shirt-fronts are white and there is white piping on their tails. They are beautiful birds against the snowy background. It seems to me that it takes a storm to bring them down out of the woods. Then they come wheeling in—gliding in, really—by the flock. I almost welcome a snowstorm simply because it brings the snowbirds. Or juncos, if you insist.

JANUARY 13

I am writing this in the winter, and I am tempted to say the reason for those obvious and rhythmic changes we know as the seasons of the year is to demonstrate the cycles of persistent and pervading life. And to go on and complete such an absurd statement by saying life is concentrated in the year, a single circuit of the sun—birth, growth, maturity, and the pause between generations.

But I know perfectly well that nature has no such purpose. Nature is an infinitely complex series of facts; it is not an object lesson, and it is not a ready-made sermon on conduct or morality. Those are matters man has contrived and established to ease and somewhat simplify his social relations with others of his own kind. Any lessons to be learned in the world and the cosmos where we live are a result of man's own need for understanding.

Yet the question persists: If I have the intelligence to seek, may there not be some power of reason and order, some source of design, beyond my knowing? Is man's intelligence unique, or is there some vast, remote, ultimate source of reason which man can approach and in which man, to a slight degree, participates?

JANUARY 14

I slept on yesterday's questions, but no answers came in the night. The best I can do is sum it up by saying, "I do not know."

All I know, really, is that there is a clock of time in the stars, and a clock of the year in the earth and in all the life of which we are aware. It is even in the radish seed and the onion bulb. And it is in me, when I allow myself to be aware of it. For there is a common denominator among all us earthlings—life, and the condition of its beginnings and its continuance.

Let's rest on that for today.

JANUARY 15

Sperm whales, what few are left of them, are now migrating northward up the California coast and off the New England coast. In the old days, fortunes were built on hunting sperm whales, the source of the oil for our lamps before kerosene took that market. Nantucket and New Bedford were the great whaling centers of the East Coast. Now the sperm whales pass there almost unseen, certainly little noticed.

Only the bulls migrate. They travel in pods of a dozen or more and go to the polar seas for the summer. Next fall they will come south again and join the cows and the calves for the winter. While by no means the biggest of whales, the sperms are huge animals, the biggest bulls as much as sixty feet long, the average forty-five or fifty. The blunt, square head of a sperm whale is enormous; it sometimes constitutes as much as a third of the whale's total length.

Melville's Moby Dick was an albino sperm whale.

We have now gained twenty-two minutes of daylight since the winter solstice and we continue to gain about two minutes a day. Since the first of the year the gain has been seventeen minutes in the evening, thanks to later sunsets, but only two minutes in the morning. The sun is a slugabed.

JANUARY 16

There were deer tracks around the house this morning. Two deer had come down off the mountain and across the home pasture, evidently looking for something to eat. They nibbled at the yews at the corner of the front porch and they chewed on weeping willow wythes blown from the big tree beside the garage. Slim fare, and those deer must be very hungry. The winter is relatively young, yet they had to come down out of the woods to eat yew and willow.

Deer live on browse most of the winter, and browse consists of leaves and twigs. It hasn't much nourishment, very little compared to grass or even to summer leaves, but it is better than nothing. White cedar is one of their favorites, and another is hemlock. That is one reason venison taken after the first snowfall is likely to make poor eating—it soon begins to taste of cedar or hemlock needles. Deer can eat and survive on maple twigs, witch hazel, sumac, aspen, either yellow or black birch. But they will starve to death on a diet of red cedar, and I imagine that red cedar is the easiest thing for them to get on the mountain now. That is why they came down here last night. I wish there was some way to tell them they are welcome to come back.

JANUARY 17

This is the day the ancient Druids observed as their New Year, the beginning of another annual cycle. Why they should have chosen today is a mystery to me. I can find no natural reason, no cyclic event that might have been responsible.

The Druids were the priests of Celtic Gaul and Great Britain. Since they left no written records, what we know of them comes principally from old Irish sagas and what such Roman writers as Julius Caesar set down. They constituted a priesthood but they also wielded great political power. At their annual meetings, probably at or near present-day Chartres, France, they arbitrated private and tribal disputes.

The Druids were the core of resistance to the Romans in Gaul, and although the Romans finally conquered Gaul, the Druids weren't really displaced from power in western Europe until the arrival of Christianity. Well educated, they served as teachers of the young as well as priests of a highly ritualized religion. They believed in an immortal soul and its transfer after death to some nonearthly body. Had they written down their learning they might have left us important knowledge at which we can now only guess. It is generally agreed today that Stonehenge and other "Druid circles" were not Druidic at all. They are now believed to be even older than the Druids.

JANUARY 18

I hesitate to say there is any great significance in it, but the proportion of water to solids in the human body is almost the same as the proportion of water to land on the earth's surface—71 percent water, 29 percent land. But these proportions might be said to point to man's origin in some form of aquatic life, some sea creature that learned to live on land. Certainly water remains an indispensable element in the maintenance of life.

Water is one of the simplest compounds, two atoms of hydrogen and one atom of oxygen. It is present everywhere on earth in one of its three forms, as a solid, a liquid, or a vapor. We usually think of it as a liquid, but right now it impresses itself on our consciousness as a solid— ice and snow. In its vapor form it is all around us all year, though seldom noticed. The water vapor in the earth's atmosphere tempers both the heat and the cold. If there were no clouds—all clouds that are not dust or smoke consist of water in some form—our daytime temperatures would be intolerably hot and our nights as cold as nights on the moon. And if there were no vast oceans and no ice caps in the polar regions, there would be no rain. Since all life depends on water, there would be no life.

JANUARY 19

This place where I live is a small portion of the Housatonic valley in the lower end of the Berkshire Hills. The Berkshires were once high mountains, among the earlier upthrusts that eventually shaped this continent. There are rocks here that date back, I am told, to the Cambrian period, some 550 million years ago. Those Cambrian marbles contain fossils which paleontologists identify as among the oldest on earth, fossils of primitive forms of shellfish that were here long before any creatures developed backbones and long before there were any forms of plant life on the land.

The mountains are younger than the rocks, perhaps 150 or 200 million years old. When I try to look back down that corridor I begin to lose all sense of time and most of my perspective. I can almost envision a million years, which is ten thousand centuries. But when I get to the billions, I am lost. A billion years is ten million centuries, and to me that is like trying to count the raindrops in a cloudburst. When a geologist tells me that the earth is four or five billion years old, I am tempted to ask how he knows his figure is correct to the nearest million. Then I make a mental calculation and hold my tongue: an error of one million in five billion would be an error of .02 percent, the equivalent of one cent in fifty dollars.

But apparently the earth is about 4.5 billion years old, and it spent half or more of that time settling down into a relatively solid planet of rock and water. For another billion years it underwent convulsions before any massive land form emerged. And it was not until 200 million years ago that the beginnings of the continents as we know them took shape. Another 50 million years or so, and the basic mountain ranges of northeastern America had risen. Then came the rough outlines of this continent. And about a million years ago the forces that shaped this land somewhat as we know it began to work on comparatively stable land masses. That was when what we call the Ice Ages began.

JANUARY 20

We seem to have begun our January thaw, with the temperature in the low forties this morning. It won't last, I know, but it is always welcome. It breaks the hold of winter. And it reminds me of the great thaw that must have taken place when the Ice Ages began to end.

Most scientists now believe there were four major advances and retreats of the ice. The latest one is the one we know most about. It came down over much of Europe and northern Asia and the northern half of North America. Glaciers became vast ice sheets, in places a mile and a half thick, and as they slowly pushed down across the land they scarred and scoured everything in their path. All of Canada and the northern half of the United States were covered by the ice. Every mountain in the way, including the Sierra Nevada, the Rockies, and the Appalachians and Adirondacks, was gouged and rasped away, often to the core of the ancient rock. But besides the gouging and the scarring, which scooped out thousands of lakes ranging in size from Lake Superior to the pond just over the mountain behind my house, there was the complex effect of alternate freezing and thawing, advance and retreat, of the ice sheet. Vast quantities of sand and gravel and broken rocks and other debris were dumped over the land, and oceans of water flowed away, the melt from the ice. There was a whole series of advances and retreats, so this erosion by flood and flowing water, with its consequent deposit, was repeated time and again.

Lakes hundreds of miles across were formed. Tremendous rivers went roaring across the land, ripping their way to the oceans, stripping topsoil and baring the bedrock, forming vast deltas and alluvial flats. The major drainage systems of the United States—not to mention Europe and Asia—were formed. Our whole Midwest was a shallow sea, a northward extension of the Gulf of Mexico. My relatively placid Housatonic was probably an awesome torrent flowing several hundred feet above its present bed, and the whole of Connecticut was covered with glacial debris which the streams gullied deep and carried as silt and gravel and dumped in huge quantities just beyond their mouths. Some of that debris, carried away by those torrential streams, helped form the big sand-and-gravel bar we now know as Long Island.

Finally the ice sheet was melted back and did not return. The date of this retreat varied from place to place, but there had been repeated advances and retreats and the Ice Ages had persisted for several hundred thousand years. The ice went away and we were rid, at last, of the final major force that greatly shaped the land. Then the lesser forces, wind, rain, frost, flowing water, went to work. They are still at it, trying to level the hills and fill the valleys. And every time we have a January thaw we get a faint echo of the Ice Ages of long, long ago. As I had the echo today.

JANUARY 21

Yesterday's thaw continues. The temperature was in the forties all night and up to fifty by noon. But I suspect a change. I have been watching the birds, which have been busier than usual at the feeder and less quarrelsome.

Birds undoubtedly feel changes in atmospheric pressure. Their hollow bones, which contribute to their lightness of weight and ease of flight, must respond to pressure changes. This would give them a definite physical reaction. They probably can forecast—or, as we say, "feel"— changes in the weather. They are, in effect, living barometers. I don't set much store by the notion that people can "feel" a storm coming by pains in their joints. If anyone's joints should be receptive, mine should; and I can't tell anything except that the day is raw and damp-cold, by the ache or lack of one in my knees and shoulder that have been broken. I watch the wind and the sky, take a look at the barometer, then watch the birds. If the birds are eating as though they didn't expect to get another meal for a week, if the barometer is falling, if the sky is red at dawn, then I have a hunch we are in for bad weather, and soon. All those signs were here today.

JANUARY 22

The night was mild but the temperature began to drop by midmorning. It was down to twenty degrees by noon, the wind shifted to the northeast, and by 2:00 P.M. there was fine snow in the air. By dusk it was snowing hard and the temperature was down to fifteen degrees. The birds were right. So back to the water I was talking about before I got into the Ice Age and the big thaw.

The fact that 71 percent of the earth's surface is covered with water is only a part of the story. Our best evidence indicates that wherever the earth came from and however it was formed, when it began settling down into its present shape it had approximately as much water as we know today. Apparently we have lost little or no water over the eons. We explain this by saying that when water vaporizes from the oceans and rises in the atmosphere, it is cooled and condensed and returns to the earth as rain, snow, or sleet. Thanks to gravity, it cannot escape.

Geologic evidence indicates that during the first few hundred million years the earth was completely covered with water. If there had been no internal stresses, which heaved great land masses upward and created the continents, it would still be covered with water to a depth of almost 8,000 feet, a mile and a half. Since the average elevation of the land now is about 2,500 feet above sea level, the oceans must have vast and awesome depths. That is exactly what our oceanic surveys have shown, tremendous undersea canyons, valleys, and low-lying plains. In other words, the height and extent of habitable land on this earth are minor compared with the depths and expanses of the ocean beds. There is far more water than exposed land on this earth.

JANUARY 23

There is a great deal more water on the surface of the globe than there is land, as I was saying. But man, as a terrestrial animal, knows best the land and its relatively minor waters. You know best the hilltop town, the lowland farm, or the waterfront city where you live. I know best this valley with the brooks and river that mark it. It is the dominant geographic feature of my life, though because there can be no valley without attendant hills I am also keenly aware of the mountain that flanks my side of the river.

The river is flowing water. It rises in the hills to the north and it flows to the ocean a hundred miles to the south. Like all streams flowing into the ocean more or less at sea level, my river is salty for some distance above its mouth because the salt water of the ocean intrudes with every tide. But I live well above tidewater. The river I know day by day is freshwater, carrying only a normal amount of sediment and minerals in solution—and the customary amount of pollution found in American streams.

But this river, pollution and all, is typical of all rivers in many ways. I get pleasure from having it close by, and I profit from it in minor ways. It somewhat tempers the climate, both winter and summer. In summer it is the source of heavy dews that help water my fields and my garden. Any stream does these things. Because it is flowing water, it helps create eddies in the air along the whole valley. These eddies create wind currents. In summer, for instance, there is nearly always a breeze in the valley, especially at night. On the other hand, on a hot, still summer day the whole valley may swelter under a blanket of vapor—we call it high humidity, which means the same thing—from the river. In winter the river's humidity can add authority to low temperatures and make a chill wind bitter. Occasionally its slight warmth changes a snowstorm into slush or cold rain. There have been times when higher land only two miles away but out of the river's direct influence received four inches of snow and this valley got rain but no snow.

All these minor matters of weather are a result of the flowing water in the river and the vapor that rises from it. Just across the mountain to the northwest lies a small lake, a deep pool of still water created by the Ice Age. It, too, affects the weather in its valley. Summer nights along its shore are cool and breezy. Mild weather continues somewhat longer there than it does here, just across the mountain, because the lake's deep, still water tempers the air longer than does the flowing water here. But when deep cold strikes and the lake freezes over, it acts as an outdoor refrigerator for its whole valley. Its ice persists weeks longer than does the ice in my flowing river, and its shores have a later spring.

Since the lake and the river are less than two miles apart at this point, the differences in their seasons and weather are striking proof of the contrasting effects of standing water and water that flows. Large rivers and large lakes create even more pronounced differences.

JANUARY 24

The weather has eased somewhat, though it wasn't really mild today— the temperature at 2:00 P.M. was only twenty-eight degrees. But I found three ladybird beetles out and basking on a windowsill at the south side of the house. They had come from under the shingles on that wall, where they spend the winter with quite a few of their kindred. By late afternoon, when the sun had set behind the mountain, they crawled back into their hiding places. We never bother them. We encourage them, for they eat aphids and are an asset in our garden.

Most of us know the old rhyme:

Ladybird, ladybird, fly away home;
Your house is on fire, your children will burn.

Sometimes another couplet was added:

Except little Nan, who sits in a pan
Weaving gold laces as fast as she can.

Those verses go quite a way back into English rural history. Farmers grew hops, the hop vines were infested with aphids, the ladybird beetles came and ate the aphids. After the hop harvest the vines were burned, and if the little spotted ladybird beetles didn't get out in time they were burned too. As for little Nan, she was the pupa of the ladybird. She probably had left the hop vines by then and sheathed herself in a yellow cocoon elsewhere. The name ladybird, or lady-beetle as it sometimes occurs, goes back to the Middle Ages. These little beetles were common in monastery gardens, and even then were known to be enemies of garden crop pests. They were the gardeners' friends, and the monks dedicated them to the Virgin and called them "the Beetles of Our Lady."

JANUARY 25

Watching a blue jay this morning, thinking what a Dresden blue he was against the snow, I wondered about the function of color. Not two minutes later a male cardinal appeared, as though to emphasize the question with his brilliant red coat of feathers.

Color is there, in nature, a matter of wavelength in the light we see. But why, then, do only a relatively few animals have color vision? Of the mammals, only man and some of the primates can see color. Our dogs and cats have no color vision; their world is wholly a world of black, white, and tones of gray. The horse, the cow, the pig, the sheep—all lack color vision. Yet day-active birds and most reptiles see color, and so do some fish that have been tested. Frogs and salamanders evidently are without color vision. Yet some insects seem able to distinguish a color from any shade of gray; bees can, for example. And a number of crustaceans have some degree of color sight, as do the squid and the octopus. It is possible, of course, that some insects can distinguish color by means other than the sense we use. Insects are a kind of law unto themselves—grasshoppers, for instance, hear with sensors in their knees. It may be that they can detect differences in light wavelength by senses of which we are not aware.

The color-sensitive bird's eye is more like the human eye than most other animal eyes except those of the apes. But the birds' exceptional vision—and it is so acute that it has been called telescopic in some instances—comes in large part from the size of those eyes. Some hawks and eagles have eyes larger than human eyes. Even starlings have eyes which weigh 15 percent of the total weight of the bird's head. A man's eyes weigh only about 1 percent of his total head weight.

JANUARY 26

Most of the water we know and use every day is freshwater, distilled from the oceans by the sun. Vapor rises from the oceans and is carried by the great air currents constantly flowing around the earth. It forms clouds that meet cold air masses flowing down from the Arctic regions, the clouds are chilled and the vapor falls as rain or snow. Only about one-fourth of the rain that falls on the land flows back into the oceans through the rivers. The other three-fourths is vaporized and makes more rain clouds or it is used by plants before it is transpired by the leaves into the air again.

Evaporation from the oceans is so vast in quantity that few of us can comprehend it. About six and a half feet a year is sucked up by the sun from the Atlantic between eight and thirty degrees north latitude, which includes Mexico and Central America. In the same belt of the Pacific about four feet of water is vaporized every year. Much of it returns to the ocean directly as rain, but the United States receives rain which, if spread evenly over the whole country, would be almost thirty inches each year. It isn't spread evenly, though. In one area of Washington State they get ten feet of rain a year. Where I live we get almost three and a half feet, a little more than forty inches. In eastern Colorado, where I grew up, the yearly average is less than half that.

Pure water is almost unknown in nature, simply because water is one of the best natural solvents there is. Water vapor is relatively pure, but even the water in rain clouds contains minerals in minute quantities because fine dust floats in the air and its mineral content is absorbed by the vapor. Rain that falls through a pall of smoke frequently contains a trace of sulfuric acid because it picks up sulfur from the coal smoke. We speak of rain water being "soft" because it seldom contains the lime that "hardens" most ground water.

The spring water we use is relatively "hard" because it comes from seepage through a variety of rocks, including limestone. This is a limestone and marble area. But that rock also contains minute amounts of iron, copper, and other minerals, all mildly soluble in water. It is these minerals that give water its taste. Distilled water, which is free from such minerals, tastes flat and insipid. Well water, no matter from what depth it comes, always has a certain amount of mineral content because it flows through layers of rock or sand to reach the point from which it is pumped.

If you would know the mineral content of the water you drink, look at the scale that collects inside the tea kettle. Take some of that scale to a laboratory and have it analyzed and you will find that it contains a whole spectrum of minerals, though most of it is plain calcium carbonate, or lime.

JANUARY 27

Ice is nothing but solidified water. We happen to live on a planet where the normal temperatures keep most of the water in a liquid state. But this same normal temperature keeps another chemical compound, steel, in its solid form, and thus makes possible our whole industrial establishment. Steel happens to freeze into a solid at between 1100 and 1200 degrees Centigrade, whereas water doesn't freeze until it reaches zero Centigrade.

Ice forms crystals that are six-sided. In that sense, ice has some remote relationship to granite, the crystals of which are also six-sided. But the most familiar ice crystal formations are snowflakes, those fragile, feathery, evanescent flakes that come piling down out of the sky; flakes that piled up well over a foot deep only ten days ago right here. I went out in that storm and stood for fifteen minutes watching those flakes as they fell on the sleeve of my dark coat. There were no two alike. I didn't expect to find two alike, for those who have studied snowflakes for years say they never have found two exactly alike. This infinity of patterns with a common basic form, the six-sided crystal, is awesome. I marvel at it every time the snow begins to fall, and I wouldn't think of trying to explain it. I doubt that there is any explanation. It is merely another example, one that is at hand every winter, of the enduring mystery of even the simplest things.

When ice forms, even in the salty ocean, it forms as almost pure water, leaving most of the ocean's salts behind. Whaling ships short of fresh water, in the old days of unmechanized whaling, renewed their supplies and saved the lives of their crews by finding pools of melt on icebergs and barreling it for drinking water. Polar explorers melt polar ice for their indispensable water. I have never seen a satisfactory explanation of this capacity of water to rid itself of mineral salts by freezing. But I know it happens, even in my own house.

A few years ago we bought a refrigerator with an "automatic" ice-maker, which had an endless belt of plastic cups into which water from the household supply was fed and then carried through a series of coils which froze it into cubes that were emptied from the cups into a bin. It worked perfectly for perhaps six months. Then the cubes began sticking in the cups, water overflowed from the ice-filled cups, and the whole arrangement had tantrums. We tried various cures, but none worked, simply because when the "hard" water froze, it precipitated lime that formed a rough coating in the cups, and the ice cubes failed to fall out properly. When we found that the lime from the water was doing it, we gave up, removed the "automatic" ice-maker, and went back to the old system of trays you empty by hand. They, too, occasionally get lime deposits, but they can be scoured out.

JANUARY 28

One remarkable thing about ice is that water expands when it freezes. The expansion amounts to about 11 percent in volume. Few other substances expand when they freeze; most of them shrink. But because of this characteristic of frozen water, the earth is habitable by man. Since water expands when it turns to ice, the ice floats. If it shrank, it would sink and our lakes, our rivers, and our oceans would eventually be solid masses of ice. Liquid water would be a rare substance.

This expansion of water when it freezes also has been a major factor in shaping the land. Freezing water, that slow but inexorable pressure of forming ice, has gnawed away mountains and will continue to do so as long as water freezes and ice melts. Frost is the most powerful and unremitting enemy of rock and the most persistent leveling agent we know.

That expansion of frozen water also can create trouble aplenty for people who live in the country and have water pipes that are insufficiently protected. One hard freeze can rupture almost any iron, copper, or brass pipe left full of water. Twice since we have lived here someone has thoughtlessly turned off the water we leave trickling into the cow trough all winter, and each time that section of the spring line has had to be dug up and replaced.

JANUARY 29

A biochemist once said to me that my blood was nothing more than seawater polluted by organic material which we call blood cells, red and white corpuscles. He smiled when he said it, but there is a large grain of truth in it. And it is true of all animal life. We are a strange complexity of flesh and bones that are bathed, irrigated, and fed internally by fluids that are in some ways like seawater. Even the sweat that soaked my shirt last summer, waste from my bodily processes that both cleansed me internally and cooled me by evaporation, was full of the same salts as the ocean.

I think of myself as a freshwater person, and my system will tolerate only a limited amount of seawater. But the affinity is there. The water I drink contains most of the ocean salts, though in minute quantities. The rain that nourishes my garden dissolves many of those salts into a form which corn, cabbages, and tomatoes can use. The grass in my pastures is similarly nourished, and it goes to feed beef such as I eat, make milk such as I drink. My house is built of timber from trees that fed on water that came from the ocean, by way of the clouds. The cotton and wool of my clothing had the same ultimate source.

Yet man knows relatively little about water beyond what his charts and maps tell him. Where it came from originally is an enduring mystery, and why it remains here can be explained only in terms of our atmosphere and the terrestrial force of gravity. Man knows the chemical composition of water and its physical properties. He can create water from two gases, hydrogen and oxygen, and he can separate water into those components. He uses water in countless ways. He can, though with only moderate accuracy, forecast when and where water will fall as rain or snow. But beyond those rather broad facts he really doesn't know much about water except that it runs downhill, that it is essential to life, and that it constitutes more than 70 percent of the surface of the earth.

And right now I know that, in the form of snowdrifts, it constitutes 90-odd percent of the landscape I can see.

JANUARY 30

The cold bites deep again, down in the single numbers this morning, only four degrees above zero here. One of those waves of bitter Arctic air has moved in from the northwest and may stay a few days. I have said in the past that we get such cold from Medicine Hat and Saskatchewan, but I am not sure this time. The weather maps indicate that this blast came out of the Rockies down in the Colorado-Wyoming area, and it seems to have gathered strength all across the midlands. Now it is here and the air fairly crackles. When I went outdoors this morning the snow whined underfoot. I doubt that it will get above ten degrees all day. But there is little wind with it, for which we are grateful.

JANUARY 31

The cold has settled in on us. It was twenty-four degrees below zero this morning by our best thermometer, announced officially by the weather bureau as twenty-two degrees below zero in this area. But, as yesterday, there is scarcely a breath of air stirring, so it is not intolerable outdoors. I had to go out on routine chores and, though I did not dawdle, I didn't feel as though I would freeze my nose if I stayed another five minutes. The air is so clean and clear, so devoid of dust or pollution, that it seemed possible to see right through to infinity when one looked up.

Most years the raccoons begin mating about now. Two years ago, on this last night in January, two big buck coons had a battle in our back yard, right under the bedroom windows. It was twice as loud as a dogfight and almost as hysterical as a cat-fight. It started on the ground. Then one of the combatants climbed the big apple tree. The other followed him and they resumed the fight twenty feet above the ground. One of them must have been knocked off his perch, and he bounced off several limbs before he struck the ground. The other came scrambling down and they went at it again, this time louder than ever. But by then the female coon that apparently was the cause of it all had wearied of watching and gone off somewhere. And both those fighting buck coons seemed to realize this at the same time. They stopped their yammering and snarling, looked around, then went away in opposite directions. And the night was unbelievably quiet.

Even mate-hungry coons have sense enough to stay under cover on a night like last night. I doubt that they will be out mating tonight, either. They will wait till this intense cold wave has passed.

FEBRUARY

FEBRUARY 1

The bitter cold that marked January's end has not abated. We still shiver, and I am grateful for a furnace. And for a roof and four walls. Give a man shelter and warmth and he can withstand a great deal of cold weather. He needs food, too, of course, being a warm-blooded animal that has to keep the inner fire going. We can't hibernate.

I haven't much evidence to go on, but I still say that the giant lizards which ruled the world before the mammals began to take charge were victims of a change in the weather. They were cold-blooded creatures, at the mercy of their environment for their sustaining warmth. They had other weaknesses, of course, including a lack of brain power. But their great handicap was this cold-bloodedness. And they were too big, most of them were, to burrow into the mud as frogs do today, and hibernate.

So there they were, big, vulnerable beasts, dinosaurs and plesiosaurs and tyrannosaurs and all the other saurs, wading around in the shallow lagoons and thumping across the hills, ruling the world. Then the earth's axis shifted, or something happened, and the climate changed. The air chilled off, there was ice on the ponds, a raw wind blew. And all those big lizards were practically stopped in their tracks. Their blood chilled and thickened and was sluggish in their veins. Their hearts labored. They gasped. Their muscles went slack. One by one they crumpled into the muck and on the darkening hillsides. Some of them found shelter before they collapsed, and life, flickering in their huge bodies through the night, was warmed into slow-motion action the next day. But they were finished. Their time had run out. Some of them left their heritage in the egg, which probably hatched eventually. But only a few more generations were to endure. Great, hulking, slow-witted creatures that they were, they froze to death in temperatures that we warm-blooded inheritors of their old kingdom would consider no more than topcoat weather.

FEBRUARY 2

This is that secular occasion known as Groundhog Day, when a remarkable combination of guesswork, superstition, tradition, and error is taken for divination. The groundhog, or woodchuck, is supposed to waken from hibernation, emerge from its burrow, look at the sky, and foretell the weather for the next six weeks. If the sun shines enough to cast a shadow, the groundhog will return to its burrow and we will have six more weeks of winter. If there is no shadow, the sun hidden by clouds, the groundhog will remain out and winter is at an end. So runs the old belief.

First off, let me say I put no faith in any animal afraid of its own shadow. Second, this is an old, old myth that has taken many forms. Most early peoples believed animals could forecast weather. Early Egyptians turned to bears for prophecy. Continental Europeans chose wolves as their seers. The English left it to the otters and the badgers. The badgers were called groundhogs by many English countrymen. When early English colonists arrived here they mistook the big American marmot for a badger, called it a groundhog, and pinned the Candlemas superstition on it, substantially as it had been handed down in England with the badger as the shadow-watcher. And just to round out the packet of errors, the name "woodchuck" comes from the Algonquian word "wejack," which to the Indians meant the fisher, a large member of the weasel family, and no kin whatever to our present-day woodchuck.

So take the old belief or leave it, as you will. But it does bring up the matter of the woodchuck's hibernation, which is of more than casual interest.

The woodchuck is a warm-blooded mammal, close kin of the squirrel and other large rodents. Yet it has this unique ability to throw itself back, in a sense, to cold-blooded beginnings far back in the mists of time. In late summer it fattens, increasing its weight sometimes by a third. When hard frosts come, it retreats to an underground den, closes the entrance behind it, and relaxes into a comatose state where its heart beats only once every four or five minutes, its respiration almost ceases, and its body temperature sinks from a normal summer level of around ninety-seven degrees to as low as thirty-eight degrees. And thus it remains for as much as four or five months, sustained by its body fat and never wakening. Then something, perhaps the sun's angle or the day's length or some mysterious message that can penetrate the soil, rouses it. Sometimes it emerges to a snow-clad end of March or early April and has difficult going. More often it comes out into the balmy air of early spring. Maybe it actually looks at the sun and at its own shadow. I wouldn't know. But if so, it does so only in passing. Weather is of minor importance to it at that time. It has two big hungers, for food and for sex.

If those big lizards I was talking about yesterday had found some way to hibernate, the whole history of life on this planet might have been different.

FEBRUARY 3

This whole matter of hibernation is touched with mysticism for a warm-blooded biped like me. It is suspended animation that is deeper than sleep, deeper even than a coma, for it involves a slowdown of all the bodily processes to a point far below normal. It approaches death without quite going over the threshold. That spark of life is still alive, though it is only a spark and no longer a flame.

The cold-blooded creatures are the hibernators—with only a few warm-blooded exceptions. Snakes, salamanders, frogs, toads, lizards, turtles, some fish—they all hibernate. Some insects hibernate, usually selectively. Queen bumblebees, mated and full of fertile eggs, hibernate, though all the other bumblebees die in autumn. Most insects, however, leave their spark of life in the eggs which hatch a new generation the following spring or summer. Some insects hibernate in caterpillar form, notably the little moth *Isia Isabella* which becomes the woolly-bear caterpillar. Woolly bears find hiding places in barns and sheds and under bark on trees, where they freeze solid, and yet thaw and come back to active life in the spring, pupate, become moths, lay eggs, hatch into caterpillars, and continue the cycle. I have taken a woolly bear from a beam in my woodshed in January, when it was frozen as hard as a pretzel, put it under a jelly glass on my desk, and watched it thaw, come to life, and look around for food. When I put it back on the exposed beam where I found it, it curled up and froze solid again, apparently with no ill effects.

I wonder if there aren't stages of life and hibernation that we haven't yet properly classified. What would you call the germ in a bird's egg? Isn't it a form of life suspended, waiting proper conditions to rouse and grow? Or how explain the remarkable stages of any moth or butterfly? In the winged stage it feeds and lays eggs which hatch into some form of caterpillars. The caterpillars eat and shell themselves in as pupae, another stage of suspended life akin to hibernation. The pupa bursts and the winged moth or caterpillar is released, to start the cycle all over again.

What is the seed of a pumpkin or a sunflower, say, but a form of life suspended—hibernating?—which needs only the right conditions of light, warmth, and moisture to rouse and become a thriving plant?

Life goes on, generation to generation, pausing, growing, pausing, growing; even human life, in the dormant ovum and the dormant sperm which, brought together under the right conditions, become another entity, able to pass along that spark of life to still another generation, and another.

We have various terms for its various manifestations—hibernation, estivation, dormancy, coma, sleep, unconsciousness, somnolence, dozing, daze, stupor, and the ultimate, death. But, short of the ultimate, they are largely matters of degree, of the borderline area that separates full wakefulness and total lifelessness.

FEBRUARY 4

Some years I can find skunk cabbage poking its greenish brown hoods through the ice in the small bog down the road by now. Earliest of all spring flowers, it occasionally appears in January. That strange, primitive-looking hood shields an even more primitive flower stalk, a fleshy, thumblike core on which many small blossoms appear. These blossoms exude the odor of rotting flesh and attract a species of fly, one of the earliest insects. They fertilize the flowers which to some people have an overtone of garlic smell, much like that of a skunk. This odor appears whenever a stem or leaf of the plant is broken; it marks the juice.

Skunk cabbage is an arum, cousin of the jack-in-the-pulpit. All arums are perennial, all have peppery juice and need damp footing. But only the skunk cabbage pokes its snout up through the ice.

I have heard some people boast that they have boiled and eaten skunk cabbage leaves. I advise against trying it. Another plant, rankly poisonous, is sometimes mistaken for skunk cabbage and if eaten could have serious consequences. And skunk cabbage itself has an element, difficult to remove even by repeated boiling, that is poisonous to some people. It has an unusually apt botanical name, *Symplocarpus foetidus.*

FEBRUARY 5

For a long time I was baffled by the early appearance of skunk cabbage, particularly the plant's ability to penetrate the ice in the bogland. Then I learned that all plants at the time of blossoming generate heat, what we would call "running a fever." This undoubtedly is akin to the mammal's estrus period, which is accompanied by a degree of fever and is often called "being in heat." Skunk cabbage has intense vitality, the shape of the emerging hood concentrates that inner heat, and the result is sufficient to melt ice. Measurements have shown that an emerging skunk cabbage hood sometimes has as much as twenty-seven degrees more warmth than the surrounding soil and air. That is why those sheaths coming up through the ice, even in February, are surrounded by a small patch of melt. I find something of the same effect in my own garden. The first shoots of crocus, daffodil, and tulip create small areas of melt in the snow crust or the frozen soil around them. They, too, have their fires of spring. They burn the food within them, somewhat as my body burns the bread and meat I eat, and energy is created. It is released as heat in them. It warms my blood.

FEBRUARY 6

All winters are difficult for birds, but I doubt that their problems are as serious or as painful as we sometimes think. Man has a habit of attributing human thoughts and feelings to nonhuman creatures, and wild birds and animals live and have experiences on another plane from ours.

For the normally migrating birds that occasionally winter-over here, winter provides at best a marginal existence and some of them fail to survive. Those that patronize the bird feeders, dependent on charity, probably make out fairly well. But if they are going to spend the winter here they must be rugged. That demand is a part of the natural selection process.

The birds that normally live here the year around probably are doing as well as usual. They are equipped for our weather. They are well upholstered with feathers, they live on diets that can be had in the winter woods and fields, and they know how to conserve energy during prolonged cold spells. Take the ruffed grouse. They eat a great many buds, which are never completely covered with snow, and they eat wild berries even though they are dry as raisins. They are well clothed, even their feet. I have been told, and I believe it, that the grouse's feet are not feathered in a mild winter. I know that in years with little snow I have seen them in late December with feet as naked as those of a chickadee.

Owls, of course, have no speical winter problems. Cold, in fact, forces rabbits and mice into the open for food, so the owls have plenty to eat. Crows and jays are omnivorous and truculent enough to take good care of themselves. Both invade barnyards for waste grain, and crows eat small animals killed on the highways. The small woodpeckers, the downies and the hairies, will not starve as long as there are trees and insects that live on trees. They are steady customers at the suet cage, but they can do very well without handouts.

Life is somewhat difficult for the little birds, chickadees, juncos, sparrows, goldfinches, and the like. But for every one that lives on handouts at the feeding station there are thousands that work for their living all winter long in old pasturelands, fencerows, woodlots, meadows, and anywhere that weeds and grasses grow. All of them spend much of their time feeding on weed seed in such places, which are almost never wholly covered with snow.

Ice storms are the worst of all hazards for birds. They not only seal in the food but they can ice up the feathers and make flight difficult or impossible. Most winter kills of birds occur during or soon after an ice storm.

FEBRUARY 7

Rain today, but not really a February thaw. Only rain, and February rain is cold and cheerless. It smells of ice and it has a touch of sleet even when it does not freeze as it falls. The temperature today stays right around forty degrees, not warm enough to melt the ice, not cold enough to freeze the rain. It falls from a gray sky and it drenches a gray and frozen earth. It runs swiftly down frozen gullies that have no song in them. February rain even spills from the eaves without one musical note in its drip and gurgle.

There is, I grant, something like promise in it, the promise that April lies ahead, with rain that can whisper and chortle and even sing. In April, but not in February. There is also the minor comfort of knowing that an inch of rain in February will run off, even if it turns to ice somewhere tomorrow. That same amount of moisture in snowflakes would be a foot deep and would lie on the ground until late March.

I can even like February rain, as long as it doesn't turn to sleet. By now I am very tired of shoveling snow.

FEBRUARY 8

My barometer reminds me every day that I am a peculiar kind of finless, gill-less fish living at the bottom of an ocean of air. I cannot swim in it, as a fish swims in water, but it is my element; as I move about on this air ocean's floor I am partially supported by it and its oxygen feeds the fires of my life. Theoretically, I could move more freely in a vacuum; but my body would explode in a vacuum even before it suffocated. Air pressure holds me together.

I cannot see the air around me. It is invisible to me, and I cannot even imagine the kind of eyes that could see the atoms that compose it. A fish cannot see the water, either. I do see drops of water in the air, and the fish sees bubbles of air in the water, but we are in a sense equally limited. We both, however, have learned to live with such limitations.

The ocean of air which surrounds the earth acts in many ways like an ocean of water. It has waves and eddies and currents and tides. But because the air is a gas and water is a liquid there are also profound differences. Water is much heavier than air; otherwise rain could never fall from the clouds. Water is almost the same density from top to bottom, except in unusual depths. Air is much more dense at sea level than it is even on a two-mile-high mountain, and it thins away to almost nothing at extreme heights. And air is a mixture of gases which varies from place to place and changes completely at different altitudes. At sea level the air generally is composed of about 78 percent nitrogen, 21 percent oxygen, and small amounts of water vapor, carbon dioxide, and occasionally hydrogen and helium—not to mention the pollutants generated by cities, internal combustion engines, and industries. At high altitudes the oxygen is displaced by hydrogen, and at extreme altitudes even the nitrogen is displaced by the hydrogen. About seventy miles above the earth the atmosphere consists almost wholly of hydrogen. From there on out the hydrogen thins away into empty space.

We sometimes think of it as a fortunate circumstance that oxygen is heavy enough to permeate the atmosphere down here where we live.

That, of course, is nonsense. We are here because this is true. We evolved as we did, and all life exists in its present form, because the oxygen is here, not the other way round. The oxygen wasn't put here for us to use. We just happen to be a form of life that grew in an atmosphere rich in oxygen. It takes a bit of imagining, but there may be other forms of life elsewhere in the universe that live on hydrogen or some other gas, even one toxic to us.

FEBRUARY 9

Because the air is invisible we usually forget that it has substance. But it does. Otherwise there would be no wind. If air had no substance, neither birds nor airplanes could fly. They can't fly in a vacuum, not as long as they are within reach of the earth's pull of gravity.

It is the substance of the wind that makes a sailboat possible and operates a windmill. A windmill is nothing but a turbine driven by air instead of water, steam, or some other fluid or vapor. And because warm air is lighter, less substantial, than cold air, the winter wind is stronger than the summer wind. Tests prove that a wind of the same speed exerts 25 percent more force in January than it does in July. That is because there is more body, more substance, to the air in cold January than in warm July. That is also one reason a dog pants and a workman breathes faster in summer than in winter. They have to get more air into their lungs to get the same amount of oxygen from it.

The substance of the air is also responsible for sound. Sound is vibration, and vibration sets up rhythmic motions in the air which are picked up by our ears. Sound travels faster in thin, warm air than it does in thick, cold air, but it sounds louder in cold air because more of the vibrations are transmitted. At zero Centigrade sound travels 1,000 feet per second at sea level, and its speed increases about two feet per second with every degree of rise in temperature. There are other variables, such as humidity, but they are minor. When I see a flash of lightning five seconds before I hear the thunderclap I know it was about a mile away. If I catch the tingling scent of ozone after a lightning flash I don't have to count; I know the bolt was too close to suit me. Ozone is another form of oxygen, three atoms of oxygen in one molecule, formed by a flash of lightning or other electrical discharge shot through the air. You don't smell ozone when the lightning is a mile away.

FEBRUARY 10

There used to be a country saying that you had to earn spring, you had to work your way through January and February for it. By mid-March, or whenever spring arrived, you had done enough winter penance, shoveled enough snow, toted enough wood, to entitle you to it.

By now, many of us are inclined to agree. The bright sheen of winter has worn off. Whether there has been much snow or little, there always has been enough cold, particularly for old bones. But there are, as always, a few signs. Robins have been seen. They are robins that wintered over here, of course, and they simply come out of the thickets onto somebody's front lawn on a sunny day, hoping to find green grass and some form of insect life. It really isn't the robins that are the good sign; it is the willingness of someone to believe that migrant robins could possibly have arrived. However, I do find faint signs of life in a half dozen giant mulleins on a south-sloping hillside where the snow has melted. Give them a couple of weeks of warm sun and they would show new leaves. They prove to me that one of these days, though not tomorrow, hepatica will bloom.

The unfailing sign comes every evening, at sunset. The sun now sinks, officially, forty minutes later than it did a month ago. And it rises almost half an hour earlier in the morning.

FEBRUARY 11

It is remarkable how the human body adapts itself to the air around it. Indians who live in the high Andes, where the air is thin and the oxygen content low, not only have larger lungs than lowland Indians but their blood has more red corpuscles. Red corpuscles carry oxygen from the lungs to the rest of the body. So these high-altitude Indians not only have bigger bellows, lungs, but they have more oxygen traps, red corpuscles, to catch and carry the oxygen to their tissues. Apparently this change, this adaptation, is a natural means of meeting the local needs of their environment. But it remains a flexible arrangement. When one of these high-mountain people is taken down to sea level the number of red corpuscles in his blood gradually diminishes to about the same proportion found in sea-level natives. He doesn't need those extra oxygen-carriers, so his body dispenses with them. But when he returns to the mountaintops the red corpuscles increase again.

The ability of the blood to absorb oxygen from the air in the lungs comes from the presence of hemoglobin in the red cells. Hemoglobin has a loose affinity for oxygen, captures it in the lungs, and carries it throughout the body. As it distributes the oxygen, the hemoglobin picks up carbon dioxide and other waste material and carts them away.

Hemoglobin—really its chemical basis, which is called hemin—has a structural resemblance to chlorophyll. Chlorophyll is the active green substance in leaves which takes water and carbon dioxide from the air and, powered by sunlight, converts them into a starchy form of carbohydrate the plant needs for food. The principal chemical difference between the chlorophyll of the leaf and the hemoglobin of human blood consists of a few atoms of iron in one and of magnesium in the other. Both substances use the air as the agency for their vital processes. One uses the oxygen from it, the other uses the carbon dioxide.

Here, then, considerably simplified, is the fundamental difference between a man's body and a stalk of corn—a few atoms of iron in the vital fluid within the man.

FEBRUARY 12

To know the February full moon as it rises in the brittle eastern sky is to know both awe and shivering wonder. It is round as a medallion, bright as burnished brass, but its light has no more warmth than the frost cloud of a man's breath. It is a false and lifeless sun that makes false daylight of the night. It kills the lesser stars and reduces the constellations to fundamentals. It burns the darkness with neither heat nor smoke, strewing the snow with charred skeletons of the naked trees. No wonder the Indians knew the February full moon as the Hunger Moon.

Tonight the moon's edges will be frostbitten and it will rise an hour later. Tomorrow night it will be still another hour laggard and its rim will begin to crumble. And night by night more stars will creep back and begin to claim the darkness. Day by day the sun will move a fraction of a degree toward March and the equinox. The Hunger Moon will have passed its prime.

FEBRUARY 13

I sit and watch the open fire and think that the Greeks, who called fire
one of the four elements, were more nearly right in a fundamental way
than those who later insisted that fire was only a chemical reaction. Our
earth must have been born in fire, it was shaped in fire, and without the
inconceivably hot blaze of that swirling mass we call the sun there would
be no life on earth. We even have our share of fire within us, at the core
of our own vitality, where the oxygen we breathe is burned. Whether
fire is an element or not, it is elemental.

When I study the history of man I am repeatedly reminded how
closely man and fire are linked. Not earliest man, who was a beneficiary
and sometimes the victim of fire but had not yet tamed it and made it his
own. But man somewhere along the early path of misty speculation,
before he left the caves but after he quit the treetops, somewhere along
the route to the most primitive stone implements.

A paleontologist turns up a fossil bone and traces of charcoal carbon
from a fire, and he tells himself he is on the track of ancient pre-man.
This creature used fire. That sets him apart, makes him different from all
other creatures. For fire, that fourth element of the Greeks, was and is
man's unique possession.

FEBRUARY 14

Valentine Day as commonly observed, as an occasion for romantic messages and sentimental gifts, has nothing whatever to do with the saint for
whom it is named. Valentine was a priest in Rome at the time Claudius
II was persecuting Christians, and Valentine openly ministered to the
martyrs. For this he was arrested, urged to renounce his faith, and, when
he refused, condemned to death. He was beheaded on this day about the
year 270.

Quite apart from this event, the Romans at about this time of the
year celebrated the Lupercalia, which were feasts to honor Pan and
Juno. One feature of the Lupercalia was a drawing of the names of
young women by the men who participated, for partners at the feast.
Pastors of the early Christian church tried to eradicate pagan practices,
or to adapt them to Christian ritual, and they tried to give as many

festivals as possible the names of Christian saints. The festival of Lupercalia began about the middle of February, so the new Christian festival, established to supersede Lupercalia, was named for Saint Valentine. However, it was almost impossible to blot out any festival of the common people, so all that happened, really, was that the old romantic trappings of Lupercalia were continued under the saintly name of Valentine, the martyred priest.

So now we have a day of romance and love notes named for an early priest who was bound by vows of chastity and died helping Christian martyrs.

FEBRUARY 15

When and where man obtained fire is one of those mysteries that will probably remain forever unsolved. It was available to anyone, of course, and had been available since the beginning. But man was the first form of life to capture it and put it to his own use. All other forms of life either avoided it or perished in it. Fear of fire is instinctive. Yet somewhere back at the beginning, man captured a spark of fire and made it his own, perhaps at first using it only to defend himself from those enemies who never learned that fire could be tamed. A fire at the mouth of a cave was as effective against natural enemies as a wall would have been, perhaps more so because snakes could not penetrate nor insects pass through fire with impunity.

The legends hold no clue. Primitive people believed that fire was the possession of the gods and that it was stolen for man by some mythical hero like Prometheus, or a friendly animal such as the coyote. To the ancients, fire was sacred, as an earthly manifestation of the sun. The early Greeks worshipped it. Vesta was the goddess of the hearth and the vestal virgins were committed to guard the sacred fire. When a new colony was established, fire from the sacred fire in the metropolis was taken there, thus linking the colony to the mother city in a practical as well as a spiritual tie.

But Greece came late in human history. There were centuries of man's mastery of fire before the first Greek was born, and we know little about those centuries except that man and fire were linked, that man's progress must have been along a path warmed and lighted by fire. He learned early to strike fire from stone, perhaps by accident in chipping his earliest stone implements. Not too long after that he must have learned to create fire by friction, for the fire drill reaches far back into the mists of antiquity.

With fire, man could move out of the caves. He could carry fiery walls of protection with him and he could somewhat fend off the cold. He could move about the earth, for fire gave him safe mobility as well as strength beyond his own sinews. In time, it gave him his first advance beyond the raft for water travel—with controlled fire he could hollow a log, make his first primitive boat. And fire gave man eyes to see in the darkness of night.

One must marvel at the courage of the first man who held fire in his hand. How did it happen? Did he see a tree struck by lightning, and then discover that the flame at the far end of that broken branch could be carried away? Lightning seems a more likely source than the volcano, which rained death as well as fire. However it happened, that first man to capture fire and hold it at arm's length conquered not only his own impulsive fears but the even deeper fears of punishment by jealous gods who owned all fire.

FEBRUARY 16

My life depends on the temperature of the fire within me. That, of course, is the quiet fire of life, the burning of food in the oxygen of my intaken breath. If the temperature of that inner fire drops only a few degrees for any length of time, my body begins to die. Raise it five degrees and I am critically ill; raise it ten degrees and my life processes burn out and I swiftly die. Starve those inner fires of oxygen for a few minutes and they begin to flicker.

This is true of all forms of animal life, though the temperature of normal living varies from species to species. Regardless of outside temperatures, the human body maintains a temperature level of approximately 98.6 degrees F., though that varies somewhat from one individual to another. The normal temperature of a horse is 100 degrees, that of a dog 101.5 degrees, that of a sheep 102.3 degrees, that of a rabbit 103.1 degrees. In birds the temperature is consistently higher, as high as 108 degrees in some species.

Bird temperatures fluctuate from day to night and to some extent throughout the day. Birds are so active and have such a high metabolism that they have to stoke their inner fires almost constantly. At night, when they are at rest, their temperature may drop four or five degrees. In the hummingbird, which is so small and so active, there is a kind of hibernation at night, when the fires burn low and all bodily processes go into low gear. Whippoorwills and some other birds that live entirely on flying insects have the ability to go into semi-hibernation where the fires of life are dampered, the body temperature drops, the pulse relaxes, and they can live for days on a minimum of stored fat.

This capacity for diminishing the vital fire is attributed by zoologists to what they call "imperfect warm-bloodedness"—a kind of regression to an intermediate stage of the evolution from reptile cold-bloodedness to the warm-bloodedness of birds and mammals. Most warm-blooded animals, including man, have reached an evolutionary point of no return. Our fires glow continuously. We can't turn down the thermostat.

FEBRUARY 17

Sitting in front of our Franklin stove last evening, I wished I could thank old Ben for his invention. He didn't really "invent" the stove, of course. Like most inventors, he took ideas already in use and rearranged them into better working order. But he found a way to get twice the heat from firewood that I would get with a fireplace—to use fire more effectively. The same fire, basically, that I have been talking about; but here it is the outer fire, the one that burns wood.

The inner fire uses carbohydrates for the major fuel, with oxygen, as always, the burning element. Like any fire, these inner fires yield energy in the form of heat. But the heat of the body seems to be less for personal comfort than for swift and efficient progression of vital chemical processes. The warm-blooded creature may be said to live swiftly. Much of the heat and energy is produced by nervous impulses, the remainder of it probably by muscular tension. These dictate the metabolism, the intensity of our chemical processes. When we say we are "burning up energy" we come close to literal truth. We are using nervous and muscular energy that is created by the inner fire. That fire, however, continues even when we sleep, although nerves and muscles are presumably at rest, or almost so. But our vital organs are still at work and, to some extent, the nerves are still on the job. Our sleep is not hibernation.

One might say that here is the basic necessity of life—the continuing inner fire. All living creatures are constantly undergoing combustion, burning up. Yet there is a constant replenishment of the fuels for that fire—just as I replenish the logs for the fire in my Franklin stove—so that until disease interrupts or old age slows down the process of replacement we are never actually being consumed.

Man has long dreamed of a perpetual-motion machine, some contrivance that we could set going and expect to go on forever. But man himself is such a machine. So is every form of life we know, which consists of some combination of substances animated with the vital spark and endowed with the inner fire of energy. Grass and all vegetation live on and on, lit by the flame of life and passing on that fire by seed and germination. Birds are such "machines," perpetuating life and motion in the fertile egg. And man, energized all his own life by that inner flame, passes it on to each succeeding generation with his own seed, the ovum and the sperm, out of which grows another sentient individual, another complex heat machine that eats and grows and thinks and reasons only because of that quiet inner fire.

FEBRUARY 18

We haven't had any fresh snow for almost a week and the skunks have been out and about their private business—which tends to become very public at times. They are mating, and when two male skunks meet now, they tend to be truculent. A truculent skunk makes his presence known. Twice in the past three nights we have been wakened by the fetid odor of skunk. Our back yard and our garage apron seem to be crossroads in the skunk highways. Last night we not only smelled them but heard them snuffling angrily and scuffling about.

I don't mind having skunks as close neighbors, though they do have a deplorable habit of digging holes in the lawn to reach fat white grubs. I suppose that if I got rid of the grubs the skunks wouldn't dig for them, so in a way the fault is mine. Skunks also catch and eat a great many insects that are pests to me. And they are not really unfriendly; I have never known one that was hostile if I kept my distance. Some people make pets of them. Some people make pets of snakes, too. One winter a skunk took up quarters under our front porch, which wasn't so bad until it resented our living here. Then it had to be dispossessed. Otherwise we live in a prolonged truce. But I do wish that sex-hungry skunks would congregate elsewhere than in our back yard. There's plenty of room for them out in the lower pasture.

FEBRUARY 19

In the beginning there was life, simple, single-celled life that undoubt-edly lived in the water because water is the natural habitat of the most primitive life we know. The beginnings of life are mysterious, and so are almost all its early changes. We can only speculate about what happened. But there is every probability that the very earliest form of life was not yet committed to being either plant or animal. It was in that unresolved state where the balance could tilt either way. Eventually, some of the individuals in that welter of uncommitted life turned one way and be-came animals, some turned the other way and became plants. Some never made the commitment; they persist even today in that anomalous state which defies the classifiers but does provide evidence of the way life may have been many millions of years ago.

Broadly speaking, those which became plants found a way to man-ufacture and store food from elemental substances, and those that be-came animals found that they could subsist by eating plants or other animals. The plants became manufacturers. The animals became con-sumers.

In a sense, plant life and animal life complement and even sustain each other in a remarkable manner. Plants, making food by photosyn-thesis, consume great quantities of carbon dioxide and give off great quantities of oxygen. Animals, in the simple process of breathing, con-sume oxygen and constantly give off carbon dioxide. We might call this a fortunate circumstance, because it provides the essentials for both forms of life. Or we might say the two forms of life evolved simply because the essentials for living were available and it is life's way to use what is at hand. This, of course, leads straight into that thorny philosophical thicket labeled the "meaning" or "purpose" of life, and I have no inten-tion of getting lost in it. I am quite sure that no one really knows either the meaning or the purpose of life. I am content to accept life as a fact and go on from there.

FEBRUARY 20

Looking up an old saying this morning—"An apple a day keeps the doctor away," it was, and it is totally anonymous—I found two others that I had forgotten and was glad to recall. The first is a rhyme for a horse-buyer, which I first heard in my youth in the ranch country of Colorado. It goes:

> One white foot, try him.
> Two white feet, buy him.
> Three white feet, look well about him.
> Four white feet, go without him.

I never owned a horse with four white feet, but the saddlehorse of my boyhood had three white feet and had to be watched every time I got on him. He would spook at his own shadow.

The other saying is an old New England maxim that I first heard from my grandmother in the West and didn't hear again until I settled in New England years later. It goes:

> Use it up, wear it out;
> Make do, or do without.

Needless to say, this advice was swept out the door when the modern age of built-in obsolescence arrived. If it were only partly observed now we wouldn't be frantically looking for some place to put our personal, community, and national trash.

FEBRUARY 21

Looking up those old sayings yesterday I also ran onto the text of "Turkey in the Straw," which if I ever knew I had forgotten. I know the tune very well indeed, but the words were something else again. Here are the first stanza and the refrain:

> Went out to milk and I didn't know how,
> I milked the goat instead of the cow;
> A monkey a-sittin' in a pile of straw
> A-winkin' at his mother-in-law.
>
> Turkey in the straw, turkey in the hay,
> Roll 'em up and twist 'em up a high tuckahaw,
> And hit 'em up a tune called Turkey in the Straw.

Why the switch was made from monkey to turkey, I have no idea. But it might just as well have been called "Monkey in the Straw."

Two lines from the sixth stanza caught my eye because they have provided titles for at least two good novels:

> Sugar in the gourd and honey in the horn;
> I never was so happy as the hour I was born.

FEBRUARY 22

By the calendar in use at the time, George Washington was born on February 11. The American colonists did not adopt the Gregorian calendar and make the eleven-day correction until twenty years later, in 1752. Inevitably that change made confusion about birthdays and anniversaries and many older people refused to change their birthdays to conform to the revised calendar. For some time, those who changed the date noted the change by writing the letters NS after it—February 22 NS, for example—to indicate that the date was "new style." Where the old date persisted, it often was identified as OS, old style.

And now it has become legal to change such anniversaries as Washington's birthday to the nearest Monday for observance as a holiday. Thus, in 1971 Washington's birthday, February 11 OS, February 22 NS, was observed on February 15. If that doesn't confuse matters utterly, I can't imagine what would.

FEBRUARY 23

The sap is climbing in the maples, life starting to rouse. Traditionally the maple sap begins to flow in my area on Washington's birthday, and about three years out of five it does flow by now. I am quite sure that if I were to bore holes in my maples and insert the spiles, the faintly sweet drip would begin. It would continue as long as we had mild days and frosty nights. Chilly days stop the flow. For several years, early in our tenure here, we tapped our trees and made our own syrup. But our equipment was makeshift and it took too long to boil the sap down. We finally gave it up and now we buy our syrup. But every year I am reminded of the remote beginnings of plant life that finally produced such a masterpiece as a sugar maple tree.

Among the earliest traces of plant life we find are fossils from the Cambrian rocks, close to 550 million years old. Those plants were a form of algae, simple water-dwelling plants. We still have algae, which form the basis of most of the green scum that gathers on stagnant water in late summer. The earliest fossils of land plants come from the Devonian period, about 350 million years ago. Some of them have neither leaves nor roots, though they definitely are land-dwellers. They resemble sea-weed in many respects; seaweed is generally considered the ancestor of all the plants we know today. Some of those early plants consisted only of underground stems and a few uplifted shoots, on some of which were borne spore cases. These have been identified as plants in transition from algae toward ferns.

The transition was relatively swift. Land plants soon began to show leaves like elementary fern fronds. Then they grew swiftly in size. There was a kind of explosion of plant life, the vitality too tremendous to be contained in one or two types. Hundreds of variants appeared, some of them of great size. By the Carboniferous period, some 300 million years ago, there was a profusion of towering fernlike plants, some of them trees twenty feet in circumference and 150 feet tall. Some had long, grasslike leaves that grew in spirals up the trunk. Some were much like giant forms of the running pine and ground cedar that grow today as creepers in my own woodland.

The reasons for this profusion of form and gigantic growth are obscure. The time was just before the rise of the giant reptiles, the dinosaurian families. Clearly, some combination of conditions favored life as never before, life in many forms and reaching giant size. Perhaps there were obscure but benevolent radiations. Perhaps there were newly available salts in the earth, the water, even the air, that prompted such growth.

Among the plants of that era were gigantic horsetails, much like the Equisetum, or scouring rushes, that grow today along my riverbank. Today's scouring rushes seldom are more than three feet tall, but the giants of those ancient days were taller than my sugar maples. They reproduced by spores. But among those long-ago jungle plants were a few seed ferns, venturers in a new direction. The original plant line was diverging. My maples at last were a possibility.

FEBRUARY 24

Frosty last night, but up close to fifty today. Ideal sap weather . . .

After the appearance of the first seed ferns there was a moderately slow divergence of the two major plant families—the spermatophyta, or seed-bearers, and the thallophyta, or spore-bearers. That change marked the beginning of all the flowering plants we know today. The next great change came during the Jurassic period, which began about 155 million years ago. In fossils of that time are trees closely related to the ginkgo of today and others closely related to our sequoias. But even more important was the appearance of many smaller plants and bushes that were beginning to show flowers and something like today's seed-bearing devices. Those plants were the forerunner of the daisy in my meadow and the laurel on my mountainside.

Again the evidence is obscure and there are many gaps, but it seems clear that another explosion of plant life was beginning. The form and habit of trees, bushes, and lesser plants were changing swiftly, in terms of geologic time, and the varieties were proliferating. Perhaps it is worth noting, though there may be no clear connection, that by then the first birds were flying and the early mammals, small as rats, were scurrying through the underbrush. Animal life, too, was changing swiftly. Giant ferns were thinning out or vanishing and the giant lizards were specializing toward their doom and disappearance. In the animal world, placental birth and the mammalian way of life were about to take over, and among the plants the blossom and the seed were beginning to dominate.

The blossom is difficult to trace, but it probably evolved from the early cycad cone, which had both pollen and ovules. But somewhere between those primitive cycads and the primitive pines of the next period, the Cretaceous, which dates from about 115 million years ago, the explosion of plant life abated. Fossils from Cretaceous rocks show not only the early ginkgos and sequoias but also trees and shrubs clearly belonging to families familiar today—magnolias, cinnamon trees, oaks, sycamores, maples, poplars. And most of the modern flowering plants by then were established and recognizable.

The links between those plants, evident in rocks of more than 100 million years ago, and the primitives of only 35 million years earlier, are almost completely missing. The line of descent from the Cretaceous plants down to the present is relatively clear. What happened between that early cycad cone and the primitive magnolia blossom, nobody really knows. But eventually it was the seed-bearers, the flowering plants, and the mammals, who inherited the earth.

And that, to sum it all up, is the way those sugar maples got here and the reason they are, right now, dripping their vaguely sweet sap into the buckets of the maple-syrup makers.

FEBRUARY 25

We are always impatient for the first migrant birds to return, mostly because their arrival means that seasonal change is at hand. We start looking for them about now, though we know it is too early by two or three weeks. Only the rarest of early springs would bring them north this far the last week in February. But almost every year I see a flock of migrant red-wing blackbirds in the trees along the river before mid-March, and soon after them there is a flock of migrant robins in the big pasture back of our house.

All migrant birds wait for hospitable weather. Robins and red-wings rather closely follow the northward advance of the thirty-five-degree isotherm. Watch the weather map, and when that isotherm approaches you can begin to look for the birds. Apparently it takes that temperature to bring out the insects on which they feed. No bird will migrate into a starvation area, even if it won't freeze to death there.

Spring migration always is slower than fall migration. Apparently they want to get out in a hurry when they feel or sense winter nipping at their tail feathers. But they take their time about coming back. Among the smaller birds, most of the seed-eaters prefer to migrate by day and rest at night. The insect-eaters, such as robins, usually make migrant flights at night and feed in the daytime. This may be because insects are more active and easier to find in the daylight. Swallows and other birds that catch and eat insects in flight are an exception. But once at their destination, they all revert to their normal habits.

Observers watching migrations by radar or telescope have found that the heaviest night migrations occur between 10:00 P.M. and 1:00 A.M., with the busiest hour between 11:00 P.M. and midnight. There seem to be few flights after 4:00 A.M., perhaps because of the approach of dawn.

In the fall migration the young birds are sometimes the first to go south—and please don't ask me how they know where to go or how to get there; I don't know. I've never found anyone who does know. The youngsters are followed by the females, and the males go last. Except among ducks and geese, which have their own rules. In the spring the two sexes usually migrate together most of the way. Then, the last couple hundred miles or so, the males often push on ahead. We see this most clearly among the red-wing blackbirds, with the males here and making the air echo with their somewhat raspy but very vernal calls at least a week and sometimes two weeks before the quieter and less conspicuous females arrive.

FEBRUARY 26

All birds had reptilian ancestors. So did I, so we are, in a sense, distant cousins. But the birds long ago learned the art of flight and clothed themselves with feathers, though they continued, like reptiles, to reproduce by laying eggs. My kind became bipedal mammals with dextrous hands instead of wings, and with no feathers.

Nobody knows why one branch of the reptile tribe long ago became birds and another branch became mammals. Something happened, and it cannot be wholly explained by any theory of natural selection. Selection helped, after the commitment was made and the direction of change chosen. But before selection came strongly into play there was this basic diversion from the reptilian form and way of life. And that divergence, significantly in both instances, bird and mammal, was in the direction of more brain power. The bigger, more effective brain was of more enduring importance than wings or manual dexterity or even placental birth.

Details of evolutionary change are not always obvious until the change is more or less complete. We have to guess at many intermediate steps, and some of those steps are vitally important but completely mysterious. For instance, the change from cold-bloodedness to warm-bloodedness was a basic alteration, yet we have no evidence of how it began, or when. The reptiles were and still are cold-blooded, dependent on the temperature of their environment. Mammals and birds are warm-blooded, relatively independent of environmental temperature.

We speak of this change as high achievement and sometimes we think it enabled birds and mammals to move freely about the earth. We sometimes say it provided warm-blooded animals with more energy than cold-bloodedness. But when we make such statements we overlook the insects. Insects are cold-blooded, but they are numerous beyond counting and they live almost everywhere. And insects have more energy per ounce than any other creatures alive.

I have also heard it said that warm-bloodedness enables its possessors to live longer, more active lives. Both reptiles and insects disprove that statement. Turtles are notably long-lived and, in the tropics at least, very active. And some insects live in the larval stage for years. The larvae of the periodic locust, for example, live far longer than most small warm-blooded animals and longer than most small birds. Insects are slowed down by cold weather, and warm-blooded creatures continue active. There are a few warm-blooded hibernators, such as woodchucks; but virtually all insects hibernate in some form, egg, larva, or imago.

I should say that the biggest advantage of warm-bloodedness is that it produces nervous energy. Nervous energy is basic to intelligence, to thought. No one has yet discovered much brain power in any cold-blooded creatures, perhaps because of this lack of nervous energy. Most of the cold-blooded ones, including both insects and reptiles, are dependent on instinct and reflex rather than intelligence. Instinct does not require a brain of any consequence. A few ganglia or nerve centers suffice to prompt the muscular reflexes.

FEBRUARY 27

The big changes from reptilian life to avian life can be stated rather simply. First was the development of a heart that supplies the body with pure blood, blood already circulated through the lungs, cleansed, and supplied with oxygen. The cold-blooded reptiles circulate mixed blood, blood only partly purified in the lungs. So the first major change was in the heart, which in the bird pumps impure blood to the lungs for purification and aeration, and sends only that purified blood through the body. This promotes energy.

The second major change was to warm-bloodedness, about which I was talking yesterday. It is important for activity around the clock, both the clock of the day and the clock of the year. But in many species this change remains incomplete, for the nestlings are cold-blooded at the time of hatching and will die if not kept warm by the mother for the first few days. It takes those few days for their own warm-bloodedness to establish itself.

The third change was the development of feathers. Feathers apparently are an elaboration of scales, common to reptiles. Birds have scales on their legs and feet, sometimes on their beaks, but elsewhere they are covered with feathers. Nobody knows how the feather evolved, but as we know it today the feather is a remarkable achievement with many different forms, from fluffy insulating down to protective outer feathers and to strong, movable wing feathers for flight. Feathers protect the bird's body, streamline it, and provide the variable wing for flight. The bird's wing is quite different from that of the bat, for instance, and different from that of the prehistoric "flying dragon" from which birds may have evolved. In both the bat and the "flying dragon" the flight foil was a stretched membrane, not a variable member such as a feathered wing.

The fourth major change was in the bird's skeleton. Most of the ancient lizards had heavy bones, necessary to support their huge bulk. The bird's bones are hollow and light in weight, with tubular strength. And the whole body of the bird is designed for muscular strength to drive the wings.

Finally, and in some ways most important of all, the birds achieved bigger brains, relatively, than any of their ancestors. Along with the brains came acute senses, particularly vision and, in many instances, hearing.

FEBRUARY 28

In almost all birds the power of vision is excellent. It is highly developed in some. The kingfisher, for example, has a kind of double vision, one for seeing in the air, the other for seeing under water. Both are combined in the same pair of eyes, and both are acute, thoroughly efficient. Some insects have acute vision, but it is limited in range. The ant, for instance, can see clearly only about three feet and has only about six feet of useful vision. Yet vision probably is the most efficient of all insect senses except the sense of touch.

The bird's eye, like my own and those of all vertebrate animals, is essentially a sphere of transparent membrane filled with liquid. This creates a lens that transmits the image to the optic nerves. Insects and other backboneless animals have compound eyes, a series of small lenses formed from layers of the skin, which focus light on sensitive nerve cells but do not produce any single clear image. Each lens is in effect a single eye, and the creature sees a whole series of somewhat blurred images.

The large, single-lens eye is not new with the birds, but its high development is. And that is part of the whole brain development. This is also shown in the acute sense of hearing in birds. But few birds have much sense of smell or taste. Nor is there any strong sense of touch, generally, among the birds. They have no antennae, like insects, or fingers, like men. Antennae and fingers are peculiarly sensitive to touch.

In most reptiles the brain is very small in relation to the size of the animal, small even in proportion to the size of the skull. In birds it is large. The old epithet, "bird-brained," has no basic truth. A bird's brain is small only in comparison with the brain of a man, not in relation to the bird's own body. And it is the development of this brain, particularly in birds and mammals, that baffles the evolutionists. Nobody knows why the bird family and the mammal family diverged from the original reptile stock, and nobody knows how the brain multiplied in size, or why.

But along with this remarkable brain growth, or perhaps because of it, the birds and mammals developed in their own ways and degrees a whole series of impulses and mental capacities that were unknown to the reptiles. The insects evolved a few parallel instincts, but never achieved the capacity for thought. And that, in the end, is the real measure of the difference—thought.

FEBRUARY 29

This is Leap Day and occurs only once every four years. But it gives me a chance to say a few more things about birds.

Birds have notable skills in flight and song, and they are capable of using those skills to express what must be emotions. When we go out on the river or the lake in a boat on a summer evening and the swallows gather there to feed, they often engage in what must be play. I can find no other explanation for their gyrations, their follow-the-leader tactics and their games of tag. I am sure they are not chasing insects when two or three of them, sometimes half a dozen, come sweeping in toward the boat, usually in line, and spiral and climb and utter peeps that have every aspect of cries of pleasure. I have sat on the bank and watched them and seen no such maneuvers; then I have gone out in the boat and they have staged the aerial circus around the boat, as though showing off just for me. Perhaps I am interpreting too much, but if I am not actually an audience I am some kind of creature of which those swallows are aware and in front of which they play their games.

And I have watched, from indoors and out of sight, the play of blue jays in my apple trees. They, too, play tag, through the tangle of un-trimmed branches. And this happens in the fall of the year, not at mating time. Mating and nesting are then ended for the year. The jays are more self-conscious than the swallows. When I appear, the game ends abruptly. They prefer to play alone.

And as for song, if birdsong were only a kind of elaborate mating call, why should the house wren be so full of song after the fledglings are hatched and gone? The wrens that nest regularly in our big spruce are singing virtually all summer, and their July dawn songs are ecstatic. The same is true of the orioles that nest in our maples. They sing for song itself, or I am no judge of song. So does the brown thrasher which celebrates, morning and evening, from April till mid-August. So does the wood thrush that makes the evenings throb with simple melody.

I am tempted to say that man learned song from the birds, that song expresses emotions common to both even if not quite comparable. But such a statement could be wholly wrong. It may be that the emotions prompted the song in both instances and independently. Perhaps it is best to say only that song is an expression of emotion both in men and in birds. But that requires the further statement that, of all animals, only birds and men have achieved both the emotions and the song to express them. Some mammals other than man, notably the dog and possibly the cat, express both joy and pain with a range of vocal sound; but they have never achieved the full ecstasy of song. We have diverged, the birds and my own kind, a long way from the emotional poverty and the oral limitations of the reptile tribe from which we sprang in the remote past.

I am grateful for that. But most of all I am grateful that somewhere back there along the way the nodes of nerves in our craniums began to grow and complicate, began to evolve into brains that can wonder and wish and learn and remember.

MARCH

MARCH 1

The really important thing about the first few days of March isn't the temperature, or the wind, or the rain or snow, or the clear blue sky—when it is clear and blue. The important thing is the sunlight, almost eleven and a quarter hours of it now between sunrise and sunset. Right there, in that sunlight, are the potentialities, the beginnings, actually, of spring and summer and autumn, of sprouting and growth and ripeness.

I can participate in this only emotionally and through my senses, because I am of a kind that had other beginnings than a seed in the soil, and I will outlast this year's four seasons. But I can and do partake, perhaps out at my nerve-ends or through the soles of my feet, or even through mysterious senses that nobody has yet isolated and named.

I lack roots, I cannot fly on my own wings, and I do not burrow into the earth. But I am a part of something vastly bigger than myself. I am a part of the enduring force, of life itself. And the great surge of life occurs every springtime. It is this that I am made aware of now.

MARCH 2

The grass begins to show signs of life on the sunny side of an old stone wall, a few green shoots reaching up from the brown mat of last year's withered growth. And I think of the way the grasses have helped shape this earth, the everlasting grasses.

A river comes flooding down to the ocean, spate of a March thaw, and drops a load of silt at the river's mouth. Over the years that silt becomes a sandbar. Seeds lodge there and marsh grasses grow and slow up the flow of water, making it drop even more silt. The bar widens, becomes an island. The grasses grow, die, form humus, the substance of fertility. Birds bring seeds in their droppings and bushes take root, then trees. What was first a sandbar, then an island, becomes a barrier at the river's mouth. It creates a marsh. The marsh traps more silt, fills with decaying vegetation, eventually is a new part of the mainland, simply because grass came and took root there.

Wind whips the sand at the shore of an ocean or a big lake, piles it into dunes. The dunes begin to spread inland. A dozen seeds from perhaps ten miles inland are carried there by the wind or on the feet of birds. They sprout, take root, grow. The grass creeps up the side of the dune, slows the wind, and begins to anchor the sand. The blades give it a sparse green cover. The roots begin to form a mat. The grass traps dust. A covering of humus and topsoil is created. What was a dune becomes a grassy hillock and the spread of the dune is ended.

A brook in my pasture rips a gash in the soil in a spring flood. For a few weeks the gash stands raw and open to the weather. Then the grass begins to reach with its roots, down over the face of the flood-torn scar. The roots take hold. New stems rise in the March and April sun. By summer's end the grass has softened and clothed the scar and the new roots have begun to form a new network that will help anchor the soil. It eases the bite of fall rains and the erosion of winter's ice. Another spring and the grass will spread down to the brook's edge. It catches the seeds of mustard and wild geranium and watercress and wild mint. What was a scar becomes a tangle of green and urgent growth that I must watch or it will spread out across the pasture as a new "weed patch." All because grass roots reach out to occupy the vacant soil.

MARCH 3

Give a grass seed a root-hold and it grows, even on a rock. I have seen grass on a ledge where three years earlier there had been nothing but a patch of lichen. The lichen caught drifting dust and formed a film of soil. Moss came and occupied the soil, caught more dust, made more soil. Then a grass seed fell there. It penetrated the soil with its roots, found sustenance, endlessly searched for a crack in that fundamental rock. Rootlets eventually would find a hairline crack, work their way in, fatten, slowly wedge at the rock. Moisture would follow the roots, and frost would find the moisture, turn it to the most powerful, most persistent of nature's small wedges, the ice crystal. The rock would be pried apart. That is the sequence in rocky places—the lichen, the moss, the grass, then a bush, a tree, a crumbling rock. Thus are ledges reduced to rubble, to stones, to gravel, to sand, to silt, to soil that fills the valleys and nurtures the fields of man, the harvests of man's chosen grasses, the cereal grains.

The living habits of grass are, in one sense, much like those of the social insects. Grass grows in communities wherever possible, usually in communities of literally millions of individual plants. Unlike social insects, however, grass makes no division of labor and has no social organization within the colony. Each grass plant is complete unto itself, a unit capable of doing all things necessary to its own processes of successful life. It simply is a plant that colonizes, as trees colonize a woodland. One rarely finds a lone grass plant, and if one does, he may be sure there will be others soon, for grass is prolific. Where one plant can live, more will follow.

Grass spreads in a multitude of ways. Some grasses multiply by underground stems which send up new shoots at every joint. Some multiply by runners above the ground. But most of them spread by seed. Grass seed often is so small that it can easily be carried by the wind. Often grass seed has tiny, buoyant hairs that catch the air currents and ride them surprising distances. Investigators gathering insects and other forms of life from airplanes have trapped grass seed almost a mile above the earth. One grass introduced into Louisiana from South America sixty years ago now is found from Virginia to California, gone wild and spread by its own devices.

MARCH 4

Nearly all plants have a strong capacity for self-renewal, but grass is outstanding in this respect. Break off or cut one stem and another stem will soon rise to take its place. Mow a hayfield and within a week there will be new growth from the shorn grass plants. Even such relatively temperamental annual grasses as our cultivated cereal grains—wheat, barley, oats—will persist in growing and coming to seed if they are cut or grazed off early in the season. Corn, which probably is the furthest removed from its wild sources of all cereal grains, is the least adaptable in this respect, but I have seen field corn eaten partway off by cattle early in its growth still recover and produce a crop of ears.

The wild grasses are notably persistent. I have cut quack grass down to the root repeatedly through the season, and still it sends up a few stalks and comes to its own fruition. One year's damage seldom checks the next year's growth of a perennial wild grass. Even when rooted out by dust storms or apparently killed by overgrazing, the wild grasses try to recover. A few roots remain, or a few seeds, and they send up hopeful shoots at the first favorable chance.

It is this persistence of life and growth that has enabled the grasses to take and hold such large areas of the earth. Every spring I marvel at the urgency of all green things, but I have a never-ending wonder at the vitality of grass, all grasses. Their simplicity of flowering, their toughness of seed, their essentially simple organization of parts, all are remarkable and contribute to their persistence. But it is this indomitable insistence of growing and seeding and multiplying, this indomitable urge to live, that impresses me. The grasses are as ubiquitous as the insects, and they have that same tenacity of being. If one can say that any one form of visible plant life possesses the earth, that plant is grass.

MARCH 5

Living in a dairying area, I have been specially interested in a treatise on "cowes" by Conradus Gesner, a sixteenth-century Swiss zoologist, which I found in *The History of Four-footed Beasts,* published in London in 1658. It says, in part:

> In the choice of Kie, you must observe this direction, you must buy them in the moneth of March, let them be young, not past their first or second calf, their color black or red, seldom brown or white, bright colored, especially red, brown legs, blackish horns smooth and beautiful, high foreheads, great eyes and black, hairy and grisly ears, flat nostrils like an Ape, but open and wide, their back bones bending somewhat backward, black lips, long and thick necks, most broad fair crests descending from the neck, well ribbed, a great belly, the back and shoulders very broad, the buttocks broad, with a long tail hanging down to their heels, and their neather part in many places crisped and curled, well set and connected, legs rough and short, straight knees, and their bunches hanging over; their feet small, not broad but round, standing in good distance one from other, not growing crooked or splay-footed, their hoofs smooth.

Mr. Gesner also has other things to say about Cowes:

> The Cowes of Arabia have the most beautiful horns, by reason of abundance of humours which flow to them, feeding them continu-

ally with such generous liquor as naturally doth encreate them. . . .
The principal benefit of Cowes Milk is for making Butter, for the
Milk itself, the Cheese and Whey, are not fit for the nourishment
of Man, as are those of sheep. . . .

It is reported as a wonder of nature, of the rivers Milchus and
Chardeus, running through the city of Patrae that all the Kie which
drink of them in the spring time do for the most part bring forth
males, wherefore herdsmen avoid those places at that time. . . .

These beasts are very lustful and do most eagerly desire the company of their male, which if they not have within the space of three
hours after they mourn for it, their lust asswageth till another time.
In a village in Egypt called Shussa they worship Venus under the
title Urania in the shape of a Cowe, perswading themselves that
there is a great affinity between the Goddesse and this beast; for by
her mournful voice she giveth notice of her love, who receiveth the
token many times a mile or two off, and so runneth to accomplish
the lust of nature; and for this cause the Egyptians picture Isis with
a Cowe's horns. . . .

The Pyrrhean Kie . . . do give at one time seven or eight gallons
of Milk, of Wine measure, and they are so tall that the person
which milketh them must stand upright, or else stoop very little;
neither ought this seem incredible for it is evident that the Cowes
of Phonesians were so high that a very tall man could not milk them
except he stood on a footstool.

MARCH 6

In the book from which I quoted yesterday is a long section on the
Horse, and toward the end is a discussion of "the medifines arifing out of
Horfes." (Throughout the book the long "s" is used, incidentally; I have
modernized it in my quotations.) Here, then, are a few notes about the
place of the horse in sixteenth-century medicine:

We do also find that the flesh of the Horse, being well boiled, is
very medicinable for divers diseases. Moreover, it is very usuall and
common with the women of Occitania to take the fat or grease of
Horses to annoint their heads to make the hair multiply and increase;
and certain later Physicians do mingle the marrow of a Horse with
other ointments for a remedy against the Cramp. . . .

The teeth of a male horse not gelded, or by any other labour
made feeble, being put under the head, or over the head of him

that is troubled or starteth in his dreams, do withstand and resist all unquietness which in time of his rest might happen unto him. . . . The teeth also of a Horse is very profitable for the curing of Chill-blanes which are rotten and full of corruption when they are swollen full ripe. . . . If a childe do kiss the nose of a Horse, he shall never feel pain in his teeth, neither at any time shall he be bitten by the Horse.

If you anoint a comb with the foam of a Horse, wherewith a young man doth use to comb his head, it is of such force as it will cause the hair of his head neither to decrease nor any white to appear. The foam of a Horse is also much commended for them that have either pain or difficulty of hearing in their ears, or else the dust of Horse dung being new made and dryed, and mingled with Oyl of Roses. The grief or soreness of a man's mouth or throat, being washed or annointed with the foam of a Horse that hath been fed with Oates or Barley, doth presently expell the pain of the soreness if so be that it be two or three times washed over with the juice of young or green Sea-crabs beaten small together; . . . The foam of a Horse, being three or four times taken in drink, doth quite ex-pell and drive away the cough, or consumption of the lungs. The same being also mingled with hot water and given to one who is troubled with the same disease, being in manner past all cure, doth presently procure health, but the death of the horse doth instantly ensue.

I grew up with horses, but this is the first time I ever heard such stories. Offhand, I would rather have the herb doctors tend me.

MARCH 7

There is a faint stirring of life in the small bogland just down the road. Out of that stirring will come full-blown spring, then summer: bud, blossom, and seed; egg, nestling, and bird; caterpillar, pupa, and butter-fly. In a way, the history of this earth and the life upon it will be recapitulated, but with all of today's life here and in being. Actually, of course, that life has been evolving for millions of years. The earliest life we know of today seems to have been that anomalous one-celled entity that could have been either plant or animal. From that earliest form of life evolved, more or less in succession, seaweed, sponges, small worms, shellfish, primitive fish with backbones, early amphibians, and insects. From the amphibians came the first reptiles, and after them came the dinosaurs and their kind. By the end of their age, birds and early mammals had appeared. Finally, perhaps two million years ago, perhaps three million, man appeared.

Not all this, of course, is going to happen down in that small bog this spring. I don't expect to see dinosaurs there, and I am quite sure there will be no Neanderthal men. But the feeling of potentiality, of all things possible, of limitless scope of change that has already marked life, is inescapable. And I have a feeling of strangeness there. In a sense, I and all my own kind are still strangers here, newcomers trying to fit ourselves into this environment, learning to live with our own kind and all the other forms of life around us. Slowly learning, very slowly. Our tenure here is unpredictable, and even while we are here our life depends on a thousand variable conditions which really are beyond our own control.

MARCH 8

Each spring when I watch the renewal of life after the time of winter rest I realize once more that life as we know it and participate in it is a consequence of many balances and compromises. The spring we see is evidence of the effect of these conditions, but the basic facts of the season we call spring are few and simple. Spring comes when there is a rise of a few degrees in the average temperature from one week to the next, when there are a few more minutes of daylight than of darkness, and when the angle of sunlight shifts a fraction of a degree. These things are a result of certain predictable movements in the planetary system to which the earth belongs. They are a part of a cosmic rhythm that apparently governs every planetary system we have yet discovered in the remoteness of space. Reviving life, as we see it in the form of opening buds, growing stems, nesting birds, birthing animals and blossoming flowers, depends on these essentially minor changes, which are so slight that we would be unaware of them, certainly unaware of day-to-day change, if there were not a response in all the forms of life around us.

Man has nothing to do with these conditions. They were here and they governed life long before man appeared, and they undoubtedly will be here for a long time to come, whether man is or not. The best man can do is chart spring astronomically, then cooperate with it when it comes. Of all the machines ingenious man has invented, not one can create a living flower. We can incubate birds, we can artificially inseminate cows and even our own women, we can force buds into bloom, we can grow lettuce and tomatoes in a greenhouse. But in every instance we have to start with a natural germ of life, and we must abide by basic rules that have governed natural reproduction and growth since far back in the unknown past. Man cannot change the rules.

MARCH 9

I think of spring as a beginning only because the human mind and habit tend that way. Human creatures like to count. They like matters to be neatly parceled, with beginnings and endings. That is one reason we devised the calendar and invented the clock, and one reason we call sundown the end of the day and sunrise the beginning. But few matters have such neat beginnings and endings. There is a continuance, a progression, or at least a continuity. Spring is a quickening, but it is no more a beginning than is high noon or mid-July. It is only another aspect of that which is continuous.

There are, to be sure, annual plants and seasonal insects as well as those that live on from year to year. But annual plants grow from seeds, and the insects come from some egg form. The seeds and the eggs are no more than capsulated life carried over from one generation to the next. Somewhere along the path of evolution those plants and those insects found it would be more advantageous to entrust their precious germ of life to an egg or a dormant seed than to try to hoard it in a root or a body over the winter. There are also such plants as the bristle-cone pines of California that have lived as growing trees for at least 4,600 years. And there are periodic locusts that live in the ground as grubs fifteen years or more before they emerge, acquire wings, eat, mate, create a din, lay eggs, and die, all within an adult life of only a few weeks. They merely prove that spring is but one point in the vastly larger rhythm of life and time.

Spring happens to be the obvious time, the season of spectacular change, of growth and flowering and hatching and birthing in a multitude of ways, since life is almost infinitely varied. We see life burgeoning. We are made aware of life and sometimes we celebrate its existence. More often we merely celebrate our own existence and indulge our pride in being what we call a superior form of life.

MARCH 10

We had a couple of robins out in the side yard today, and just the sight of them warmed up the whole day. They weren't migrants. The migrant flocks haven't yet returned from the South, though they could arrive almost any day now. These two were from the small flock, no more than eight or ten, that wintered here. I saw them from time to time in the small bog down the road, and several times two or three of them came up here on a mild day to poke around in the bare grass under the big Norway spruce and in the circle out there where the septic tank is situated. That circle is a kind of hot-bed, warmed by water from sink and bathtub, and crocuses appear there two weeks before they show up anywhere else.

When those robins appear here in January it only makes the day seem even colder, somehow. Maybe I shiver for the birds. But in March there is something about a robin that denotes spring.

MARCH 11

The trees are slowly, persistently working toward leaf and blossom. Maple sap began to flow more than two weeks ago, and the syrup-makers have been busy. There is yet no maple leaf or blossom in sight. It will be late April before they shed their bud scales and the first maple blossoms of the year will appear, to give the lowlands a vivid coat of rouge first, then to make the upland maples look almost lacy with their greenish yellow tassels.

Every year when this happens I am once more aware of my kinship with all living things. The compulsion for life which animates the world around me created humanity as a species. We all have a kind of racial desire to live. Leave purpose to the theologians, if you wish; you still must face the biological fact. There it is, something more than this animate compulsion in man, something that has endowed my species with powers of reason and emotion, thought and speculation. As much a part of man as his powers of vision and locomotion is his impulse to create; and I speak not only of procreation, so much a part of all animal life in the vernal season. I speak of that rarer impulse, the impulse to think, to build, to record, not for oneself alone or for now, but for others unborn, for tomorrow.

This attribute apparently is unique in man. The bear marks a tree with his claws, only to prove his existence here and now, not to impress future generations. The wild mother, mink or robin, feeds her young that they may survive, not as extensions of herself but as individuals; and she does it by instinct, not by reason or by social pressure. But man creates his works and sets down his records at least in part because he hopes that life may be easier or better or more purposeful for his own kind after he is gone. Whether he succeeds in his purpose or not is beside the point, which is the innate aspiration of the species. And those who call this pointless and futile are the exception to the race thought, the race impulse, the racial compulsion. They are at war with their own kind and they deny their own racial inheritance.

Two things mark humanity as a species to me: this impulse to build and perpetuate and improve, and the emotional quality we know as compassion. The ironic thing is that among my own race the most pessimistic of the intellectuals recognize these impulses and yet belittle them. They, like the damnation-crying theologians, are a product of this peculiar human possession, yet they refuse to accept its big implications.

Maybe the trees are better off. They have neither preachers nor philosophers.

MARCH 12

Trees as we know them came relatively late in the scale of living time. There were vast forests of big trees in the Carboniferous period, 300 million years ago, but they were mostly tree ferns, alien and exotic to man and now known only in fossils. The early conifers, ancestors of my pines and hemlocks, did not appear in abundance until about 200 million years ago. And it was not until about 100 million years ago that recognizable ancestors of my modern maples, elms, hickories, sycamores, willows, and birches were here. The flowering plants, including most of today's trees, were first numerous enough to leave a substantial fossil record in the Cretaceous period, which began about 120 million years ago. That was the recognizable beginning of the forests of today.

Botanists group plant families according to similarities in essential elements of their physical structures, and a good many of these families include trees, shrubs, and lesser flowering plants. The rose family, for instance, includes the wild rose in my fencerow, the wild strawberry, the cinquefoil, and the meadowsweet with the pinkish plume. And the pulse family, in botanical terms, includes the garden peas we eat, the clover in my pastures, the vetch at the roadside, and the locust trees that make a thorny tangle up on the mountainside.

MARCH 13

In terms of the big spans, it was the primitive trees that made possible the kind of life man knows today. There is no need here to speculate on whether primitive man originated in the forests as an arboreal animal. No doubt the ancient forests provided shelter for primitive mammals, but man's particular phase of evolution is a little too misty to relate to the trees. The point I make here is that trees were the original substance of all the coal beds, and what we call civilization, the age of the machines, was built on the latent heat in coal, the stored carbon energy of those Paleozoic forests. Man started on the path toward power-driven machines when he first found that coal would burn with more intense and more enduring heat than a billet of wood.

But along the way toward the Power Age, man was sheltered and comforted by the trees. Whether he went from the trees to the caves or not back at his beginnings, he eventually went from the caves to the woodlands. Trees provided him with roof and walls. They gave him his first raft, his first boat, eventually the ships in which he roamed the rivers and shallow seas. The trees provided his weapons, the club, the lance, the bow, the arrow. Its resins and other juices gave him medicines and glue and crude chemicals. Bark clothed him and gave him cordage. Sap provided syrup, nuts provided oil, the flesh of fruit fed him. Man never was in dire need as long as he intimately knew the forests. And when he deserted the woods they still gave him the materials with which to build his villages, towns, and cities.

MARCH 14

The most primitive of all existing trees are the cycads, of which the best known of America's four species is the sago palm. The ginkgo tree, now native only to China but grown here as an ornamental, possibly is older than the sago palm, but it probably changed more in structure than the cycads over the eons since its beginning.

Next after the cycads and the ginkgo came the conifers—the pines and all their kind. They inherited the cooler regions of this earth. Only one among them, the tamarack, adopted the deciduous habit of shedding its leaves each autumn. The others cling to most of their leaves the year around. But all conifer leaves have been reduced to—or never advanced beyond—the familiar needle shape. The very earliest trees had scalelike leaves, something like the scale leaves on today's cedars, and apparently these were adapted into such leaves as the long, thin needles on my white pines.

After the conifers came those trees that bear catkins, though the post-conifer sequence is not certain. The willows, the poplars, and the birches are among the catkin-bearers. Sometimes the catkins are bisexual, having both male and female organs. Sometimes they are unisexual, producing either pollen or seeds but not both. In some species there are trees that bear only male catkins and other trees that bear only female catkins. The similarity of the catkin to the cone is not too obscure. I see it most pronounced in the alder bushes that grow in the lowlands. The alder's seed catkin, the female, looks much like the small hemlock cone when it is ripe with seed.

After the first catkin-bearer, though the span may have been relatively brief, came most of the fruiting trees, those with true blossoms. Among them are the maples, the oaks, the hickories, the lindens, the whole rose family of apples, peaches, plums, cherries, etc. Most of the true flowering trees were in existence about 100 million years ago. Virtually all of them were here by the beginning of the Tertiary period about 60 million years ago. These dates are significant primarily in relation to man. One of the earliest dates given for primitive man's appearance has been two million years ago, and more often the figure is given as one million. In either case, trees were well established, were very old in fact, before man appeared on the scene.

MARCH 15

This is the famous, or infamous, Ides of March, the day when Julius Caesar was assassinated in 44 B.C. The Ides was one of three days used each month in calculating the date in the early Julian calendar. The other two were the Kalends and the Nones. The Kalends always fell on the first day of the month. The Nones and the Ides varied from month to month. In March, May, July, and October the Nones fell on the 7th and the Ides on the 15th. In the other months the Nones fell on the 5th and the Ides on the 13th. Dates were calculated as so-and-so many days before the Kalends, the Nones, or the Ides; or they fell on one of those calculation days, as the well-remembered Ides of March.

This is also a day when I look for violets. It is a tradition in our house that there are violets for the lady. So I go and look, and I never find them where the violets grow and bloom in great profusion a month from now. So I go to the florist's and find them. The florist knows there must be violets and provides them, year after year, on this day.

MARCH 16

Forests essentially the same as those man has always known were here when the great Ice Ages came. It is a tribute to the tenacity of the conifers that they persisted through those cold centuries, for the ice sheared off millions of them in the series of glacial advances from the north. Conifers seem always to have preferred the colder regions of the earth, so they were the first trees in the path of the advancing ice. But somehow the conifers did persist, and so did all the other trees we know today. They learned to grow in an altered climate, and each time the ice retreated, the trees enlarged their range again. Life, all life, both plant and animal, ebbs and flows with the conditions, and even plant life moves from place to place. Slow growth and lack of legs with which to run may impede the movement of trees, but they migrate just the same. I have but to look at the constant encroachment of brush and trees on any abandoned farm field or pasture to know the persistent truth of this.

When, at last, the great ice sheets melted back and did not return, the trees followed the ice northward. They had new land to conquer, a wholly different aspect of hill and valley. Most of the ice-scarred land was stripped of topsoil. The New England where I live was a desolate place, a landscape of shorn rock and vast heaps of glacial debris, threaded by rushing streams carrying silt-laden ice melt down to the oceans.

The scars of those times remain today here on my own acres. Perhaps 15,000 years of insistent, benevolent growth have clothed the rocks somewhat with soil, and the valleys are silted in many places and rich with plant-grown loam. But the topsoil is thin. In geological terms, there has been little time for the trees to mellow the land. My own valley is filled with silt and that silt has an overlying layer of natural humus. That is what gives it its fertility. But if I dig down only a foot or so into this valley soil I come to sand with only the slightest trace of humus. In all those centuries, the trees and lesser plants have laid down only a few inches of organic matter over sands that date back to the Ice Ages.

When ecologists and conservationists talk about waste and spoliation of the soil, that is what they are talking about—those relatively few inches of topsoil. In the Midwest, which was formed by the silting-up of vast, shallow seas, the topsoil is several feet deep. Even there it has been washed and eroded, allowed to go down the vast floodwaters of the Mississippi and its tributaries. But it is that layer of topsoil, whether it is inches deep or feet deep, that supports the green life of this earth. That makes all animal life possible, actually, yours, mine, and every cow and deer and fox and dog and weasel and mouse.

MARCH 17

When the first white men came to America, they found a land of trees. Old records show that the Hudson Valley when Henry Hudson first saw it was one vast stand of towering white pines. Most of the early settlements of New England were hemmed in close to the shore by the forests, dark and forbidding, the people said. By that time much of England and western Europe was an old land with few virgin forests. But the legends persisted. Deep woods were full of terrors and danger.

The conquest of America was accompanied and even paced by the rhythm of the ax. For years the sky of the near frontier was darkened by the smoke from burning trees. At the very best, the trees were a nuisance to the farmer. He girdled them, killed them, cut them, burned them, that he might plow the land. Wood, for lumber or for fuel, was anyone's for the taking, and the game that lived on the woodland margin—the deep woods were seldom the place to find game animals—provided a community larder. But the forests had to go before the settlers could possess the land, and that was their deep, determined purpose. Only the fugitive and the frontiersman, the leather-clad hunter and trapper, ever made peace with the trees.

MARCH 18

The forests dictated the early pattern of settlement, not only here but all over the world. The first farmers lived in villages, and those villages were in natural clearings beside the streams. They only slowly and cautiously extended their farmlands, wresting them acre by acre from the forests. And when the farmer finally cleared a field beyond sight of the village and went there to live, he was a man of courage and remarkable independence. But he set his house in the midst of a clearing and he extended that clearing as swiftly as ax and fire could do it. He seldom regarded the forest as anything but his enemy.

I can remember my own grandfather's words, the first time he saw the Great Plains with their horizon-wide treelessness. "A man could plow a furrow here a mile long," he said, "and never have to go around a tree or a stump." He said it in awe. He had spent all his life till then in timbered country, fighting trees and stumps. And he had spent that life in Missouri and Nebraska, 1,500 miles from the Atlantic Coast. In my great-grandfather's day there had been forest all that distance, interrupted only by a scattering of farms and towns carved out of the woodland.

It is difficult today to understand this warfare between man and trees, yet in essence it has been nothing more than an example of the eternal competition among living things for living space. As long as man remained a primitive creature he could dwell in relative peace with the trees, occupying a kind of niche in the habitat, which is nature's lot for most animals. But when man began to multiply and insist on having more living space, when he tamed grasses and created field crops, the woodlands became his enemy. There could be a truce with the trees only when man had asserted his dominance over whatever land he thought he needed. He was no longer content with his niche in the forest. And as mankind proliferated and his way of life became more and more complex, the very simplicity and the basic insistence of trees had to be brought under man's control. Whatever truce was reached had to be on man's terms.

Man had begun to dominate the environment. He had dreamed the dream of omnipotence.

MARCH 19

I live in a house built of lumber cut on my own mountainside. Yet that mountainside still is a timbered place. The old stumps are all surrounded by middle-aged trees, self-sown. Even in the dry grassland of the Great Plains where I grew up there were a few cottonwoods and a few stunted willows in the valleys where water flowed from time to time. Now and then one of the cottonwoods was felled by lightning, but always there were new seedlings to take its place, and at least one of them seemed always to survive.

The first tree grew out of the primeval muck at least 300 million years ago, a new adventure in plant life. Animals came and went. Species vanished. Eventually man appeared. And the trees persisted. Without arms or legs or brains or eyes or ears, they still persist. And richly endowed man still has achieved no real victory over the trees. The best he has been able to do is arrive at an armistice with the forest, keep it away from the door of his house; but it is an uneasy truce that will end ten minutes after man goes away. The trees will win in the end.

MARCH 20

This is the day of the vernal equinox when, according to astronomical calculations, winter ends and spring begins. But the seasons down here on the ground follow only approximately the seasons in the almanac. There have been times when the equinox found us, here in this valley, with a foot of snow still on the ground. There have been other times when the red-wing blackbirds were celebrating their return to the trees along the river and I was out in my shirtsleeves cleaning up some of the winter's trash and litter.

But I never yet have seen an equinox when there wasn't some sign of spring. Even with snow on the ground, the maple sap is almost sure to be flowing. If there is no snow, I often can find the white-veined leaves of crocuses and sometimes even open crocus blossoms. And the pasture brook that cuts across the corner of the vegetable garden is always flowing by now and usually has a touch of green on its banks, the first grass and the first leaves of winter cress.

When I watched the sun rise this morning, due east, I felt that the universe, the solar system, the earth, the year, the season, the day, were all in order, no matter what stupidities man might achieve today. It is good to know such things about the place you live. It is good to know that there are certainties.

MARCH 21

The frost is out of the ground and the soil looks as though it had been sprinkled and then fluffed. Frost does that to soil. I had to go out this morning and pick up a handful from the garden, just to feel its grit and strength. And when I drove to the village I saw my neighbor down the road out in his field scuffing with his heel and picking up a handful, just as I did. It is that time of year when a man must renew contact with the source of all growing things, even though he knows it won't be planting time for another three weeks.

In that soil is the food of life, all life, waiting only for the warmth of sun, the moisture of rain, the planting of seeds. Then it will produce again the miracle of growth and ripeness. There is something eternal about the soil, eternal and yet perennially eager.

It was not by chance that somewhere in all folklore is the tale of how the first man was created from the soil of the earth. The ancients, even though they were hunters and herdsmen, knew the soil and knew it as the great source. It was Mother Earth, and Mother Earth it still is, no matter how far down the road of science and rationality we travel. It is our yearning and instinct to touch it now and hold it in our hand. And when the time comes, we shall bow down to it as we plant.

MARCH 22

It was a mild morning and out on the front porch, where the sun was making it feel like late April, I saw a spider spinning a web. I watched for ten minutes, fascinated, aware of that vast, unbridgeable gap between us. We both participate in that great common inheritance, life; but our kinship is so remote and so strange that I have difficulty understanding its occasional parallels. Some of those parallels even rouse a kind of resentment in me, in large part because there is so little of what I call "feeling" in that whole vast world of spiders and insects. The skills of a spider, an ant, a bee, or a wasp are amazing, and the social organization of bees and wasps is grimly efficient; but their kind of mental activity and their range of emotions, if they really are emotions and not mere reflexes, are so wholly different from mine and those of the other animals I know that we live in almost totally different worlds.

Yet we share this earth, those other creatures and my own kind, and we share this common heritage, life. We are, both of us, breathers of air, we eat and digest food, we multiply, and our kinds persist. We belong to the same brotherhood of living things.

But the spiders and insects, in their line of evolution, went one way, and my kind went another. They long ago perfected a way of life concentrated on one object alone, perpetuation of the species. Apparently they did this by perfecting certain instincts and suppressing others. And somehow their brains never developed far beyond the capacity needed for survival. Long ago they learned the necessary techniques for their kind of life and never advanced beyond that.

MARCH 23

This world I know is more populated by insects and other small exoskeletal creatures—animals with their entire skeleton outside rather than inside the body—than by any other form of visible animal life. Some naturalists put the number of insect species at more than 600,000, ten or fifteen times the number of known species of fish, amphibians, reptiles, birds, and mammals combined. Others put the number still higher, around 750,000. The total number of individual insects, of all species, is beyond even rough estimate.

Scientists make clear distinctions between insects and members of the spider family. An insect is an air-breathing animal with three body parts, head, thorax, and abdomen, one pair of antennae, and six legs. A spider is an air-breathing creature with only two body parts, a cephalothorax and an abdomen, no antennae and eight legs.

Spiders are arachnids, a Greek term meaning spiderlike creatures. They are even older than the amphibians. Fossil evidence indicates that they were here close to a million years before the first backboned creature crawled out onto the land and learned to live at least part of its life out of the water. The oldest fossils of spiders, scorpions, and harvestmen, or daddy longlegs, date back approximately 300 million years. Fossil bees and ants date back only about 150 million years.

Nobody knows precisely what was the origin of either insects or the spider family. The supposition is that they diverged, many millions of years ago, from some early form of aquatic life. Theories about their beginnings reach back to various forms of shellfish, most of them small and most of them having a larval stage in their development. There is speculation that insect wings evolved from external gills in a very early ancestor, but nobody knows.

There is one strong clue to the origin of the spider family. That is the creature we know as the king or horseshoe crab. It is not a crab. It is an arachnid, closely related to the scorpion, and it is a kind of living fossil. It exists today in almost exactly the same form it existed, by fossil evidence, close to 200 million years ago. There is strong evidence that it was at least one of the links between the marine creatures and the whole spider family. Where the change came, however, and when and how, are enduring mysteries.

MARCH 24

To the experts it may be a dubious clue, but to me there is a strange coincidence in the fact that spiders, insects, and crustaceans all have shells or external skeletons composed of the same substance—chitin. And chitin occurs nowhere else in nature except, of all places, in a member of the plant world, a certain fungus.

Chitin is an amorphous, horny substance that looks and feels something like my own fingernails. Chemically it is not like either my fingernails or any animal's horns. It is simply chitin, a tough substance composed chemically of carbon, hydrogen, nitrogen, and oxygen. It forms the claws of lobsters that I crack to reach the meat inside. It is the substance of the shrimp's papery shell. It is the beetle's many-colored shell. It is even the fragile outer skeleton of the housefly, the mosquito—and the spider.

MARCH 25

The bodily structure of a spider is so efficient, so near perfection for its purpose, that one must admire it. It is also so complex and so fully equipped with specialized organs that one would think it was the result of long evolution. Yet the earliest fossil spiders and scorpions show substantially the same perfection of organization we find in living spiders and scorpions today.

The spider has eight eyes situated in the upper front of its head. It has a pair of palps on the under surface of the head, a kind of combination of fingers and jaws. It has a lung with sheets of lung tissue like pages in a book; they open and close as air is drawn in through an opening in the abdomen. It has a heart which circulates very pale blue blood, almost colorless; its faint color comes from copper in the blood rather than the iron which makes my own blood red. It has glands called spinnerets through which a liquid is secreted to form the familiar spider silk. And any one of its eight legs, each seven-jointed, can be sacrificed without injury to the spider. The lobster, too, can sacrifice a leg without injury, and like the spider it will eventually grow a new leg or a new joint of a leg to replace a lost one.

Spiders come in all sizes, from that of a pinhead to that of a dinner plate. And, despite their seeming awkwardness, spiders are swift on their feet. They can run, comparative size considered, about five times as fast as a human sprinter. They have an acute sense of touch, apparently in the hairs on the body and in the palps on the head. No one knows whether they can hear or not, but it is supposed that they feel vibrations through the body hairs and thus have an equivalent of a sense of hearing. They probably have a sense of smell. And they definitely have a sense of taste.

The spider's brain is not much more than a nerve center, and there seems little doubt that no spider has more than a glimmering of intelligence. Kept in captivity, spiders will learn to come toward the person who feeds them, but this appears to be only a conditioned reflex. It would indicate some degree of memory, perhaps, but it is no proof at all of rational intelligence. There is no such proof, so the conclusion is that spiders do not think.

MARCH 26

The spider's accomplishments are quite remarkable, but I wonder at the use of that word "accomplishments." An accomplishment, to me, implies conscious purpose and a degree of planning. That comes close to intelligence. So I shall amend the statement. I shall say that a spider can do remarkable things. I am convinced that most of those things are done by instinct because young spiders as well as old ones can do them, and there is no training of the young by their parents.

A spider, for instance, can spin a silken line 1/250-thousandth of an inch in diameter. Such a line is stronger than a steel wire of the same diameter. Baby spiders, fresh from the cocoon, spin such lines a few feet long, use them as sails and parachutes, and ride the breeze for surprising distances. Spiders so borne have been found five miles above the earth, and they have been found two hundred miles at sea. That apparently is the way they have traveled all over the earth, for they are found not only in the tropics and the temperate zones but well up inside the Arctic Circle and 22,000 feet up on Mount Everest.

The spider uses this silk in many different ways. It makes webs in which to trap insects for food. It makes trapdoors of silk to protect underground nests. It weaves cocoons in which its eggs are protected until they hatch. It weaves waterproof cages in which it can live under water.

The orb spiders, those which weave the beautiful webs that deck the weeds and grass near my house and seem to be studded with pearls on a misty morning, have long been credited with well-developed mathematical skills. Actually, even the best orb-spider web is a rather haphazard piece of construction, mathematically speaking. The foundation lines form a quadrangle, usually, but they never are a perfect square or even a perfect parallelogram. And the cross lines, the spokes or radii, never have equal angles at the center. No spider has yet qualified as a mathematician, or even an elementary geometrician. Instinct tells them to make webs and how, in a rather specific way, to build them. But that instinct does not know how to count or how to measure an angle. And the orb spiders are the only ones whose instinct tells them to make a superficially symmetrical web. The webs of most other spiders are random masses of silk, more like a tangle of thread than a designed structure.

MARCH 27

Spiders have no social instinct. They do not even live or travel in pairs. Their mating processes are peculiar, almost unique. The male spider excretes his seminal fluid, takes it up in one of his palps, and seeks a female. Sometimes he performs a kind of courtship dance, but on other occasions he approaches the prospective mate with stealth. There is no evidence of anything like affection between them. The male impregnates the female with his sperm-laden palp. And sometimes, but not always, the female thereupon kills and eats the male. In any case, there is no further association between the male and female.

After mating, the female spins silk and shapes a cocoon in which she lays her eggs. The number may vary from a few to several thousand. The black widow spider sometimes lays only twenty-five at a time, and she sometimes stuffs a cocoon with as many as nine hundred; and the black widow may produce nine cocoons of eggs in a season. Spiders make sure they leave a new generation behind them.

The eggs hatch in a week or so—black widow eggs take ten to fourteen days. In most species the hatchlings remain in the cocoon at least a week, sometimes six weeks, eating leftover food from the eggs from which they were hatched. Then they leave the cocoon, miniature spiders but already equipped with a full set of instincts and organs, everything they need for spider life except sex glands. They begin to grow and molt, shedding their constricting chitin skin from time to time and growing a new one. Black widow males are sexually mature after five molts, females after seven or eight. But before the second molt most spiders spin a silken line and launch themselves on a breeze, airborne on their way to a new home.

Nobody tells the spiderling when to leave the cocoon. Nobody tells it what to eat, when to molt, how to spin a thread of silk, or what to do with that thread. Nobody teaches a young orb spider to weave a web or any spider how to shape an egg cocoon. They know these things, instinctively, as a hatchling fish knows how to swim. And they know how to kill an insect with their poison fangs, how to hide from enemies. But they don't know how to think, and to the best of our knowledge they know neither happiness nor sorrow.

A spider, in other words, is a completely efficient small machine endowed with a spark of life. It is such a machine from the time it hatches from the egg, needing no instruction, complete with all necessary instincts and reflexes. In some way, it is aware of being alive. It has hungers and it has the instinct to mate and multiply. It has no awareness of death. It has little awareness of others of its own kind, apparently, except as rivals for food. It may have eaten other spiderlings in the cocoon before it emerged—many kinds of spiders are cannibalistic from the time of hatching.

MARCH 28

I can explain the spider by saying nature has an infinite variety of life forms and that each one is, in its own time and place, sufficient unto itself. But that does not answer a persistent question: Why, then, has there been the kind of change that eventually created my own kind, man? If spiders were a satisfactory form of life 250 million years ago, why weren't fish satisfactory? True, fish are still fish, but some of those ancient fish became amphibians, and amphibians became reptiles, and reptiles became birds and mammals. Change persisted. But not for spiders.

The scorpion, for instance, is only a step or two, broadly speaking, from the horseshoe crab. The harvestman is little more than an awkward, long-legged spider. None of them traveled far on the road of change, and they have traveled virtually no distance at all in many million years. There they are, a family of creatures that achieved a form and a way of life that was, for them, sufficient. They achieved it early, and the forces of change passed them by.

The arachnids, the spider family, participate in this common inheritance, life, as I said earlier. But they are not even remotely of my own kind. Except that they move about and eat only organic matter, which makes them a part of the animal kingdom, they are almost as remote from me as the weeds in my garden. Yet they are closer kin than the thistle or the pigweed, for they *are* animals, and so am I.

MARCH 29

Whatever adaptation the arachnids have made seems to have been in the slow process of what we call natural selection. Those best fitted to survive in a certain environment have survived and multiplied. If large size was important, the large ones grew larger until they reached the maximum size tolerated by their environment. If minuteness was called for by some special environment, the small ones became still smaller. All without subjective plan or knowing. And always, apparently, the ratio of brain to body, of capacity for thought, remained at the minimum needed to carry out the orders of inherent impulses and reflexes.

The spider clan has its place in the complex organization of this world's life, and it clings firmly to that place. Without the spiders there would be an immediate upset in the balance that is so persistent and, at times, so baffling to man. Some spiders catch fish, some live on birds and small mice, but for the most part they live on insects, which are closer kin to them than any other living creatures. But both spiders and insects live in a world that is enduringly strange to man. They surround us, they outnumber us beyond calculation, they are in terms of life itself related to us. But they remain alien, mysterious in origin and understandable only as themselves, not as links or even as theoretical changelings in the big chain of life that stretches so far back in time.

MARCH 30

Spring is here! I heard the peepers this afternoon, down at the little bog at the bend in the road. It has been mild the past few days, the temperature up to fifty both yesterday and today. That is what it takes to rouse the spring peepers from hibernation. They work their way up out of the mud, crawl up on an old cattail stem or into a red-osier dogwood bush at the edge of the muck, dry off and warm their blood in the sun, and begin to call. It chilled off this evening and they stopped, but if it is mild tomorrow they will be at it again, that shrill call that is a combination of life celebrated and sex urgent. It is both a mating call and a cry of triumph. Or so it seems to me. Anything that can spend the winter down in that muck and emerge alive and eager deserves to be calling triumph.

The red-wing blackbirds are here, too. And there was a big flock of migrant robins out in our home pasture this morning. Everything seems to be happening at once. Crocuses are in bloom. Bees are out and making a great to-do over the pollen in the crocuses. Daffodils are up and showing buds, especially the greenish double ones that seem to be the earliest of all we have, both early and very hardy. They were here twenty years ago when we came, and I have divided and transplanted them a dozen times. Now most of them are across the road on the riverbank, and they make a fine showing there, early.

MARCH 31

The silence has ended, with the peepers calling, the robins and black-birds singing, if you can call a red-wing blackbird's notes anything like a song. It was a long silence. It began with the last rough scratch of the last katydid out in the back yard. It progressed with the crisp rustle of leaves in the road when the winds of November began to pick up speed. It became even more noticeable when the owls hooted in the deep night, and when the foxes barked. And by late December the hush was so complete that I could hear snowflakes nudging each other in a kind of whispery lisp as they fell.

Now even the brook chatters at night, in the little waterfall across the home pasture from the house. I lie and listen to it, and know that the winter's ice is still seeping out of the ground up on the mountain.

But no insect voices yet. Few insects, for that matter. The robins have to search to find any. The first big insect hatch comes just when the first hatch of nestlings open their mouths and demand that the parent birds stuff them. Thus does nature provide—newly hatched birds need the rich diet of insects to grow properly. Without the insects the birds would starve. Without the birds, the insects would eat us alive. Where-fore I thank every god in nature for the sound of birdsong. May it never diminish!

APRIL

APRIL 1

The world is full of beginnings now, and beginnings are often more interesting, sometimes even more important, than what follows. The vernal change has started. The color will return, the bright pennants of spring, the blossoms of a fresh, new world.

But the great change comes now, before the full flowering. Now is the deep wonder, for the bud itself is the miracle. To watch the upthrust of a daffodil, to see it take form as a flower-to-be, to see the bud grow and take on the warmth of color—there is the very synthesis of spring. But once open, it is a flower, color, perfected beauty; and once open it begins to fade, imperceptibly but also inevitably.

Thus it is with a bud, all buds. Spring is there in the flower within the bud, but the miracle is in the beginning, the way that bud opens. You see a birch on the hillside, its buds fat against the sky. You watch the slow deliberation as it comes to that moment when the first pale leaf-tips appear, when the tree stands in all the delicacy of April's green mist, no longer in bud, not yet fully in leaf. Or the way bloodroot comes to flower, opening that fat green bud. Or the way a violet lifts its buds for the sunlight to warm and slowly unfold. That, to me, is April, the swelling bud, the beginning.

Today I went up and saw April among the birches.

APRIL 2

The bees are specially busy now, hungry after the chilly, changeable days of March and eager for any pollen they can find. They swarm at the crocuses, which still are in full bloom, and they buzz around the daffodils, even those in tight bud.

Only four kinds of animals, as far as we know, ever learned to fly—the insects, the now extinct flying lizards, the bats, and the birds. The insects were the first to take wing, before any of the others even existed. Quite possibly the power of flight enabled them to persist through thousands of centuries, for it made them able to escape earthbound enemies. Fossil insects almost 200 million years old have been found, and among the most ancient insect fossils are wings with no traces of the bodies that bore them.

Insects seem to have changed little over the eons. Many fossil insects are almost identical with those we know today, particularly cockroaches, dragonflies, certain beetles, ants, and bees. Some of those ancients, I am sure, would be completely at home in my own woods and fields. There is every probability that ants and bees, at least, have been the kind of creatures they are, social instinct and all, as far back as we can trace them. And it is this social instinct that makes them of special interest to men. Special, that is, beyond the fact that they are examples of life, living creatures. And it is this social instinct that marks the distinct line between insects and the spider family, if we ignore the anatomical differences so important to entomologists.

APRIL 3

The social instinct is by no means common to all insects. Authorities in the field say that only twenty-four separate families of insects ever developed what are called "insect societies," and of these the best-known ones today are the bees, the wasps, the ants, the termites, and the beetles. A society calls for teamwork, some enduring instinct and ability to act as a group toward a common project. A swarm of flies or mosquitoes definitely is not a society; it is merely an unorganized group in which every individual is working for itself. A hive of bees or a hill of ants is a community, with assigned tasks for every member of the colony and an organized system of labor and existence.

Nobody knows how many species of insects there are, and the number of individuals in each species is incalculable. A few years ago I estimated the number of ants marching in a forage column from a nest at the edge of the pasture. It was so inconspicuous a nest that I had never noticed it until the column marched out, one morning, to attack another ant colony about two hundred feet away. The attackers marched steadily for almost six hours in a column roughly five abreast, and I estimated the numbers at almost 25,000. I have no idea how many anthills there are on this farm, but if there were 25,000 ants in that one inconspicuous colony there must be many, many millions of ants within a hundred yards of the house.

Yet ants may not be the most numerous of the insect species. Probably the various beetles outnumber them, for there are about 22,000 *species* of beetles in North America alone and beetles live all over the world. And who could begin to estimate the number of houseflies, say, or mosquitoes in even one small area? I doubt that we have comprehensible numbers to count them.

APRIL 4

In the sense of sheer survival and proliferation, the insects probably are the most successful of living creatures. There are various reasons. They have perfected a means of extracting oxygen from the air that is more efficient, for their purpose at least, than the lung-breathing of larger animals. Insects have a network of air tubes through their bodies which swiftly purifies their blood and provides them with quick, constant energy. Their power of flight and quick movement enables them to escape from many enemies. Many insects live on plants, and there is a great variety of plants; hence, the insects have profited by a diversity of opportunities for food and shelter. Insects, by having their skeleton on the outside of their bodies, are able to compress all the necessary organs for life into a very small space, so they can take advantage of the ecological gaps, so to speak, between the living space and the vital needs of birds and quadrupeds. And, finally, insects have remarkably well-developed instinct.

It is this instinct that enables insects to react so quickly. They don't have to think what to do, as long as the situation is not too unexpected. Being unable to reason, they simply react as instinct tells them to. And instinct is built into them, as definitely as are their eyes or their antennae. They don't have to learn what to do. They simply know—or their nerves and muscles know.

And here we get over into the fascinating area of the social instinct of certain insects. I have never seen this discussed, but I am sure it is not new or unique: Can it be possible that man's social instincts and actions came, not from the insects, but from some common source? We don't know the source, but possibly it was the urge for common survival, for preservation of the species. That, at least, seems to be the purpose of the social instinct in social insects.

Such a notion, of course, raises many other questions. If ants and bees had this instinct millions of years ago, why did it not appear with any noticeable strength or persistence in the early amphibians, for instance? And why did not other insects than those relatively few species who build colonies today have it?

And, further, if this instinct was strong enough to shape the lives and habits of social insects for many million years, why did it fail to evolve in them some advance in intelligence, some noticeable increase in reasoning power? The brain of an ant or a bee or a wasp seems to be ready-made, complete with instincts, as soon as the ant or bee or wasp emerges from the larval stage. It doesn't have to be taught anything. It cannot, in fact, be taught anything, not in the sense that we know teaching or learning. It is born knowing all it needs to know, and it learns little from experience.

APRIL 5

Insects are remarkably efficient, more so than most of the higher animals. The mouth of an ant or a bee, for instance, is perfectly equipped to do anything an ant or a bee has to do. Possibly the insect learns to use that mouth more skillfully by practice, but from the very start it can do satisfactorily all it really needs to do. My own hands can do many more tasks than an ant's mouth can do (in a sense they are equivalent, since the ant's mouth-parts are its nearest approximation of fingers), but my fingers are not adept from birth, and an ant's mouth is. I have to learn to use my hands. I, a man, am initially limited in my capacity and my skills, but eventually I become not only more adept but more broadly skillful. I, too, have instincts and reflexes, but to these have been added reasoning power and the ability to learn, to acquire new skills.

In many ways, insects are the most skillful of all nonhuman animals. Wasps knew how to make paper long before man evolved, and the paper nests of the hornets are insulated against both heat and cold as well as being waterproof. Mud-dauber wasps are expert at building mud structures—insect adobes, you might call them—though they have little sense of design beyond the patterns of crude utility. Ants made the first apartment houses, the first underground communities. Dung beetles make almost perfect spheres, balls in which they lay their eggs and which provide food for the young. Some wasps even know how to use tools; they use a large grain of sand to tamp down the earth over a cavity in which they have laid eggs. Some ants are farmers, masticating leaves into humus, planting fungus spores, and harvesting food from the resulting growth. Bees make beautifully proportioned hexagonal cells in which to store honey and hatch eggs, though the precision of their hexagons is something less than perfection.

These skills I recognize and admire, but I know they are a result of instinct, not reason. They are not acquired skills, and they never are really improved or perfected much beyond what they were when the insect was hatched. The things they do, the things they make, have no mark of the individual on them, nothing to show that one insect rather than its neighbor did or made that thing. And this is a fact to remember when one considers the even more fascinating habits of social insects.

APRIL 6

The social habits of bees and ants particularly have held man's interest and inspired his admiration for a long time. These insects seem so efficient! They know precisely what to do and how to do it. Their whole life seems completely dedicated to the community. Man has from time to time so admired this efficiency and dedication that he has wished he could achieve equal strength and unity in his own society.

But history indicates that this is not what man really wants. When he sees what it means, his intelligence rejects it. The purpose of the ant and the bee and the way of life of such insects, admirable as they may be in some ways, are not enough for man.

There is a rigid caste system in almost every ant colony. Most of the members are infertile females. They do most of the work of the colony, from gathering food and building the complexity of nests and tunnels to caring for the eggs, the pupae, and the larvae. The males are drones and they generally are tolerated only because eventually one of them will fertilize a new queen. Sometimes the males are also the colony's soldiers, the fighters. The queen is the heart of the colony, pampered, petted, fed, and kept prisoner inside the nest. She lays all the eggs.

Periodically, new queens are hatched. At a proper time the queens and the males grow wings, are released from the colony and take flight. The queens are mated in the air, return to the earth, nip off their wings, and find sites for new nests. The males die soon after the nuptial flight.

Each solitary queen digs her way into the ground and begins to lay eggs. She tends them until the first ants are hatched, a generation of sexless females. They go to work, enlarge the nest, care for the queen, who never again emerges into the open, tend the eggs that the queen lays, feed the larvae, and live out their brief lives. They work themselves to death in a few weeks and are replaced by the next generation of sexless females.

APRIL 7

Scientists seem to agree that most ants have some capacity for pleasure and anger, that they apparently are elated at times and depressed at other times. They have keen senses, with good eyes that apparently cannot detect color but can see ultraviolet rays, which are invisible to man. They have "touch hairs" on the body that are sensitive to vibrations, which probably include sounds. It seems likely that they can communicate with each other by means of their antennae, though their communication may be limited to news of food or danger. They are sensitive to heat and cold. There is no evidence that they feel pain; an ant with its whole abdominal section cut off will continue to eat honey with apparent relish.

There is evidence of intense community loyalty. Ants make raids on other communities for "slaves," and they fight battles in defense of their own nests. In such battles they are ruthless. They dismember each other, apparently with little effect until the maimed ant is left helpless. I have seen two ants, each with legs missing, push and tumble and nip at each other as though still whole. But if one cuts off the other's antennae, the victim seems helpless. It stands dazed, it runs in circles, it staggers about nipping the air. But it is out of the battle, utterly defeated.

APRIL 8

One researcher has said that 95 percent of an ant's actions are purely instinctive, that 4 percent are a result of habit formed in the community, and that only 1 percent can be credited to anything like reflection or subintelligence. This 1 percent, he adds, can be perceived only by long observation. Another researcher says he trained an ant to come and eat from his finger. Still another reported that he had taught an ant to cross a bridge to reach its nest. But such instances are of virtually no consequence and verify, if anything, the statement that ants have trifling intelligence.

In every instance that I have ever seen—and I find no exception in researchers' reports—when an ant nest is disturbed the workers rush to save the pupae, the undeveloped young of the colony. They do not hurry away to save themselves. Self-preservation is not high among their instincts. Safety for the next generation is. And that probably is one reason the ants, as a species, have persisted for millions of years. The colony comes first, always. And that is true of all social insects. It is almost as though there were no individuals, but only cells or separate small parts of the colony, and the colony itself were the true individual.

APRIL 9

The disconcerting part of any discussion of social insects is that apparent parallels keep intruding. It makes no difference that many of those parallels are more apparent than real. Mankind's society has a superficial resemblance to that of the ants. It is a community, a group of individuals living together and having a more or less common purpose, the welfare of all its members. Why, then, would it not be a good thing to emulate the ants?

The flaw in such thinking is thought itself, the capacity for thought in man and the incapacity for it in the ant. Man is an individual as well as a member of the community. The ant has no individuality; it is merely a member of the community, a kind of cog in the great machine. The machine may have its own complexity, but it is essentially a complexity of numbers, not of ideas. And it is based on instinct, not thought. The ant has no inkling of ever being anything but an ant, a bundle of instincts and reflexes. The unsexed female worker can never become a queen or a mother. She is fixed in status, unchangeable. She is a minute animal, a kind that has not changed in millions of years, and she has a routine of unchanging and unchangeable tasks.

Man, on the other hand, is another kind of being entirely. He is capable of thought. He is more than mere animal, knows it, refuses to accept such status. He has a capacity for learning; for change, in other words. He has instincts that prompt his survival, both as an individual and as a species, but he also has intelligence which tells him that mere survival is not enough.

APRIL 10

We have had a couple of good April rains and bright April sunlight. Maybe April showers bring those May flowers, as the old saying has it, but I say it is April sunlight that brings April flowers. They aren't the kind of flowers that send us dashing to the meadows to admire or pluck, but they are blossoms and the bees appreciate them.

Down along the river and beside the bogland the willows are in bloom. The treasured pussy willows have turned to blossoms that nobody would pick and put in a vase in the living room. That silvery gray coat has vanished and instead there is a tuft of stamens tipped with yellow pollen that spills off at a touch. Neat householders want none of it, but the bees consider it a great treasure.

Nearby are the swamp maples. They were gray and stark all winter and all through March, in fact. Now they are opening bud and dangling those tassels of crimson florets, proclaiming their right to the name, red maple. The florets are red, the young leaves are red as they first begin to appear, the twigs are red, the seeds are red, and in October the leaves turn red. The sugar maple, or rock maple, is a little later, and its basic color is yellow.

Spicebush's tiny blooms give a greenish yellow mist to the undergrowth. Shadblow is like a spurt of white steam in its blossoms. Birch catkins are reddish brown and polleny. So are those of the aspens and poplars.

April's flowers are high-hung, for the most part, blossoms on the bough.

APRIL 11

Foresters scorn them, but I have a soft spot in my heart for the gray birches. They have neither the dignity nor the durability of the big white birches, the pungent essence of the sweet or black birches, nor the bronze beauty of the yellow birches. They are the rabble of the birch family. But they reclaim waste places and open the way for maples, pines, and oaks.

Strip a New England hillside, with ax or fire or even with bulldozer, and leave it for five years, and it will be clothed with seedling gray birches thrusting up through the weeds. That seems to be the purpose of the gray birch, to clothe the naked places, to grow swiftly, lose leaves, twigs, even trunks, rot and form humus, create soil. And as long as the persistent roots are there, new shoots will grow, adding to the shade and enriching the soil.

Loggers pass them by. Farmers are forever warring with them in their pastures. Small boys swing on their tall, slim boles. Woodpeckers mine them for food. They are of little importance in man's economy, though they do make acceptable firewood while still green—dry, the logs rot over a winter. But nature's economy needs them. And in the spring they are beautiful. The green haze of young gray birch leaves is the very color of woodland spring. It is in the making right now.

APRIL 12

By all the logic of survival, the insects should have inherited the earth long ago. They are prolific beyond belief. A single aphid, for example—aphids are parthenogenetic, able to reproduce without mating—is capable of producing several tons of offspring and descendants in a few weeks, if all were to survive. Many insects care for their young as well as do any of the larger animals. They can live in almost any environment that any form of life can endure. Not as a group but as individual species they have adapted to the whole range of natural conditions and to every change that has occurred in millions of years. Their food supply covers the whole range of organic material. They prey widely upon one another, they eat almost every type of vegetation, and they are parasites upon each other and on other animals. Some of them hibernate. Some can go months without food.

Yet the life span of the individual insect is relatively brief. Few of them live as long as a year and most of them no longer than a single season. True, the periodic locust spends fifteen or more years in the larval stage underground, but it emerges as an adult insect for only a few days, to eat, mate, lay eggs, and die. Worker bees live only about six weeks during the summer. The adult form of the mayfly lives only a few hours, does not eat, mates, lays eggs, and dies.

Evidently this is enough—for an insect. And maybe that is the ultimate difference—it isn't enough for a human being.

APRIL 13

We picked marsh marigolds today, for greens. We have already had a cooking of winter cress, one of the very earliest of all the wild greens. But today we went around the mountain to a brook that flows into the lake over there, and we found the marsh marigolds just right for picking, in bud but not yet beginning to open. We picked enough for one meal, being careful not to pull up the plants by the roots. They grow in shallow water and are easily pulled and thus destroyed. By plucking the tips we left the plants to grow and spread and be there next year and the year after.

They aren't really marigolds, of course. The name means only that they are marigold yellow when they come to flower. They are also called cowslips, though they have no botanical relation to real cowslips. They are cousins of the buttercups, members of the big and varied crowfoot family. Botanically they are *Caltha palustris,* Latin for marsh-cup. They have round or kidney-shaped leaves with blunt teeth, the stems are brittle and succulent, and the flowers resemble meadow buttercups magnified to an inch and a half diameter.

Marsh marigolds were one of the favorite spring greens of the early settlers. We find them good fare, boiled briefly and eaten with salt and butter. They grow in the same damp places where we find the big marsh violets in May.

APRIL 14

The red-wing blackbirds have been back three weeks, and now the females, which look so much like big sparrows and so little like the resplendent males, have also arrived. They are setting up housekeeping, I assume. But just listening to the *ka-ree*ing of the males in the trees beside the water takes me back to my boyhood in a land of little rain. There they meant water, cattails, cottonwood trees, shade in a place where shade was rare.

Each trip we made from the homestead to the town on the South Platte river where we bought our groceries once a month I saw and heard the red-wings as soon as we came to the irrigated land a few miles from the river. They lived in the reeds along the irrigation ditches and in the tall cottonwoods. Now and then a great flock of red-wings and yellow-headed blackbirds took to the air as we approached, glistening black speckled with red and gold. Memorable!

Later I knew the red-wings along the Rio Grande in New Mexico, where they again were symbols of shade and water. I knew them along the Green River in the desert country of eastern Utah. Then I knew them along the lower Mississippi, near Shreveport, where they were detested because they pillaged the rice fields. And in the Carolinas, where they again were regarded as a pest species.

Now I know them here, and they make me think of shade and cool water, even in this land of shade and plentiful water. They are welcome to nest along the pasture brook, or anywhere they please. And they do just that. They are building nests there right now.

APRIL 15

The woodcocks have been putting on their aerial performance the past few nights, I am told. We haven't been out to watch and listen. We have seen and heard it several times, and we will again, probably by accident. That is the way it usually happens for us. We can hide in the alder brush, lie in the wet grass, spend countless hours watching and waiting and not see a thing. Then we go out some night on another errand, make no attempt to be quiet or invisible, and down in a low meadow we see and hear the whole performance.

There is nothing quite like it. Usually it happens at dusk, usually at the edge of an alder thicket, usually on a night of full moonlight. But there are no absolutes. The male woodcock, grotesque bird that he is, courts when he pleases. And it is always an astonishing performance, a whirring, spiraling flight almost straight upward, then a spiraling downward. And it is the sounds, a series of *peents* before the flight, a high whistling presumably made by the wings during the upward spiral, and a short, melodic song repeated several times at the climax of the upward flight. Then those same notes repeated, soft and haunting, as the downward flight begins. And more *peents* on the ground again.

Reduced to words it doesn't sound like much. On a moonlit night in April it is memorably beautiful—you, and this astonishing bird, and the spring night. Something of the beauty of creation itself is revealed, made manifest.

APRIL 16

The spring peepers, which actually are tree frogs, were loud last evening, and so were the leopard frogs with their guttural, rumbling *gr-r-r-r-ock,* rolling those middle "r's." I thought I heard a wood frog. And I am sure I heard the high, musical trill of a toad, quite different from the chiming trill of the peepers. That would make four species of those spring-voiced amphibians. It was a good night to hear them, moonlit and mild. But no *harrumphing* of the bullfrogs. That comes later.

Some years ago the *New England Naturalist* assembled a timetable for the first frog and toad calls. It was timed for the Boston area, and because of the difference in altitude and distance from the ocean the dates would be about two weeks later for the western Connecticut area where I live. Compensated, then, for that difference, the schedule runs this way:

Spring peeper, March 24; leopard frog, March 28; wood frog, March 31; American toad, April 1; pickerel frog, April 3; green frog, April 7; Fowler's toad, April 15; Gray's tree frog, April 28; bullfrog, May 20.

My records show that the earliest I have heard the spring peepers was March 20, and the latest date I have for them was April 15. Most years I heard them between April 5 and April 12.

APRIL 17

Sometimes they are called sugar maples, sometimes rock maples. The name is apt in a variety of ways, for this is a tree of slow growth, stout fiber, firm substance. It can stand up to a storm. Find a well-crafted chair or table made of rock maple and it will outlive you and all your family. Plant a rock maple in your dooryard and it will be growing when you are gone, casting its shade each summer, offering its sap to those who have the wisdom and the patience to use it, proffering a small nursery of seedlings each year for those who appreciate its value.

The sugar maples respect this land's frosts. They open bud in their own time, come to flower and fruit, and spread their leaves. They will sigh comfortably through the summer. I will waken in the night and hear the rain pattering in their leafy branches, and I will hear them talking to the wind and whispering to the breeze. But there will be no moaning from them, and no such clatter as comes from the poplars in the gusts.

October will come, and as the sun moves south it will bestow its own glow on the sugar maples. Most of them will be golden. A few will be orange, a color no other tree achieves. Some will be particolored, some even crimson, aping the soft maples in the swamp. But mostly they will be full of sun, so full that even on dark days they will cast sunlight on me when I stand beneath them. And when the leaves come down they will stand strong and proud in great golden drifts as crisp as beaten foil of gold.

APRIL 18

After a winter of relatively light physical activity I am always annoyed at how unwilling my muscles and sinews are to exert themselves. I shovel snow, in moderation and taking my time, but my slack muscles still complain when I start the spring clean-up. But I now have picked up and disposed of the dead limbs the storms brought down and have tried to bring a semblance of order out of the natural clutter. Out in the yard yesterday it occurred to me that nature never bothers to clean up and set things in what man considers proper order. Nature is not very tidy. It thrives on litter and unfinished business, as I cannot fail to see every time I go to the woodland. Without the fertility of its own past, nature produces scrawny growth. Even with it, nature takes its own time. Only man wants everything tidied up in neat packages and disposed of now, today.

That tendency seems to have grown upon us. We want instant everything, from coffee to calculations, from cake to cures. We have achieved instant devastation, so now we must achieve instant antidevastation. If instant decisions go wrong, that is going to be just too bad; but there won't be many left to question. Probably not much of anything will be left except a few trees and a great many insects. Insects and trees don't ask questions. They will go right on, deliberate as always, and start to repopulate the earth.

Maybe I should shovel more snow.

APRIL 19

Raking litter and dragging dead branches to the brush pile the other day, I thought of the way this land was cleared and possessed to begin with. The land itself was the challenge, and that challenge made men strong in body and spirit. It broke some men, true, and it was an unbearable ordeal for many women. But it bred a stout, resolute race.

Life is easier today, physically easier, at least. But was ease the goal? Not really. If it had been, this country would still consist of a prosperous fringe of colonies along the Atlantic seaboard, and an equally prosperous margin of ranchos and missions along the Pacific shore. Maybe it would have been better that way; but this is not the day for that debate.

The challenge of the land has led the way as far back as we can trace our own beginnings. Biologically speaking, man's remote and primitive ancestors faced the challenge of survival in a world dominated by giant reptiles. An evolving brain equipped man with the wit and wisdom to meet the challenge of fang and claw. Once up on his hind legs and armed with fire and a stone ax, he accepted the challenge of his habitat.

The long story of civilizations is a repetitious chronicle of challenges met, mastered, and followed by periods of ease. Ease begot weakness, and new tribes facing the challenge rose to dominance. One of the oldest stories we know, one that keeps repeating itself, is that of the conquest of effete cultures by hungry hordes of rude outlanders, barbarians.

APRIL 20

There is a haze of green and pastel pink and yellow on the mountainside. New leaves are appearing on the trees, particularly the birches and the maples. They always come from the bud in those pastel tones. Looking at them from down here in the valley, I wonder what this land was like one hundred, two hundred, three hundred years ago.

The first white men came here almost 250 years ago, and this was then a thickly timbered land. Undoubtedly there was a line of meadows not much different from those of today along the river, on the old flood plain, but the mountainsides were covered with big trees, pine, hemlock, oak, maple, chestnut, tall and bigger than a barrel in girth. The Indians who lived here grew patches of corn on the meadows, and every year set fire to the underbrush in the woodland, in part to clear it and in part to drive deer down to the river, where a few hours' work with knives could lay in a winter's supply of venison. Then the whites came and began to clear the hillsides.

A hundred years ago, much of my mountainside was laid out in fields and cultivated. It is timbered today, but when I walk through those woods I find a crisscrossing of stone walls. The farmers who cleared those fields of trees also cleared them of stones and piled them into walls to make way for the plow. In some of those walls are trees two feet through at the butt. They have grown there since those fields were abandoned.

A neighbor tells me that when he was a boy, only fifty years ago, there was a large hayfield on that mountainside, tended and mowed each summer. Today that old hayfield is a tangle of white pine and gray birch, pine big enough for saw logs. There isn't a trace of a furrow there, and there are stumps of chestnut trees two feet through which were cut for lumber for the framing and interior trim of my house. Perhaps the chestnuts stood in the hayfield, for shade, but the pines didn't. They have grown up during my neighbor's lifetime.

Man's truce with the trees on my mountainside was kept only so long as the farmers lived to enforce it. But they were mortal. They lived and worked and died. And the trees crept silently back. They kept no truce. It is their way of life to possess the land, and there is something we call patience in a tree. It can wait. It can live two hundred years, waiting, sowing its seed each season. Eventually some of those seeds will find soil that nourishes, and they will find man with his back turned. The truce will be broken without a sound louder than the scurry of a squirrel worrying a pine cone open.

APRIL 21

How much longer the daylight lingers now than it did only a month ago! I look at the tables and see that we now have more than an hour and a half more daylight than we had then. It is one of those astronomical bafflers that I won't even try to explain, but daylight and darkness were equal, twelve hours each, on March 17 instead of three days later, at the time of the vernal equinox. Yes, I know we all say they are equal at the time of the equinox, but they aren't. Not precisely.

Anyway, the sun now rises just before five, standard time, and doesn't set till just after six thirty. And, whether this is true or not, it seems to me we have a longer period of dusk, a soft twilight that fades slowly instead of simply vanishing.

The stars come gradually into sight, too, instead of bursting out in full glow. The Big Dipper rides high, almost directly above the Pole Star, and Cassiopeia and Cephus are down near the horizon. In the south Leo stands high and Scorpius and Libra are low. But all are leisurely about appearing. They can wait for frog-trill to reach its evening peak.

APRIL 22

Up in the edge of the woods this morning I saw some bird, in the deep shadow, scratching in a drift of dead leaves, and I would have guessed that it was a fox sparrow. Then I got a good look, and it was a towhee—you can't mistake the flash of those white margins of the flirting tail, the bright chestnut body color, the shiny black head and throat, the white wing bars.

We don't have many towhees, and they seldom come down to the house, but I do appreciate them. They aren't songsters, and they aren't friendly, but they are wonderful to watch, with their quick, nervous motions and their terrific energy. They are also called chewinks, from the sound of their calls, and ground robins. They are slightly bigger than a fox sparrow, smaller than a true robin. And they are finches, cousins of the sparrows. But they eat more insects than most sparrows. That is why they scratch and make such a to-do among the dead leaves—they are looking for insects and larvae.

All towhees seem to be easy marks for cowbirds, which never hatch their own eggs. One reason may be that their eggs look a good deal alike, basically white dotted with brownish lilac. Maybe even towhees can't tell the difference. Anyway, towhees hatch and raise a great many cowbirds. I wonder if they don't ever think that some of their nestlings are most peculiar-looking towhees. I wonder what Father Towhee thinks Mother Towhee has been up to when he sees those baby cowbirds.

APRIL 23

A Baltimore oriole has been building her nest in one of the big sugar maples across the road, hanging it far out where the limbs reach out over the river. I don't think much of that site, but I don't have to live there.

I have watched her for three days, and now she has the nest shaped into a recognizable pouch. Another day or two and she will have it ready for use. I have been specially interested in what she was using for weaving material. From the ground it looked like coarse horsehair, or maybe hair from a cow's tail. There is no horsehair closer than a mile, but there could be cowhair on the barbs of the barbed-wire fence around the pastures.

Yesterday while I was watching, she dropped a couple of strands and I went down the riverbank and retrieved them from a bush. They weren't hair. They looked more like coarse monofilament nylon. They were a silvery, translucent white and surprisingly strong. While I was trying to identify them, the oriole flew down to a clump of last year's milkweed stems, pecked at them, ripped a strand loose, and flew up to her partly finished nest. I went over to those old milkweed stalks and found my answer. Those strands were fibers from the milkweed stalk. I could peel them off the dry stems in long threads. I loosened a few and left them dangling, and the oriole soon found them, ripped them loose and took them to the nest.

I still don't know how she ties them to the twig to anchor the nest, or how she weaves the fabric of it, but I do know the source of at least one of the fibers she uses.

APRIL 24

I once saw a list, in a magazine article, of "basic achievements" and "great inventions" by man. In order, it listed the wheel, the lever, the wedge, the screw, the smelting of metal, writing, and weaving. It obviously was a list made by a man obsessed with technology and ignorant of the whole history of human cultures. Anyone who has even a smattering of knowledge of American anthropology can see the glaring fallacies.

Watching that oriole weave her nest made me remember how important the art of weaving was to primitive peoples, and wonder how they learned it. From the birds? Just possibly. Anyway, the variety of patterns in prehistoric American weaving and the skill with which it was done are astonishing. To me, weaving should be one of the first two or three items in such a list of basic achievements, or inventions. It was far more important than the wheel.

Another top entry, not even on the list cited above, was the domestication of plants and animals. Here in America, corn, or maize, was the great plant achievement, certainly greater than the wheel, the lever, the wedge, or the screw. Elsewhere, the domestication of various grasses to create wheat, barley, rye, oats, and rice, was of prime importance. That led to farming, to plentiful food, to settled abodes, to a degree of leisure.

Strange, isn't it, how one can lose all sense of values when one gets caught up in the gears of technology? And I haven't even mentioned the conquest of fire or the invention of speech.

APRIL 25

The ground ivy we call gill-over-the-ground is in bloom, and the bees, particularly the bumblebees, are swarming over its little lavender blossoms. The bumblebees are big, almost twice as big as those that will be gathering pollen and nectar from the apple blossoms. These are the queens, out and working for a living, for a change.

Bumblebees are quite different from honeybees. They can make honey and they collect pollen, but they are not honey-hoarders. They make no combs and they refuse to live in hives. Their colonies are small. Only the young queens survive the winter, and it is those young queens that are out there now, working. They passed the winter in some snug hideaway, probably a deserted mouse nest. With warm days they roused from hibernation, found a little pollen, probably on willow catkins, to ease their hunger, and set about making a nursery nest.

The nursery nest usually is in a small tunnel, maybe a mouse tunnel, just under the surface of the ground. The queen lines it with dry grass, builds a simple cell for her eggs, stocks it with honey-moistened pollen, lays her first small clutch of eggs, and closes the egg cell. In the same hollow she makes a small, rather crude waxen jug and fills it with honey she has made. This is her private pantry to be used during stormy weather when she cannot go out foraging.

The eggs hatch and the larvae feed on the pollen, supplemented by fresh pollen and honey if the weather is good. The larvae pupate, undergo the final stages of change, and emerge as winged bumblebees, considerably smaller than the queen but full of energy. They become the colony's workers, and as soon as they start gathering pollen the queen stays at home and lays more eggs. These first workers are all sterile females. They are the ones that will be busy at the apple blossoms.

Later in the season males and fertile females are hatched. They will be drones, both sexes of them, and those sterile workers will have to go right on working to feed them. Late in the summer those drones will leave the nest, mate, and the males will soon die. The pregnant females will find places to hibernate for the winter, feed energetically until frost comes, then tuck themselves in for the long sleep, each in a separate nest. They are the queens who are out now, feasting at the gill-over-the-ground, waiting for the first laying of eggs to hatch into workers who will feed and cozy the queens.

The big bumblers I see out late in the fall, stiff with the chill of night and often bedding down among the petals of a zinnia, are probably old queens nearing the end, or young queens who haven't enough sense to go in out of the cold.

APRIL 26

The lilacs are in leaf and in tiny floral bud. They won't be in bloom till about apple blossom time. Then they will be so full of fragrance that we can smell them inside the house.

It seems to me that I have always known lilacs, from birth in Nebraska to boyhood in Colorado, to manhood in a dozen states east and west. I have never lived in a house that didn't have at least one lilac bush in the dooryard. And last May, up on the mountain, I found a scraggly old bush with two heads of bloom, back in the brush where a house stood so long ago that nobody remembers it now and the cellar hole is just a slight hollow in the ground.

The lilac is not a native of America, or even of England, but it came to New England with some of the earliest colonists. Lilacs originated, or at least throve long, long ago, in Persia and other parts of the Near East. We can thank the Crusaders for them in the West. Those old wanderers, who repeatedly found excuses to go traipsing off to the Near East, had an eye for pretty women, fine horses, and beautiful flowers.

They found and enjoyed them all in the Near East, and they brought flowers and horses home. Go down the list of flowers native to the Near East and you will find that the best of them became known in the West soon after the Crusades. That's when lilacs were first known in England. By the early seventeenth century they were cherished dooryard flowers, so they were brought along by the emigrants.

APRIL 27

Yesterday we had a bright and shining morning, the temperature in the high forties. A fine April day. It continued that way till about mid-morning, then became overcast and chilly, and continued that way, almost threatening, till evening. There was no visible sunset—just darkness creeping in under that thick overcast. Then, just after 8:00 P.M., we had a brief but brilliant lightning display with rolling thunder that boomed and echoed from hill to hill. I expected a downpour. None came. But when I went outdoors at eight-thirty to see what was happening I walked right into a spectacular world—snow! Two or three inches of it had fallen, and it was still coming down. It was wet and clung to everything, twigs, young leaves, even the wires of the garden fence. But the roads and the sidewalks were so warm the snow melted there as it fell, though it lay like deep cake frosting on the lawn and pastures.

This morning it was still there, a good three inches of it, on grass, twigs, and wires. But the sun came up clear and dazzling, and by nine the snow was all melted from the trees. By ten it had melted from the grass. By noon you would never have known there had been a flake of snow.

APRIL 28

Bloodroot is in full bloom, and down in a damp hollow I found a big stand of purple trilliums just opening their blossoms. Wakerobin, some call this flower, which is probably the most common of the trilliums. I remember how a visitor from the city one spring thought he was doing us a favor by plucking a big bouquet of these purple trilliums and bringing them to the house. He told us where he had found them and said, "There must have been a dead rabbit or maybe a deer nearby. I kept thinking I smelled it all the way back to the house." He sniffed. "I can almost smell it now."

"You can," I said. "It wasn't a dead animal, though. It was these trilliums." And I held one close to his nose. He gasped and exclaimed, "Oh, my God! And such a pretty flower!"

Every spring I stop and look, when they open flower, but I haven't picked one in many years.

A friend over in New York State wrote to me several years ago that she had found a four-part trillium, or wakerobin—fourfold leaves, four-petaled flowers. It happens occasionally, a sport. She watched and this plant reappeared three successive years, fourpart each year. Then it vanished.

APRIL 29

When spring comes here it often comes with a rush. Not that we haven't had spring for the past month, but it has been a reluctant season, dragging its feet. Perverse, even to that thunder and lightning followed by three inches of snow only a few days ago. But today the temperature shot up to eighty degrees, and we had a blazing sun. Daffodils and hyacinths were in fat bud—we had picked a few daffodils ten days ago, in fact—and today you could almost sit and watch them open. By late afternoon we had a profusion of flowers where this morning we had a great many buds and only half a dozen partly opened blossoms.

The trees had been in leaf, but today those leaves seemed to stretch themselves and almost thicken with chlorophyll. Until now they had looked rather pale, almost anemic, one might say. This evening there is a light breeze and the maples are whispering, the big cottonwood just up the road is chattering. That's the way the change in the leaves has altered the sounds. Until today they were too limp, on both maple and cottonwood, to make much of a sound. They needed this warmth, this touch of July, almost, to put some character into them.

And out in the vegetable garden the asparagus jumped six inches, I swear. There wasn't a stalk worth picking in sight this morning, and by late afternoon we found all we could eat for supper, up and ready for cutting. From now till the end of June we will have asparagus every day, all we can eat.

APRIL 30

I saw two mourning-cloak butterflies this morning, out in the vegetable garden. Maybe one of them was the one I saw ten days ago, on a mild, sunny day. Life must be a bit difficult for them this early, since they seem to live on pollen and nectar, which aren't in great supply yet. They hibernate, the largest of our butterflies that do hibernate in the adult stage, and they emerge in April and look quite out of place. We aren't used to seeing butterflies in April.

The mourning cloak—in England it is called the Camberwell beauty, and is quite rare—has a wing span of as much as three and a half inches. The wings are a deep brownish maroon bordered with a yellow band and dotted inside the yellow border with small blue spots. There is a hint of "tails" on the hind wings. The underside of the wings is brownish black, a good color for a mourner's cloak, I suppose. The caterpillar from which it emerges looks as though it were wrapped in black velvet splotched with white dots and with a few red dots just for variety. The caterpillar makes a pupal case of brown with red points, and the fully matured butterfly emerges by late summer. The caterpillars feed on the leaves of willows, elms, and poplars, and the adult butterflies probably get a good deal of their first food after rousing from hibernation from the blossoms on those trees, all of which are among the early bloomers.

I have seen these eye-catching dark butterflies out and on the wing while snow still covered the ground.

MAY

MAY 1

There was a time when May Day had sentiment rather than social significance.

It was preceded by a week of preparation, when young fingers gooey with paste made baskets and cornucopias out of colored paper. And young explorers prowled the nearby woods and lowlands, looking for wildflowers. Not to pick them, but merely to find them. Then, on April's last day, as late in the day as possible, those youngsters went to those woods and lowlands and picked handfuls of dogtooth violets, anemones, and big purple violets. And Dutchmen's breeches, if any were to be found. Spring beauties, if the season was right. And the daintiest of young fern fronds. All were taken home, carefully preserved in jelly glasses of water.

May Day morning and the youngsters were up early, to choose the best one or two, never more than three, of the paper baskets, and put a few gumdrops and tiny jelly beans and a heart-shaped candy wafer with printed words of affection in the bottom of the baskets. Then the flowers went in, all the baskets would hold. And then the baskets were taken, tiptoe all the way, to the front door of the young sweetheart next door or down the street, or even to two or three front doors, and hung on the doorknob. Then the doorbell was rung, or the knocker knocked, and the basketmaker ran, but only a little way, and he always looked back to see her open the door and exclaim in pleased delight.

That was May Day in the morning, once.

MAY 2

A few days ago I reported seeing two mourning-cloak butterflies and mentioned that I had seen one ten days earlier. I didn't mention that I saw a moth, a brownish gray moth with a wing span of about an inch and a half, a month before that, on March 2. It was a mild evening and I had turned the porch light on; when I went outside a little later, there was this moth, obviously one that had wintered over, probably under a slab of bark up in the woods.

Fragile as they are, the Lepidoptera, the scale-winged ones—moths and butterflies—are among the most baffling of all insects, to me at least. In a sense they are also the most reassuring, for though they answer few of the big questions science asks of life, they raise other questions that should bedevil anyone tempted to make glib statements.

The differences between moths and butterflies, the two major divisions of Lepidoptera, are rather tenuous except to the specialist. Generally speaking, butterflies are creatures of the day, moths creatures of the night. Butterflies have simple antennae, moths have complex ones, often featherlike. Butterflies usually, but not always, are more vividly colored than moths. Most butterflies fold their wings over their backs when at rest, and most moths rest with their wings outspread or folded close to their bodies. Otherwise the differences are not particularly obvious.

Both butterflies and moths go through equivalent stages of physical change, or metamorphosis. They lay eggs, the eggs hatch into caterpillars, the caterpillars become pupae or encased changelings, and the pupae become moths or butterflies. Among the butterflies, some adults never take food or drink and have only brief lives devoted entirely to mating and laying eggs. Other butterflies, as well as most moths, eat during the adult stage, and many of them have relatively long lives, some living throughout the year or even longer. In all instances the caterpillars are voracious eaters, often being what man considers a pest.

The differences in those stages, egg, caterpillar, pupa, and winged adult, are so striking that the caterpillar seems, offhand, to be of a quite different species than the butterfly or moth. Outwardly they appear to have no relationship, one to the other. There are other insects that go through equivalent stages of change, but nowhere else is the difference from one state to another quite so remarkable. How the Lepidoptera came to this complex and roundabout method of reproduction is a mystery of long standing.

MAY 3

In terms of geologic history, the moths and butterflies are old; not as old as some other insects, and probably much younger than the spiders, but old enough to be recognizable in some of the earlier fossil deposits.

Fragile though they are, bits of Lepidoptera wings and body parts have been found in the Tertiary rocks here in America, rocks perhaps 60 million years old. Such fossils prove that the butterfly, or the moth, was a winged creature at that time, not merely a crawling caterpillar in which was some remote possibility of flight. But the specialists hesitate to assign even a closely approximate date to the time when the butterfly presumably emerged from the broad, primitive insect family.

The wing is the ultimately distinctive feature of the moth or the butterfly. The wings of other flying insects are thin, clear membranes strengthened by ribs and veins, and they have no covering. Basically, the butterfly wing has the same structure, a thin chitin membrane supported by stiff, tubular "veins." But in the butterfly the wings are covered with minute scales arranged in an overlapping pattern, much like the shingles on a house or the scales on a fish. They also carry the coloring so characteristic of moths and butterflies, usually in the form of pigment but also, in iridescent butterflies, in the form of light-refracting prismatic ridges. As a boy I was told that if one rubbed even a few of the scales from a butterfly's wings it could not fly. This is not true, but if the scales are rubbed off, the wing is weakened and may easily be broken.

MAY 4

There are four wings on a butterfly or moth, as there are on most flying insects. The Lepidoptera, however, use the pair on each side as one wing, not separately as the dragonfly does. This is done by overlapping and by an ingenious device of hooked bristles that holds the forewing and hindwing together.

As a general rule, butterfly wings range from reds and oranges through white and yellow to green, blue, and purple. Most moths are darker colored, with much gray and brown, in keeping with their nocturnal habits. There are such exceptions as the brownish black mourningcloak butterfly and the green luna moth. Having such large wings in proportion to the size of their bodies, butterflies fly with relatively slow wing strokes, very slow compared, for instance, with a honeybee's two to three hundred strokes per second. And none of them can fly very fast. Some swallowtail butterflies can travel about twelve feet a second, at top speed. The white cabbage butterflies can manage only about half that speed. On the other hand, some of them can fly great distances. Monarchs often migrate from my area to the southern states for the winter, and large flights of Monarchs have been seen several hundred miles at sea.

Male butterflies often are more brilliantly colored than the females of the same species, though in some species this is reversed. When the female is more brilliantly colored or larger than the male, she usually courts him and even carries him when they mate in the air. In many species the male has scent patches on the wings. This scent apparently is of great importance in mating, for it attracts the females, sometimes from distances of a mile or more. All butterflies appear to have a highly developed sense of smell.

A single mating, which always occurs in the air, is sufficient for the female to lay all her eggs. In most instances the male dies soon after mating, and the female dies soon after she has laid her eggs. However, there are a few species that lay two sets of eggs each season, and a very few that survive the winter, in a form of hibernation, and lay eggs in a second season. And among the moths there are a few species that are capable of parthenogenesis, the production of fertile eggs from an unmated, virgin female.

MAY 5

Parthenogenesis is a word from the Greek words for "virgin birth." In biology it means reproduction in such a way that the ovum develops into a new individual without fertilization. Natural parthenogenesis occurs in social insects particularly, such as honeybees and ants. In both the bees and the ants, individuals hatched from unfertilized eggs are male drones, and those from fertilized eggs are sexually arrested female workers and sexually potent queens. Evidently the colony's queen somehow controls the type of eggs she lays, since she has already mated and has within her all the fertilized eggs she ever will lay.

Aphids, of course, are the most notable example of parthenogenetic insects. They can reproduce as many as twelve generations parthenogenetically, all from wingless females that never have mated.

The phenomenon of parthenogenesis was discovered in the eighteenth century and has been studied by many biologists since then. In 1900 Jacques Loeb, a noted American physiologist, accomplished artificial parthenogenesis in the laboratory by pricking unfertilized frog eggs with a needle. In some of those pricked eggs normal embryonic development occurred. Since then artificial parthenogenesis has been accomplished in most major groups of animals, though usually it has produced abnormal development. Some scientists believe that all the factors necessary for full development are present in the ovum, in some cases at least, and that the sperm only triggers the chemical mechanism which initiates embryonic growth.

The same phenomenon occurs, though rarely, among plants, where it is called parthenocarpy.

MAY 6

Most species of moths and butterflies mate in a normal male-female way, then the female lays the eggs. The eggs are laid, without exception, on or near a source of food for the caterpillars that will hatch from them. The choice of such a food source is unerring. Monarch butterflies lay their eggs on milkweed plants. Cabbage butterflies lay their eggs on some member of the cabbage family. Clothes moths lay their eggs on wool and some other animal fiber, to man's constant annoyance.

The eggs hatch, usually in a matter of days, and the infant caterpillars begin to feed. Caterpillars are incessant feeders. The caterpillar of the Polyphemus, an American moth of the silkworm family, weighs only one twentieth of a grain when it is hatched. By the time it is fifty days old this caterpillar will have eaten fifty oak leaves, about three quarters of a pound. This amounts to 86,000 times as much as the caterpillar's original weight. If a human child weighing eight pounds at birth were to eat as much, proportionately, it would consume 244 tons of food. Even if we take fifty years of human life as the equivalent of fifty days of a caterpillar's life, this would mean that the child, and the adult it becomes, would eat nearly seven tons of food a year for fifty years, almost forty pounds a day, thirteen pounds at a meal three times a day.

MAY 7

The caterpillar has no resemblance to the moth or butterfly it will become. It has six legs, true, as do all insects; but it has additional abdominal claws that serve as legs as it crawls about. It has six simple eyes. Usually, but not always, it has hairs that probably serve some sensory function, as they do in the adult moth or butterfly. It has a mouth equipped for biting, chewing, or tearing food. In most moth caterpillars there is also a gland in the mouth that secretes material for spinning a silken thread, an arrangement much like the spinnerets on a spider but situated at the opposite end of the creature. The body is quite different, both internally and externally, from that of the butterfly or moth which laid the egg from which this caterpillar hatched. It has no sexual organs. It has no wings, even in a rudimentary stage, though it does have "imaginal disks," as the entomologists call them, which eventually evolve into wings. It is essentially an elongated intestinal tract, an eating machine. Its function is to eat and grow.

The caterpillar sheds its skin as it grows. After a series of molts it becomes as big as it ever will be, and at a proper time it "hibernates." It either spins a silken cocoon around itself or it becomes encased in a tough shell called a chrysalis. Most moths form cocoons. Most butterflies form chrysalises. The cocoon or the chrysalis is usually attached to a hospitable place for the adult, the winged form, to be when it emerges.

Inside this pupal case, whether it is a cocoon or a chrysalis, the original caterpillar changes shape completely. New organs evolve. Old parts waste away, almost as though diseased. The complete form of the winged creature takes shape. Wings appear, folded close against the body. Finally, when its time has come, the pupal case splits open and this new insect appears.

The moth or butterfly crawls into the open, and its antennae, complete and ready to function, stretch out. It stretches its legs, crawls onto some support. The wings, soft and moist and useless when it emerges, begin to unfold. This new creature, fat with body fluids, pumps a large part of those fluids into the wing veins, stretches the wings, and slowly fans them in the air. The wing membranes dry and stiffen. The body shrinks, relieved of its distending excess of fluid. The large, complex eyes—the eye of a nocturnal moth may have as many as 27,000 facets, incredibly more complex than any caterpillar's eye—look around. The antennae wave, feel the air, come into full use with their mysterious senses. And when the wings are fully dry and set, the moth or butterfly flies out into the world, a new creature, something almost totally different from the sluggish caterpillar that was its immediate progenitor.

MAY 8

There is more to be said about the Lepidoptera, but it will have to wait. It can wait, but May won't.

The floral bounty of spring comes now with a rush, with warm days and warm rain and long hours of sunshine. The meadow violets are everywhere. Wherever there is an open space in a meadow or an old pasture there are bluets, frosty white, inconsequential individually but beautiful in the mass. Beside a rocky ledge in an old pasture up the road there is a magnificent patch of spring beauties, their white petals lined with dark pink veins. Who would suspect that they belong to the purslane family? Up on the mountainside and down on the sunny ledges the wild columbines are starting to open their vivid crimson-and-yellow blooms. In deep shade I find an occasional clump of hepatica still in flower; those I find now are the darker shades, light blue and lavender.

Along the road, the sugar maples are leafing out. In the edge of the woods across the river the shadblow is at its peak, glimmering white. In the middle of the river, just up the road, is the stone pier of an old railroad bridge, the bridge itself now gone. On that pier is a patch of soil, probably a hollow that caught dust and leaves and trash and made humus of it. In that patch of soil a seed from a shadberry fell, probably in a bird dropping, and it grew into a little tree. This year it is about four feet tall, and it is covered with blossoms, an astonishing sight—a kind of white Christmas tree on a stone pier in the middle of a river in May!

MAY 9

The birds seem all to be here now. A pair of catbirds are building a nest in the big barberry bush at the end of the front porch. They have done this the past two years, and now seem to think it's their private territory. If I go out there they call me names, order me away, even fly at me almost threateningly. . . . So the catbirds have that end of the porch for a few weeks.

Several pairs of orioles are nesting in the big maples. I can see two nests but know there is at least one other. And still another pair has built a nest in the big weeping willow out by the garage. They obviously like to live dangerously, for the limber branch to which they have fastened that nest whips about in the wind so much that it snaps its twigs right off.

The brown thrashers are nesting somewhere nearby, perhaps one pair of them in the big lilac bush out by the garage, which has been unpruned several years and has a fine tangle of shoots down at the base. I love the thrashers. Yesterday one was out in the side yard and I was weeding in the perennial border. I sat back on my heels and whistled a poor imitation of a thrasher song, complete with repetitions. Mr. Thrasher looked my way, curious. I whistled again. He came toward me, stopped. I kept on whistling and he kept coming until he was within ten feet of me. Then he cocked his head and seemed to be thinking that I was not a very good mimic. He flew to the top of the maple across the road and showed me how to sing a real brown thrasher recital.

MAY 10

As I was saying about moths and butterflies, the whole elaborate process, the whole series of processes by which an egg finally becomes a winged creature of grace and beauty, is well known to entomologists. Any lay-man with a little knowledge can go into the woods or fields in early spring, find a cocoon or chrysalis, take it home, and watch the whole emergence, the final act.

There is no deep mystery about it, no mystery at all except why it happens as it does, what pattern, what system or order, what rhythm of change, has dictated and dominated it. Compared to this, the emergence of a chick from an egg, itself a marvelous thing, is simple, for the chick is a miniature of the creature that laid the egg. But here we have a totally different event, or series of events. A butterfly laid an egg. That egg hatched into a caterpillar, with no hint of flight or winged beauty. That caterpillar retired into a cocoon or a chrysalis, and out of that house of change now comes a fragile winged creature of the air, a living bit of sheer beauty and imagination.

Why should this happen? Why should it happen in precisely this way? I find no explanation in the facts of evolution, none that convinces or even persuades me. In some instances, such as that of the frog, evolu-tionary history seems to be recapitulated in the changes from egg to adult. The tadpole stages seem to duplicate the fundamental changes from a minute, water-dwelling creature through tailed and gill-breathing forms up to the stage of emergence onto the land. These changes are obvious and understandable. There is a parallel recapitulation in the stages of a mammal's growing fetus. But even if I were to grant that, eons ago, a crawling caterpillar did become a fragile, winged butterfly by some mysterious command of change and evolution, I would still be baffled by that pupal stage, the amazing transformation that occurs, without exception, inside the chrysalis. I can see no recapitulation of evolution at that point. It is sheer mystery, even though the specialists have investigated it and have their own explanations. The explanations tell what happens, and in a sense they tell how it happens. But I look in vain for any word of why it happens.

MAY 11

There is another factor in this matter of moths and butterflies that seems to have no explanation that really satisfies. This one is further back, in the egg itself. Ignore, at this point, the purpose of the egg and the process of its origin and fertilization. Simply look at the egg.

Moth and butterfly eggs are small, some so small they can be identified by the naked eye only as egg masses. Others are the size of a pinhead or somewhat larger. They have membranous shells or outer coverings, which protect them from cold or desiccation. They come in many shapes. Some look like miniature barrels, some like simple rods or bars, some are cones, some are hemispheres, some are like cheeses and some like turbans. The shape varies with the species, but it never varies within the species.

On the surface of these minute eggs are patterns. Some of them can be seen vaguely with the naked eye but most require the help of a ten-power glass or even a microscope to be seen clearly. On some of these lepidopteran eggs are ridges, or grooves, or indentations. Some have patterns of raised lines, in a network of geometrical design. Some are like miniature carved jewels. And they are of many colors, blue, brown, red, green, yellow, white. Sometimes they are marked only by ridged lines, but sometimes they are patterned with color, usually microscopic dots. And in every instance the lines or dots are in symmetrical patterns.

There is no evidence that these lines or ridges are lines of cleavage when the eggs hatch. On the contrary, the intricate patterns tend to fade and vanish as the eggs approach the time of hatching. There seems to be no physical purpose for these details of color or shape or decoration.

I can understand the coloration of birds' eggs, at least up to a point. The eggs of shore birds are particolored in a way that makes them look like seashore pebbles, and there is protective coloration, or at least coloring that to some degree matches or blends into the background of the nesting place. But why are the eggs of the Lepidoptera not only colored but decorated, often "carved" like the most minute cameo work? Why are they patterned in the most intricate and even microscopic detail and perfection of design? Whence came those patterns, and do they have a purpose?

There are other patterns in nature, utilitarian as in seeds with spines, hooks, and spurs, protective as in birds, snakes, fish, insects, even animals, and in crystals of minerals such as we find in rocks. But I can find no reason, utilitarian or aesthetic, in the decorations and patterns of the eggs of moths and butterflies. Aesthetics, of course, are of human invention, an intellectual or emotional response to color, shape, or form, so that factor can be canceled out. But that leaves only function, and there seems to be no functional reason at all.

Perhaps I should not ask for a reason. Perhaps the fact is enough. Maybe that is the reason for butterflies and moths—to remind us, now and then, that there are mysteries we can't unravel.

MAY 12

The whippoorwills have returned to the valley. I heard one calling last evening. It seemed late until I looked in my records and found that the earliest I ever heard one here was April 24 and the latest was the last week in May. So May's second week seems to be about average.

We have had whippoorwills every year that we have been here, though there have been fewer as the years pass. Just over the mountain from us, however, they seem to have no whippoorwills at all. I don't know why. We certainly have no monopoly on the night insects on which whippoorwills feed. I suspect that they come down here at night because the lights in the house attract insects, particularly moths. But there are houses over there, too.

Usually I am glad to have the whippoorwills around. Now and then they come down too close to the house and sound off too long and too loudly, particularly at 3:00 A.M. One of them, a few years ago, chose to perch on the woodshed just back of the house and call for half an hour at a time at that infernal hour. But the past few years they have all kept to the woodland and even when I waken and hear them I can go back to sleep. Sometimes I count whippoorwill calls instead of sheep. My record is 546 calls by the same bird without more than momentary pauses for breath. John Burroughs once counted more than 1,300 calls in such a sequence.

MAY 13

Even where there are quite a few whippoorwills, most people know them only by their voices. They sleep most of the day and their coloration is so skillfully blended with the shadows in the brushy woodland that one has almost literally to kick one out of the brush to see it. And their nests are merely a few twigs and dead leaves where the female lays her eggs and broods them. Only once have I seen a whippoorwill nest and eggs, and that was by chance, when I almost stepped on it and the female flapped aside, clucked angrily at me, and fluttered in the typical broken-wing routine.

When a whippoorwill calls close at hand you can hear a kind of *cluck,* almost a hiccough ahead of each complete call—*cluck, whip poor will!* This apparently is a quick intake of breath, though from a distance it sounds as though the bird never pauses for breath. But there will be variations in tempo, for reasons I can't explain. One night I listened to one for ten minutes at a slow, steady rhythm, as steady as the tick of a clock. Then he paused half a beat and raised the tempo about one quarter of a beat. That went on for maybe another ten minutes. Then he raised it again, to a pace so fast one call seemed almost to overlap the next.

The voices vary, too, from bird to bird. Some are almost shrill, some altos, so to speak, and some are almost bass. If you have several around, you get to know them by their voices before the summer ends.

MAY 14

This is a day when I choose to quote from something I wrote some years ago. It goes thus:

We all have our summation days, when we draw a figurative line and tot up both the year and the years. I am not summarizing today, however. I am thinking how fortunate I am, how much any child of mid-May has to be thankful for. When he is young he can say: "The robin sings for me, and the oriole, and the lilacs bloom today. The trout are eager in the brook. Summer is not yet here, but close at hand. My years begin with song."

When he comes to middle age he can say, "Another winter is over and gone, and the earth resumes its vigor. My years are like the season, at their flowering, new growth on old stems and the strength of maturity in the trunk."

And when the years amount to age he can say, "I have seen the season turn with the sun, all my days, and each year I feel the growing warmth as my world turns green. My years are spring, all of them, spring returning like a promise and a fragrant fulfillment."

MAY 15

For years I have planned to keep an orderly record of when the wild-flowers bloom in my area, but I never have done it. I go out poking around the woods and their margins and in the meadow the first few days of March and come home and set down my notes in my journal. A few days later I go again, and forget to make my entries. April comes and I make a list of what I see, knowing that I missed half a dozen entries I should have made. Then May is here and the best I can do is note that I have seen all these flowers in full bloom, though I am not sure exactly when.

So, as now, I leaf back through the journals and find odd entries. "May 15: Saw the first meadow buttercup. Columbines about to open." And I know that must be wrong because columbines, in any normal year, are in bloom by May 10. Or, "May 16: Dogwoods in bloom, clouds of them in the woods like white butterflies." Still another year: "May 15: Jack-in-the-pulpit everywhere. Anemones make the ledge white. Yellow violets out." Still another year: "May 16: A vicious hailstorm brought down most of the apple blossoms, ruined the lilacs which were full out."

No two years are alike, of course. But my own records really are more of an index to my lack of diligence rather than to the vagaries of the wildflowers. All they really tell me is that there are a great many blossoms in May.

MAY 16

We have a pair of bluebirds for the first time in ten years. They vanished from our valley, seemed to become scarce all through this area, ten years ago, probably from a combination of causes. There was a bad spring, with an ice storm that was said to have killed many birds; and we were then being sprayed and dusted and generally poisoned with those chlorinated hydrocarbon pesticides that were supposed to end, forever, the foraging of gypsy moths in the woodlands. The pesticide didn't kill all the pests, of course, and the pests didn't kill all the trees, though they may yet if the spray-boys keep on killing all the natural enemies of the pests and breeding insecticide-immune pests. But the sprays did kill a great many birds, directly or indirectly, and bluebirds were among them.

Anyway, a pair of bluebirds appeared here a week or ten days ago. One of my neighbors had a bluebird house that hadn't ever had a tenant, and he gave it to me. I put it up, and I made another like it and put it up, just in case there were more than one pair of bluebirds. The first pair we saw has now inspected, approved, and taken over the first birdhouse and today they have been taking grass and straw in, evidently building a nest. They watch us with interest but not with particular fear when we go out into the yard. Traditionally, they like human company. And a second pair seems to be inspecting the other bluebird house I put up, but they haven't yet decided.

MAY 17

We plowed the home pasture this spring and replanted it to grass, which is now well up and thriving. But I see, when I walk across the new grass, that field mustard has come up here and there. Black mustard, actually,

Brassica nigra. We didn't have any mustard there before we plowed it. My neighbor says that's the way it happens. Once mustard gets into a field, it is there forever. Two of his fields are "salted" with mustard, apparently, because every time he plows them the mustard reappears. He pulls it out, tediously, and is rid of it till the next time he plows. Probably the same is true of my home pasture. Anyway, I have been out pulling mustard, and I probably shall be at it, from time to time, the next couple of weeks. I want to get it all out before it flowers and goes to seed.

Curious about the life of weed seeds, I looked up the story of the late Professor W. J. Beal and his weed-seed experiment at Michigan Agricultural College, in East Lansing. Years ago he chose fifty fresh seeds from each of twenty-three different kinds of weeds, mixed them with soil, and placed them in individual bottles which were buried in a marked area, about twenty inches beneath the surface. He and his successors then began digging up a bottle every five years to plant its contents and see what would grow.

After forty years nine varieties of weeds grew from those seeds: pigweed, ragweed, black mustard, peppergrass, evening primrose, common plantain, purslane, moth mullein, and yellow dock.

After seventy years three kinds of seeds were still alive enough to grow normal plants: moth mullein, yellow dock, and evening primrose.

So if black mustard seeds will lie there forty years and still germinate when given a chance, those fields of ours that have mustard seed in them are going to be weedy with mustard for a long, long time. Every time they are plowed, mustard seed is brought up to the surface, where it has ideal conditions for growth. The best I can do is what I am doing now—pull the plants when I find them and keep that pasture in grass so it seldom has to be plowed.

MAY 18

I used to be surprised when I looked up New England wildflowers in the botany handbooks and found them listed so often as "naturalized," which meant they were aliens, not natives. I suspect that is one reason this area is so much richer in wildflowers than were the High Plains of Colorado where I grew up. Climate and rainfall have something to do with it, but they aren't the only factors. On the High Plains we had virtually no alien plants at that time. We had plants that had been carried north and south by the buffalo herds and other animals, and by birds and by wind, but they were all of this continent, American natives. There were so few settlers that there hadn't been any wholesale importation of garden plants to go wild.

Here in the Northeast there are relatively few natives among the vast assortment of wildflowers. Cranesbill (wild geranium), milkweed, robin's plantain, steeplebush, goldenrod, asters, some of the buttercups —that about exhausts the list of natives. Black-eyed Susan is American, but it was carried east from the western grasslands, probably in hay. The daisies, bouncing Bet, the clovers, hawkweed, chicory, dandelions, Queen Anne's lace—most of the common, colorful ones came from abroad. Some were imported for garden flowers, some for use in the herbal apothecary, and many came by accident, in straw, litter, packing material. As long ago as 1672 John Josselyn reported that forty kinds of weed had sprung up in New England since the English and their cattle arrived.

MAY 19

Brooks carry a surprising load of sand, gravel, and even larger stones, especially in the spring when they are swollen with melt from the winter's snow. We have several small brooks coming down off the mountain and winding across the pastures to the river, and in April and May we sleep to the music of their burbling, for they come down the mountain in a rush, plunge off a rock or a ledge in their final drop to the pasture level, then go wandering across the flatland with only a whisper or two. By June they have begun to quiet down. July, and two of them have dried to mere trickles. Then with the end-of-August and early-September rains they come to life again.

I knew that flowing water had enormous power and could carry surprising loads. I did not know until a few days ago, when I ran onto the figures in a book on hydraulics, that simply doubling the velocity of a stream's current increases the weight of the objects it can move sixty-four-fold. This seems incredible, but the figures are there, and the proof. A brook or river flowing one mile an hour can move particles of gravel, nothing more. But if a spate increases that stream's speed to eleven miles an hour, which is flash-flood speed, it can roll rocks three and a half feet in diameter along its bed.

Small wonder that a flash-flood is so devastating.

MAY 20

My brooks have no fish in them. They are too erratic and too shallow. But the river, until it was polluted too heavily by paper-mill chemicals for fish to tolerate, had a good variety of freshwater fish, from sunfish to black bass, from yellow perch to trout. And those fish, when I began studying them, took me all the way back to the first backbone.

According to the paleontologists, the earliest fish evolved about 390 million years ago. They lived in the Silurian period, when most of the earth's land was still under water and before the first land plants were here. I find it interesting, though not of overwhelming importance, that fossil evidence indicates there were spiders and scorpions here at that time, apparently the first forms of visible life that lived on land and breathed air direct.

Fish began and always were aquatic. As I read the story, somewhere along the path of evolution one of the simplest forms of aquatic life developed a central core, a rodlike, gristly form of bodily support for the glob of protoplasm of which it consisted. Then this creature, which had been absorbing oxygen from its surrounding water through wrinkles in its surface, extended those wrinkles into slits. Those slits were the first gills. And with gills and the beginning of a backbone, this ancient creature was ready to become a fish, or at least a near-fish.

This process of evolutionary change had taken millions of years, but it eventually produced the Ostracoderm. Paleontologists have tentatively reconstructed the Ostracoderm from scanty fossil clues. It seems to have been a creature with a horseshoe-shaped head covered with horny plates and with a tail something like that of a modern skate. Only the horny plates have been found among the fossils. The Ostracoderm probably was a sluggish creature that lived on the bottom of a warm, shallow freshwater sea. The supposition is that it absorbed its food, since it seems to have had no jaws.

The importance of this phase of evolution, in big terms, was the development of a gristly core, the beginning of a backbone, and the beginnings of a brain and a spinal cord. In a primitive sense, that was the origin of sharks, fish, amphibians, and the animals which eventually produced them.

MAY 21

When I go out on the river or the lake and catch fish, I am not dipping backward hundreds of millions of years into time, except in a figurative sense. Today's freshwater fish are relatively modern. Among salt-water fish the sharks, with their gristly backbones, are probably the oldest type of fish we know today, in any number at least. The very ancient ones are known, if at all, only by their rare and extremely fragmented fossil remains. In terms of time, the dragonflies that seine the gnats from the air over the river are much older in approximately their present form than any fish I shall ever catch.

The fish I catch, like all early forms of life, are cold-blooded. Their body temperature is approximately the same as that of the water around them. This is an efficient arrangement because it enables the fish to get along with a minimum of oxygen. They use relatively little oxygen to warm the body. It is a system so efficient that it has persisted in most of the life on this earth, notably in insects, fish, amphibians, and reptiles. And in plants, of course. Only mammals and birds evolved the more complex system of burning oxygen to maintain a body temperature different from that of their immediate environment.

One cannot say definitely that the change to warm-bloodedness was a step forward. All we know is that it was a change and that it may have had some purpose. The most obvious purpose was to enable warm-blooded creatures to increase their mobility and range. It also had obvious disadvantages. It made necessary the consumption of more food and more oxygen. And it demanded some means of insulating the warm-blooded body against variations in external temperatures. Aquatic mammals developed a layer of insulating fat. Most land animals developed a coat of fur. And birds developed feathers.

Fish escaped that problem. Their dominating necessity, both as individuals and as a species, was to escape other live enemies and to perpetuate the species. From the primitive bony plates, which served as a kind of external skeleton in the Ostracoderm, the fish evolved a kind of body armor, scales. In some species the scales took fantastic shapes—horns, spines, and other forbidding types of armor and armament—that made them more difficult to attack.

The nearest thing to these defenses that I find on my lake or river fish is the catfish's horns. The catfish wears a pair of sharp horns flanking its mouth and a particularly vicious horn on its dorsal fin. The sunfish, of course, and all members of the bass family, have spines on their fins, but these are essentially minor defensive equipment. Compared to some of the bristly, spiny, weirdly armed ocean fish, these freshwater fish are as defenseless as guppies. But they remind me, every time I see one, every time I gut or fillet a perch or a trout and see its skeleton and its remarkable adaptation to its environment, that though evolution is a long-enduring and continuous process, it usually arrives at a practical result. No man has ever evolved a more efficient shape for underwater travel than the basic shape of a fish.

MAY 22

The freshwater portion of my river, which I know best, probably is home to no more than twenty-five or thirty different species of fish. This is only a minute sampling of the more than 25,000 known and identified species of fish in the world. Excepting only insects, fish have evolved more variations in kind than any other form of visible animal life. And in total numbers fish easily outnumber all other species except the insects.

In fish I can see the origins of my own backbone and skeleton, and in their gills I can see the origin of my own lungs. Equally remarkable to me is the system of reproduction which, in one way or another, is typical of virtually all the animal life I know and can see. The basic factor in that system is the egg, and the basic elements are the two separate sexes.

The earliest forms of life propagated by division of themselves. This ultrasimple process never was abandoned. It persists today in such elementary forms of life as the protozoa, the sponge, and some parasitic worms. We speak of them as "low" in the evolutionary scale, though "low" may not be the correct term. They are essentially simple, but that simplicity was so efficient for their purpose that they stabilized with that system long ago and never changed it. Other forms of life, which we call "higher"—and again, that may not be the right term—evolved a variant on the self-division system, and out of that eventually came the differentiated sexes.

MAY 23

A dourish day and very humid. A day that makes me think of those ancient, watery times when life was evolving toward sexual reproduction. When, instead of dividing the original body, as the protozoa do, into approximately equal parts, each of which contained half the original nucleus, this new form of life evolved a means of separating minute parts from the parent body, each part containing a germ of new life. These minute parts eventually became what we call eggs. But the egg process was still more complex, because two parts, quite different from each other, were needed to generate life—the fractions we know as male and female, sperm and egg.

These separate parts developed early in some kinds of life. In certain protozoa we still find what zoologists call microgametes and macrogametes, the equivalent of the two sexes. At a certain stage protozoa produce both these forms. Neither by itself can develop into new protozoa, but if pairs of them come together, one microgamete and one macrogamete, they fuse and continue the life cycle as new protozoa, capable themselves of reproducing.

Somehow this process of differentiation and pairing was carried over into other forms of evolving life, and male and female appeared. The female was able to produce eggs, minute portions of her own vital center, and the male could produce sperm, even smaller parts of his own vital element. When egg and sperm came together, a fertilized egg was the result. And the fertilized egg eventually grew into a new individual.

MAY 24

Another raw, damp day, an indoor day.

The earliest forms of fish apparently had differentiated sexes and reproduced by the sperm-egg process. The fish I catch today still have it, in substantially the same form that fish have had it for many millions of years. The female produces eggs, vast quantities of them. Codfish lay two to four million eggs a year, and large cod have been taken with roes estimated to contain as many as nine million eggs. When I catch a female sunfish in late spring she usually contains a pair of roe that sometimes weigh a sixth as much as her whole body. And the male sunfish have pouches of sperm, the milt, a third to half as big as the roes in the females.

Most fish lay vast numbers of eggs because the rate of survival is so low. It is estimated that fewer than five cod eggs out of a million hatch and mature. I suspect that the hatch-and-survival rate of my river fish, even the sunfish, is somewhat higher, but I would put the figure at less than one in 10,000. If it were much higher than that, my river would be bankfull of fish in a very few years.

The ordinary fertilization of fish eggs is far from efficient. The female lays the eggs and the male spreads the sperm in a milky cloud which, if conditions are right, sweeps over the eggs, fertilizing those it reaches. But a chance current or any one of a dozen hazards can dissipate the sperm before it reaches all the eggs. Even fertilized eggs do not all hatch. Most fish eat eggs, even of their own kind. And those which hatch still face fearful hazards because most fish eat smaller fish, and so do birds, turtles, water snakes, and many other predators. The profligate laying of eggs is the only means of insuring survival of the species.

But less hazardous means of reproduction apparently have been evolving even in fish. At least, other means than the broadcasting of eggs and sperm have been and still are tried. In some fish—skates, for instance—the female has been impregnated by the male with sperm before she lays the eggs. In still others—rays, for instance, at one end of the size scale, and guppies at the other—the fertilized eggs are held inside the mother until they hatch. Sea perch have what amounts to a gestation period, almost like that in mammals, and bear live young several months old and sometimes one sixth as long as the mother.

But the freshwater fish here in my river are quite commonplace and conventional in these matters. The females lay the eggs, the males spread the milt around them, and enough of them hatch to keep the warm shallows teeming with clouds of young through the hot days of late summer. And the fish population of the river appears to be fairly constant, though some years the rock bass and sunfish are everywhere and other years the yellow perch gain ascendancy. There were, until paper-mill pollution upstream made the water inhospitable for them, a modest number of trout in the spring, probably come down from the brooks, and there were enough black bass to make things interesting.

MAY 25

Before the river was heavily polluted we watched the sunfish on their spawning beds every summer. On a warm day we would get in the boat and go upstream to a shallow backwater where the afternoon sun made the water tepid. There we would anchor and watch the fish for an hour or two.

The water was about two feet deep in that cove, and crystal-clear. Sunfish gathered there, well out of the main current of the river. The males fanned out saucer-shaped nests, hollows several times the length of the fish that fanned them out, and about an inch and a half deep. The male sunny, head up, tail down, swept out this nest with his tail, sweeping the bottom clean. There he waited, challenging other males that swam near. Slowly the water cleared after the nest-sweeping. Finally a female appeared. The male welcomed her, swam around her, seemed to urge her down onto the nest. She inspected it. If she approved, she came to rest there and began laying eggs, which were like tiny golden-yellow beads. Eggs laid, she had done her job and swam away. The male swam down, inspected eggs and nest, then released his sperm, a milky cloud of it that almost hid him before it settled over the eggs. Then he took his stand over the nest and waited for the eggs to hatch. If any other fish, male or female, approached, the owner fought, rushing, crowding, slapping, trying to drive the intruder away from the eggs.

The eggs, like those of all the bass tribe, hatched in three or four days of summer warmth. Another day or two and the young, about the size of a fragment of toothpick, began swimming about. Sometimes the parent, always the father, then led them to shallow water where they would live, if they weren't gobbled up by some invader, for weeks, growing and preparing for deeper water and a broader life. Sometimes the father deserted both nest and young as soon as they were swimming freely. That is the way of sunfish. But their big cousins, both small-mouthed and large-mouthed bass, take care of their young at least a week, sometimes as much as a month, fighting off all foragers, herding the school of youngsters from shoal to shoal, being model parents.

No matter when we watched, if it was June or July, the sunfish were in all stages of parenthood, some building nests, some waiting for a female, some guarding eggs, some ready to desert the hatch. There was always a vigorous belligerence among them in that backwater area. Some were so touchy they would snap at even a bare hook tossed among them. Before we realized that this was a nesting area we occasionally tossed a line in there just to see the action. Any warm afternoon we could catch a pail full of bluegills there. Then we found out why and we stopped fishing there. It was more fun to watch them than to catch them. Besides, the nesting area provided food for the trout, the bass, and the perch we caught, in those days, out in the main current of the river. Our help wasn't needed to keep those sunfish in check for a balanced fish population.

MAY 26

We were wakened in the night by an uproar on the riverbank, just across the road. Loud squawks, as from a duck in panic and pain, and hisses, and the sound of flapping wings and a struggle. Then silence, which sounded twice as deep as normal. A mink, perhaps, taking a duck. Or perhaps a big snapping turtle coming up under a duck and hauling it down to gurgling, drowning death. Or possibly a big fish, one of those huge bass the old-timers say used to be in the river, took a meal from the ducks that nest along the river and paddle up and down, just offshore, in the moonlight. Whatever it was, something aquatic was taking a live meal.

Lying in the darkness, after the sounds of violence had ceased, I reflected that the river's fish, all freshwater fish, are really throwbacks, because the first fish are supposed to have evolved in freshwater. They came along in the procession of life before the oceans were salty as they are now. The salt was leached out of the land, slowly, century by century, and the salt-water fish of today are of species that adapted themselves to the gradual change. Even the coelacanth, which has been called "a living fossil" because it is the only known link between fish and amphibians, once was a freshwater fish, the chief predatory animal on earth during its heyday.

Could a coelacanth, I wondered wryly in the darkness, have come up the Housatonic from some ancient ocean depth and committed the noisy killing ten minutes ago? It was a fantastic thought. The coelacanth, one of a family called fringe-fins, still persists as a salt-water fish, though it is so rare that until a few years ago it was believed to have vanished millions of years ago and was known only as a fossil.

There is a living relative of the rare coelacanth, called the lungfish, which has an air bladder that serves as a lung; it can live out of water for a considerable length of time. It also has nostrils that open into the mouth cavity, though it apparently does not breathe through them.

No, I decided, it wasn't a coelacanth or even a lungfish. It probably was a big snapping turtle. Both coelacanth and lungfish are considered remnants of the remote past, though they do indicate lines of probable evolution. The coelacanth's fins are like rudimentary limbs, even to the bone structure. Who knows but that it was the first creature with a backbone to walk ashore, on those fins? And the lungfish's air bladder is a primitive lung. These two attributes were essential for the development of the first amphibian, and the first amphibian was a step toward all the land-dwelling creatures, toward reptile, bird, mammal, and man.

But before either coelacanth or lungfish became an amphibian it was a fish, a freshwater fish.

MAY 27

Sometimes, as I did today, I go out and sit on the riverbank on a warm afternoon and watch the green banks and the flow of gray-blue water and feel that I am watching a kind of stream of evolving life in this river that flows past my dooryard. Life began in the freshwater oceans, true, but by the time it had progressed to that stage of organization where backbones and brains and vestigial limbs were at least latent in the structure of a fish, there was land and there were rivers. And those rivers and the tidal waters at their mouths teemed with life.

Fish evolved for life in the water, which then was the major element, excepting only the air that enveloped this earth. And that air was poor in oxygen, since there were few green plants to cycle the moisture and the sunlight and create oxygen from water. Life depended on water. And water, the great solvent, contained all manner of materials for life's creation and sustenance. And, through the agency of lesser life, it provided the vital food for those strange new creatures whose framework was made of calcium and whose flesh was essentially protoplasm enriched with carbon and hydrogen.

Why, I wonder, watching the river, did one of those fish choose to leave that hospitable water? What urgency was upon it to climb out into the air and onto the land? Was it to escape predatory enemies, or was it to achieve greater freedom? What was that urgency?

I don't know the answers. I doubt that anyone knows. All we know of a certainty is that other forms of life already had left the water-womb. A small assortment of primitive plants were growing in the humid air and marshy ground at the water's edge. Spiders and scorpions were there upon the land, eight-legged precursors of the insect armies that eventually would appear. But there were no other animals of enduring consequence except in the water. Yet from those fish, those early backboned creatures, came the hordes of land animals.

I sat there on the riverbank and watched the emergence, the long, slow change that evolved the first amphibian, the ages when that whole cosmos of marshland was dominated by those awkward newcomers of such a long history. The amphibians, then the first reptiles, then the age of the reptile giants. And somewhere among them, unheeded, I could see the insignificant beginnings of still another kind of creature, the mammal. Creatures no bigger than rats, but wholly land animals and no longer reptiles, were scurrying about in the background. Animals whose blood ran warm, who had bigger brains than the reptiles, who did not have to fear the chill of night. There, in those scurrying strangers, was the beginning of my own kind.

But first, I reminded myself, watching the slow roll of the river in front of me . . . first, there were fish.

MAY 28

A typical late May day, here in the hills—overcast this morning, and a light shower; then clearing, hot and humid this afternoon, and this evening warm and what we used to call "close," meaning oppressive. But we probably are past the time of frost, at last, so today we set out tomato plants, and peppers, and we planted more beans, more beets and carrots, and another lettuce bed for seedlings to transplant in two or three weeks. The first lettuce seedlings were transplanted a few days ago and we have had our first salad, thinnings from the lettuce seed bed. Such baby lettuce is almost too young to eat, but it has a subtle flavor that even the best mature lettuce cannot match. We think so, at least, though a part of it may be in our own palates, which have not had garden lettuce since last September. Anything that new and fresh—and free of chemical fertilizers or pesticides—has a special taste.

MAY 29

From the time I woke up this morning, soon after five, there was tension in the air. It was a strangely quiet morning, with few birds singing and the leaves hanging limply from the trees, not a breath of air stirring.

There wasn't a ripple on the river and the sun had a brassy look. And the day never relaxed. The birds called with a querulous, questioning note, even the robins. The brown thrashers uttered a phrase or two, repeated them, then stopped. And the catbirds flew restlessly from bush to bush, didn't even scold.

By noon the heat was oppressive, though only in the high eighties. The humidity hung like a blue haze on the hills. The plants we set out yesterday were limp and drooping, so I took old curtains out, draped them on wooden stakes, and provided shade, which did little good. By mid-afternoon the temperature was ninety-two and a low bank of clouds hung in the west.

It was almost five before there was any sign of the tension breaking. A few restless gusts of wind whipped down the valley, stirring the trees, which seemed even more listless afterward. Then there was a flicker of distant lightning. The cloud bank, steadily rising now, was illuminated with each flicker and looked like the surging foam on a flooded river.

The cloud bank rose, reached the zenith, and just before six there was a blinding flash as a jagged bolt of lightning ripped the sky beyond the mountain. I counted seconds and got to eighteen before the booming roll of thunder came bouncing down the mountainside. That bolt was almost two miles away. Before the echoes died there was another, and then another, closer now, twelve seconds, then ten.

The storm was moving up the valley beyond the mountain. Another flash, and the count was only eight. It was coming around the mountain, making a big circle. Crash! Another boom, and another crash. The house shook. Windows rattled. You could feel the jolt in the very bedrock, and the flashes were so constant, the roll of thunder so endless, I couldn't count.

Then the rain came, a roar of wind and a thunder of rain on leaves, slashing, drenching. And with it a flash of lightning so close that the thunder shook its final flare. But after that the rain seemed to quench the lightning, which passed to the east, still growling and rumbling but moving on. And the rain settled down from a cloudburst to a roar on the roof.

By six thirty the violence of the storm had passed. I stripped to a pair of old khakis and Barbara to shorts and a shirt and we went out to see what could be done for the garden. Barefoot, we sloshed about in mud to our ankles, rescued the tomato plants from their sunshades, which had been beaten down around them, and transplanted another row of lettuce seedlings, as much to get our hands in the warm, wet soil as to get those lettuce roots in. Then, wriggling our toes in the mud like eight-year-olds, we closed the garden gate, wiped our feet on the lawn grass, lifted our faces, eyes shut, mouths wide, drank the rain as it fell, and were one with grass and trees.

Then we came in, stripped to the skin, made sandwiches, took them to the sun porch and lay, naked as jaybirds, slowly eating and listening to the soft drone of rain on the roof, the gurgle in the downspouts, and the brown thrasher celebrating the cool wetness of the rain-washed evening.

MAY 30

A beautiful day, a kind of atmospheric apology for last evening's bombardment. The rain continued only a little while into the night and the gauge this morning showed .75 inch total, most of which must have come down in that first furious downpour.

The whole world looks washed and clean, and we have the first lemon lilies out and the first of the big yellow iris, the special ones. The old-fashioned yellow and purple iris, those I always called flags, have been out for a week. Those flags, of course, are the bi-colored ones, the purples more a blue, really, and with a good deal of white in them, and the yellows marked with an orange-brown, a good deal the color of the streaks in the common day lilies that will soon be in bloom along our roadside. I can remember those yellow flags from my very small childhood. My grandmother had a whole bed of them along the picket fence that enclosed her dooryard. I remember them as huge flowers and very tall, as tall as I am. Actually, they probably were about three feet tall, which must have been my own height at that time.

MAY 31

This morning, about six fifteen, I saw a big raccoon in the back yard eating something it had dragged out of the compost heap back of the woodshed. I stood at the sun porch window, which was wide open, and it obviously saw me. It kept watching me but was in no mood to run until it had finished with whatever tidbit it had. Its coat was full and glistening, indicating good health. Finally it ate its treasure, to the last gulp, looked at me again, then turned and went across the pasture toward the woods at the foot of the mountain. It was in no hurry whatever.

I wonder if this was the same coon that spent a time under our front porch last winter. I never knew why that one came down to the house, or why it took up quarters under the porch, which it entered by pushing aside one of the lattice slats on the frame that covers the gap at one end between porch floor and ground. We saw that coon almost every day for the better part of a month. It wasn't exactly tame, but it obviously considered itself the owner of this house and we were guests or possibly short-term renters. If I hadn't been careful to close the door every time I went in or out, I am sure it would have moved right in.

Just when we thought it was becoming a nuisance and would have to be dispossessed, it packed up and moved, we never knew where or why. Possibly the move was in response to the arrival of a skunk that found that place under the front porch to be a comfortable haven on a cold, windy day. We didn't welcome the skunk, but it stayed only a week or so. After that nobody lived here but we two people.

JUNE

JUNE 1

The good weather continues, and June starts off ideally. Last night we sat on the front porch in the dusk and listened to the croaking, down along the river, of my remote great-great-uncles.

I have no qualms about recognizing the frogs among my kinfolk; there is no way I can deny the relationship if I accept the basic theses about evolving life. First came the minute, single-celled water-dwellers, so small and so remote I have to take them on faith. Eventually, out of eons of change, came the first fish. And when a creature that had once been a water-breathing fish crawled out onto the new land and made an effort to live there, the first amphibian had appeared. The amphibian pioneered the way of all creatures of the land and the air except the microbes and the spiders and insects, which followed a separate line of evolution. My line led through the newts and the salamanders, and so did that of the frogs and the toads.

The frogs are still amphibious, and I am not. The line which led to me led to all the mammals and the birds. The frog's line has culminated in a kind of evolutionary dead-end. In a sense, the frog is a hold-over—a thoroughly successful one, but an antique creature, nonetheless—and one of a vastly diminished breed. There are only three kinds of amphibians left in today's world: wormlike creatures called Caeciliae or blindworms, tailed creatures that we know as newts and salamanders, and tailless ones that make up the kingdom of frogs and toads.

I have no blindworms for neighbors, and I must say that I do not miss them. They are very primitive, and of interest only to zoologists and students of the fine points of evolution. I do number frogs and toads, newts and salamanders among my local acquaintances. The frogs and toads qualify as friends, from my point of view at least; in fact, they are among the best four-footed neighbors I have. The newts and salamanders, on the other hand, stir merely a mild academic curiosity in me.

They are sluggish, unobtrusive, and at best only vaguely interesting, the newts as dry-land creatures, the salamanders as essentially aquatic.

I suppose this attitude labels me as whimsical, especially in any discussion of evolutionary trends, since the frogs are off the main track. But I do have my reasons. Although the newts and salamanders lie in the mainstream of evolution toward my own kind, they never got beyond a minor station along that great river. They are essentially the same as what they must have been many millions of years ago. To me, they represent an adventure that never got anywhere. In a way, the same is true of frogs and toads; but they seem to belong to my world, which makes them remote kin.

JUNE 2

Now and then I find a newt in a damp, woodsy hollow or a boggy spot warm and wet with spring. Nearly always it is a murky, overcast day when I find a newt, because dry, sunny days make life in the open difficult for him. His skin must remain moist or he is in trouble. His kind left the water to live on land a good part of the time, but dry land and dry air are still hazardous for his limited range of life.

The newts I know best are only a few inches long, are dull coral in color, and crawl about among the wet, decaying leaves. I find them when swamp violets come to bloom and in those moist places where such violets grow. Sometimes I turn over a flat stone on a hillside above the bogland and find a cowering newt beneath it. When I do, this dull creature looks stupidly around and wanders off on four weak legs, looking for another dark, damp place in which to hide.

I know this is no way to regard a creature which carries the remote beginnings of my own backbone and my own brain, not to speak of my own five fingers. But the span between us is too long for my impatient mind to bridge easily.

Once in a while, too, I find a salamander down along the river, and now and then I hook one when I am fishing in a shallow, murky cove. This fellow is called a mud puppy and is an amphibian which breathes both through gills and directly through his skin. Though amphibian, he spends little time on land. He never progressed even as far as the newt. All the salamanders I know are unexciting and uninteresting, primitive and dull. And they all are somehow furtive, fearing the daylight.

Frogs and toads are in a wholly different category. They are here the year round, though they do hibernate in winter. From April till November I hear and see them almost every day. They have no visible resemblance to the lizardlike salamanders and I do not think of them as true primitives. True, they are cold-blooded, they breathe a part of the time directly through their skin, and they have no immediately visible link to my kind of animal. But they belong in my world, as the fish belong, and the birds.

JUNE 3

All amphibians are generally considered an experimental outgrowth of the ancient fish tribe. Considered as an experiment, the amphibian was a success even though it was essentially a transitional stage. It led to other animal forms, notably to the birds and the mammals of today.

But the use of the word "experimental" is both arbitrary and inexact. Evolution is a matter of change in various directions, and most of the changes seem to have been dictated by some factor of environment. It is presumptuous to call any such change experimental, if only because we are not sure of the causes and we can judge evolution only by its results. There have been countless changes. Some of them have led down what seem to us to have been blind alleys because they often led to extinction. The word "experimental" implies conscious purpose, and I doubt that anyone can say either that there was or was not conscious purpose in any evolutionary change. If conscious, then whose consciousness was involved? And whose purposes? This, I know, will raise the hackles of the devoutly religious who follow a fundamentalist doctrine. But I am not here concerned with religion. I hope that doctrinal quarrels with the questions of evolution can rest in quiet. After all, Mr. Darwin died in 1882.

In any case, we now hear much talk about mutations caused by the effects of atomic radiation. Our immediate concern is with the fate of the human race, but scientists are turning up data that obviously apply to the whole history of evolution. In surveying man-made radiation and comparing it with natural forms, they sometimes come up with controversial theories, but the net result is more knowledge of what obviously has been happening in the universe for more time than man can measure. If man-made radiation can effect mutations or even affect genetics noticeably over a few generations, it is obvious that natural radiation must have been doing the same thing ever since the world took form and life appeared. Cosmic rays have long been bombarding the earth and every form of life upon it, and they still are. It is even theorized that man is a consequence of mutations that were, in a sense, blasted into being by a series of unusually violent explosions in the sun perhaps a million and a half years ago. But that is a matter quite apart from what I am now discussing and trying to rationalize.

JUNE 4

We know very little about those early amphibians, but we do find a kind of condensed version of their life and the slow processes of change in the way a modern amphibian's eggs hatch and evolve into living, adult animals. The history of a frog, for instance, shows all the changes we would logically expect in the development of a fish into an animal capable of living most of its life on land.

The egg of a frog is in many ways like a fish egg, comparable in size and structure. It is laid in the water by the female frog, and it is fertilized there by the male, much as fish eggs are fertilized. The egg hatches in about two weeks, the time depending on the temperature to a large degree.

The egg hatches into a kind of larva which has neither mouth nor legs but does have three pairs of feathery gills. Soon an opening appears for the mouth, and the larval tadpole is able to eat algae and other fine vegetable matter. Then four pairs of gill clefts open and the intestine begins to lengthen, which stretches the body. Now the frog-to-be is able to swim by using its tail.

At this stage it becomes a true tadpole. A fold of skin grows over the external gills and new gills appear inside the gill slits. The mouth acquires horny jaws. Then the gill chambers close to a single small aperture through which water taken in at the mouth is expelled after the gills have absorbed its oxygen.

The tadpole grows steadily. Small "buds" appear on its body where the legs will grow. Both pairs of legs start at the same time, but the hind legs develop first. As the hind legs grow, the lungs appear, first as small pouches opening off the gullet. When the hind legs are fully developed, the lungs are ready to work. The tadpole rises to the surface of the water and begins to breathe in gulps of open air. Then the forelegs begin to grow.

This has taken about two months, and every step of the change has been in precise order. As soon as the lungs begin to function, other internal changes take place. The major changes now are in the heart and the circulatory system. As long as the tadpole breathed only through its gills it had a two-chambered heart. Two chambers are all that is necessary in a fish's life, which is what the tadpole lived at that time. But when the lungs began to work, the heart developed a third chamber and the blood began to circulate through the lungs. This change in the tadpole is typical of the vital alteration from fish to terrestrial animal.

Now the tadpole is approaching its final form, the frog. The next step is to rid itself of the tail, by this time an awkward appendage and the last vestige of its fish ancestry. The blood begins to remove from the tail the materials the rest of the body can use. It is almost as though the tail had become diseased. It is absorbed from the inside and worn away from the outside. Finally it is sloughed off. Only a stub is left, and that eventually disappears.

JUNE 5

Clear, dry weather now, almost perfect weather for hay-making. And the farmers in the valley are making hay, cutting the first crop, tedding it, and letting it lie in the sun for a day of curing before they bale it. In consequence, the whole valley has that sweet, new-cut hay smell, which is like nothing else I know. There is a hint of it in the evening smell of a new-cut lawn, but blue grass doesn't smell like orchard grass or timothy, or any of the usual hay grasses. And it certainly doesn't smell like alfalfa, which most of the farmers here grow for winter hay.

The farmer's problem now is rain, not grass. If he is caught with a field of hay "down," cut and not yet cured and baled, he is in trouble. One day of rain can be taken more or less in stride, if the weather clears the next day. But a slow, persistent two-day rain followed by dark, damp weather for another two or three days means that any hay that is down is probably no good for anything but bedding. It may be mildewed, and even if it can be dried it is no good for feed.

So the farmer with hay on his hands, ready to be cut, is more interested in the weather than he is in his food, his sleep, or even his cows. He listens to the radio forecasts, he reads the forecasts in the daily newspaper, he consults the *Old Farmer's Almanac*. And in the end he makes his own guess. If he is a poor guesser, he spends only a few years on the farm. Then he moves to town and gets a job in the hardware store and tells everyone who asks that he decided there was no future in farming.

JUNE 6

The dry weather continues, and so does the haying. I suppose it is safe to go on with the discussion of amphibians, since it hasn't yet provoked a drenching rain for all those hypothetical frogs.

The tadpole, as I was saying, born of an egg in the water, was first a kind of larva, then a kind of fish, and now becomes a land animal that will drown if held too long under water. It now is a frog that will live on land most of its life, returning to the water only for safety from predators on land and to lay eggs and perpetuate its kind in the parent element, water. It breathes with lungs, no longer has gills. But it also breathes through its skin, as its ancestors did before the first fish evolved gills. When the frog works its way into the autumn mud to hibernate it will breathe entirely through its skin throughout the winter, thus reverting to the remote, primitive processes.

So there is my amphibian neighbor, the frog. That is, as near as we know, the way it became a frog, not only the frog I know but the first frog that ever was. There, too, is the toad in my garden, which differs from the frog of the riverbank primarily in being a much uglier creature, in having a warty skin instead of a smooth one, and in spending all its life on dry land except for the brief period of egg-laying and mating. There were toads even on the virtually waterless High Plains of eastern Colorado where I grew up. They dug holes in the ground to escape the blistering heat of summer days, and they emerged at night to feed. They hibernated in the ground all winter. Spring always created a few shallow pools of melt and rainwater, and the toads gathered at those pools, mated, laid their eggs, and went away. The eggs hatched and the tadpoles grew as the ponds shrank. The ponds were dried up by June, but by then enough of the toad tadpoles—which are almost identical to frog tadpoles —had grown into small toads to maintain a minor toad population in that inhospitable area.

JUNE 7

In point of evolution, the salamanders are the closest of the amphibians to the mammals and all the land animals that came after the first amphibian. But salamanders, as we know them, never advanced far as a species. The biggest achievement, it seems to me, was the salamanders' method of achieving live birth. At mating time the male salamander deposits a conical mass of jellylike substance on which, or in which, is the sperm. The female draws this mass of sperm-bearing jelly into herself and there it fertilizes her eggs. The eggs hatch and she bears live young.

This is an advance over the somewhat random fertilization of most fish eggs. Frogs never achieved it. But some fish did. So there we have a crude form of live birth and a beginning of the mating and birthing of the mammal. Neither fish nor salamander, however, achieved the next phase of mammalian motherhood, mammary glands and nipples at which the young are fed directly from the mother. That was a long step forward, and the slow-moving salamanders never achieved it.

The earliest amphibians appeared on earth about 350 million years ago, in what the geologists know as the Devonian period. They throve for at least 50 million years, perhaps as long as 100 million, all through the Carboniferous period, the Coal Age, when the giant tree ferns covered the land and laid down the materials for our coal beds.

JUNE 8

Undoubtedly there were many kinds of primitive amphibians, and they must have been of various shapes and sizes. We know the very earliest of them only by five-toed footprints they left in the sandy mud of the seashore, later consolidated into stone. Those five toes are a point to remember when we look at our own hands and feet, for we, too, are five-toed creatures.

We have clues to the later amphibians—and by later I mean those of the Coal Age—because fossil remains of them have been found. Some had heads as big as those of today's donkeys. Some had vocal cords and could make sounds in their throats, as frogs and toads do but probably as loud as the braying of a donkey. Some lacked vocal cords and were silent, as are today's salamanders. All of them must have had true lungs, or at least transitional lungs, so they could live on land in the open air. But all of them had to return to the water to mate and lay eggs. Their young had to begin life as aquatic creatures.

JUNE 9

The warm weather, haying weather, holds and the farmers have almost all their first cutting of hay in the barn loft or the silo. Some of them prefer to chop that early hay and put it in the silo, partly because then they don't have to worry about good weather failing them, partly because they think it makes better silage than hay.

First daisies are out, have been out all this week. It makes the valley look very summery to have daisies in bloom. And hawkweed, the yellow species, has come to blossom, most of it along the roadside. A few years ago I saw hay fields up in Maine that had been almost taken over by hawkweed, both the yellow and the orange. It made a spectacular showing, but I imagine the farmers who owned those meadows were greatly annoyed. Hawkweed is useless as hay.

Hesperis is in bloom, too. Some carelessly speak of it as wild phlox, but it has no relation to phlox. The flower is four-petaled, not five, and nearly all the four-petaled flowers of that type are on plants belonging to the big mustard family. *Hesperis matronalis* is the botanical name, and I have heard it called wandering lady, though the more common name is dame's rocket. It is an alien, an escape, it comes in white, pink, and deep lavender, and it grows three feet high along the roadsides. Its seeds are borne in little cylindrical pods, like all the other mustards.

Barbara saw the first baby robins out on the side lawn this morning, following the mother bird who was trying, without much success, to teach the young ones to catch their own worms.

JUNE 10

We can speculate about those early amphibians I have been discussing on a basis of those least removed from them today, the salamander and the newt. Some of them, at least, had the power of regrowth. The newts of today still have it. If a newt loses a leg, or even an eye, it can grow a new one. Sometimes the replacement is deformed, but it is a new member just the same, regenerated by the body, and it serves a purpose. This power of regeneration has come down to various of today's creatures, though sometimes in a restricted way. Most lizards can regenerate a lost tail, though a new one often is misshapen or shorter than the original one. A snail can replace a lost horn, even to the eye on its tip. A crab can replace a claw, though the new one usually is smaller than the one lost. Many worms can regenerate themselves if a major portion is left to start the process.

Man has this ability to a limited extent. If I lose a patch of skin by burn or abrasion, I can replace it. My body will grow new skin, though it will leave a scar to mark the spot. If I break a bone, it will grow back together. If I tear off a fingernail, it will grow back. But I cannot regenerate a finger or an arm. I have evolved beyond that point. Why? Probably because my body has grown so complex, and possibly because I am supposed to be clever enough and wise enough to take sensible care of myself. Nature seems to look after her own only up to a certain point; beyond that they are supposed to fend for themselves.

The frogs along my river cannot replace a leg. They, too, grew beyond that stage of self-replacement. But their tadpoles still can. If a fish nips off the tail of a tadpole, that tadpole simply grows a new tail. If it loses a leg, it grows a new leg. Once it leaves the tadpole stage, however, it loses this replacement power. It has quick eyesight, as a frog, and it has vigorous legs, and if it cannot save itself from natural enemies then it must perish. Nature went so far with it, gave it the equipment to become a mature frog, and then left it to its own devices.

JUNE 11

Fossil frogs and toads have been found in rocks 50 or 60 million years old, and those ancient frogs seem to be almost identical with the frogs and toads of today. Fossils of frogs with tails have been found in rocks 200 million years old. Except for the presence of tails, those frogs were not greatly different from those of the later periods. The frogs we know today, then, are essentially holdovers from the time when the first lizards and crocodiles appeared. That was also the time of the modern sharks' first venture, and many of the common bivalves of today emerged about then. And soon after that the great reptiles began to specialize.

Other changes did occur in frogs over the eons. There is today a tropical frog that spends much of its time in the treetops. Its feet are not only webbed but the toes are very long and the webs very wide. By spreading those broad, fan-webbed feet this frog can launch itself from a treetop and glide like a flying squirrel. It is called a "flying frog," though the name is in error. It cannot fly, but it can glide remarkable distances.

Other exotic frogs lay their eggs in cup-shaped leaves, where the tadpoles grow in pools of dew or rain. There are frogs that blow a mass of wet bubbles and hatch their eggs in that. There are toads that hatch their eggs in their mouths. There are even toads that hatch eggs in big pores on their own backs.

JUNE 12

A hot, humid day, one of those days that so often build up to an atmospheric tension that breaks with a violent thunderstorm. We got no thunderstorm, but in late afternoon it began to rain and cooled the air fifteen degrees, from eighty-five down to seventy, within twenty minutes, There was a rumble of thunder on the other side of the mountain, but no lightning here. Somehow a June shower without lightning is a little like catching fish without any bait.

The roses are in full bloom. Not the tame ones—we have no tame ones except some of the old cabbage roses, which I think are beautiful and fragrant but which last only a day or two when cut. They have been in bloom ever since the end of May, and after the first week had as many petals on the ground as in their corollas. What I am talking about now are the wild and semi-wild roses. The pasture roses, those big pink singles that have been treasured by country folk for generations, and the little white ones and their pink counterparts that were promoted a few years back for fencing. We have four or five huge bushes of them, which we never planted. The birds must have planted them. They grow into mounds six or eight feet high and sometimes ten feet across, and just now they are covered with their little white and pink blossoms. By September they will be loaded with hips, which the birds eat. The few farmers who set them out for fences ten years ago have now grubbed them out, disgusted with them, but meanwhile they have been given a foothold in many a pasture and on many a fence line by the birds that feasted on their ripe hips. They probably will become, in another ten or twenty years, one of the common wild roses of this area, for they are tough and hardy. I have been trying for five years to be rid of a bush of them that the birds planted in the corner of our vegetable garden. I have cut it down, I have dug its roots, I have used a brush-killer on it, and still it persists. Such a rose deserves to live, as a species.

JUNE 13

One of the simpler, but still remarkable, adaptations the frogs have made is that of the spring peeper, *Hyla crucifer*, which makes the lowlands loud with sound on mild spring evenings. This small tree frog has long toes tipped with round, sticky pads that enable it not only to climb trees but to cling to surfaces as smooth as glass.

One spring evening I heard a peeper calling almost at my elbow as I sat in the living room. I went out onto the front porch and searched every inch of it, I thought. Then I looked on the trees and bushes nearby, remembering that the peeper sometimes has an almost ventriloquistic ability. Not a sign of a hyla, which had been silent all the time I was looking. I returned to my chair, and within two minutes that frog was calling again, still there at my elbow. And at last I saw him, in the center of the windowpane within three feet of my chair.

How or why he came there, I have no idea. Hylas often call from across the river, but I had never before heard one within a quarter of a mile of the house. But there he was, and there he remained for an hour. I had a good look at him through the glass, saw how he puffed and made his trilling call. And I had a close-up look at those pads at the end of his toes. They were like little foam-rubber buttons, and they were so effective that he shifted his position several times on that polished glass without losing his grip. He sat as firmly as though he were perched on sandpaper. He seemed as sure-footed as a fly.

I watched that hyla and I listened to him, and I silently thanked him and his kind, including the newts and the salamanders, for three things the amphibians have contributed to me and all my mammalian kind. For lungs, with which I can breathe in the open air and live on the dry land of this earth. For vocal cords—the newts and salamanders get no credit there, however—with which I can use the air in my lungs to speak my thoughts or sing my songs and communicate with my mate and all the others around me. And for legs on which to walk and run and fingers with which to manipulate the tools of my life's routine.

JUNE 14

The black-eyed Susans, *Rudbeckia hirta,* are in bloom and make a strong contrast to the forthy white of the daisies. Neither of them, of course, is native here, though they act as though they own not only this valley but all New England. The daisies are among the old English garden flowers that were brought to these shores in the seventeenth century by the settlers. By their wives, actually, who wanted familiar flowers growing in their dooryards. They escaped, found this hospitable soil, and now have spread pretty well over the whole country.

The black-eyed Susans are native Americans, but native to the grasslands of the Midwest, probably beyond the Mississippi. They came east in the usual way, by accident. Their seeds were mingled with hay, or litter of some kind, carried in a riverboat or perhaps in one of the old freight wagons. They were unknown in the East until the waves of settlement reached well out into the Ohio country.

JUNE 15

Wild plants have a great variety of ways to distribute their seeds. That is one of the secrets of their success. The dandelion needs only a breeze, when its flowers have ripened to balls of fluff, to send its seed sailing, sometimes for miles. Much the same is true of thistles and milkweeds—they ride the wind, borne by tufts of floss.

Other seeds are notorious hitchhikers. They have hooks or spines that catch on the fur or clothing of any passer-by. Burdock and sandburrs are conspicuous examples. Less obvious but perhaps even more success-ful travelers are the various small sticktights, burr-marigolds, and the whole family of Bidens plants, beggar-ticks, Spanish needles, trifids, and the Desmodiums, all the varieties of tick-trefoils which have pea-type flowers and segmented pods covered with tiny hooks so that they break off, segment by segment, when brushed by some passer-by. Some, nota-bly the immigrant Russian thistle, *Salsola kali,* are tumbled along the ground by the wind, shedding seed at every bounce.

Some of these plants came over on the first ships from Europe. They came as seeds in the hay and litter used for livestock, and in the grain the settlers brought—there always are a few weed seeds in any bag of corn or wheat. Once here, they soon took root, and those that liked the soil and climate spread.

JUNE 16

Before the white man came, with his insistence on clearing and plowing the land, the native weeds had relatively few areas where they could thrive. The Indians were not the extensive farmers the newcomers turned out to be. The forest persisted in clothing the land whenever a flood or fire exposed the soil. Leave an old pasture uncared for even today and in five years it will have brush and young trees spreading over it from every side. Even in an area of lush grass, the white pine will take root and thrive, and once a tree has a foothold there will be other trees before long. Relatively few of the weed plants, as we know them today, whether they are natives or immigrants from long ago, thrive in the shade. A good many of them do very well in the woodland's edges, where there is a mixture of sun and shade. And it was in the woodland margins that most of the Indians' game animals fed. That was one reason the Indians burned the underbrush seasonally—to encourage that marginal growth and thus insure themselves meat.

But the white man, in the centuries he has been here, has altered the whole ecology. Not only did he plow the land he had cleared; he ripped up the vast grasslands of the Midwest and opened them not only for his own crops but for any wildling that blew or was carried there. And every road he made, from his frontier trails to his latest superhighway, gashed the countryside and became a weed bed. If you would know a country's plant life, prowl the shoulders of that country's highways.

JUNE 17

Reading some old reports on American Indian use of herbs, I find notations that throw strong doubt on the belief that the dandelion was brought to this country from Europe by the white settlers. There is every likelihood that it was native here, for it has been used by the Indians a long time. It was known by the tribes west of the Alleghenies before the first English ever penetrated that area. The Indians used the plant much the same way that it was used abroad—the young leaves were eaten as a kind of salad or they were boiled and eaten as a cooked green.

I suspect that the marsh marigold is a native, too. The Indians of the mountain West have long used its leaves and buds as spring greens, raw or cooked. In England, however, it had a somewhat less than refreshing and reassuring purpose in the pot. It was used to disguise the taste and odor of rancid meat. As one commentator of the time wrote, when you saw marsh marigold in the pot you knew that the other "vittles were at least a mite flyblown."

Milkweed, one of the unchallenged natives, was another item of Indian diet when the first whites got as far west as the Missouri River. There they found the Indians cooking not only the young shoots, as we do today in this household, but boiling the young pods with buffalo meat, then eating them as a green vegetable. They also sweetened their wild strawberries by gathering milkweed blossoms in the early morning and shaking the dew from them over the berries. Evidently the dew was sweetened by the milkweed nectar, which is notably sweet.

JUNE 18

Indian medicine men were, in many cases, wise herb doctors. Their magic and rituals were important as a part of the cure, or the treatment at least, but back of those were the herbal remedies that were basic to every medicine man's equipment. For almost every illness or malady there were several herbal remedies, even in the same tribe, because the tribes moved around, on hunting expeditions and other forays, and one must have an alternate remedy at hand. Some were dried for future use, but a great many were used just as they were found growing. Here are a few out of a long list that I have gathered from various sources:

Yarrow roots, mashed to a pulp or steeped in water, made a satisfactory local anesthetic for dressing neglected wounds or removing projectiles that had been embedded and began to fester.

Mullein, skunk cabbage, and rue were used as antispasmodics. So was gumweed, *Grindelia squarrosa*, the flowers and young leaves dried and steeped. A decoction of clematis leaves was used as a cure of intestinal cramps.

False hellebore, also sometimes called Indian poke, *Veratrum viride*, was widely used as a contraceptive. Indian women drank a daily cup of tea prepared from its fresh root. It was dangerous, however, and had to be prepared very carefully. Too much of it, or too strong a dose, would cause sterility for life. At least that was the belief. The boiled leaves of Solomon's-seal, if taken for a week, were also said to be effective. Occasionally sterility was considered necessary by the attending medicine man, and this was accomplished with skunk cabbage root or the false hellebore. In some places men were sterilized too, on occasion, by the same means.

There were also abortive medicines. Yarrow was one. Others included kinnikinnick, hops, and cedar sprouts. In the West a mother who had just borne a baby was made safe from pregnancy for a year by lying in a trench filled with warm ashes, when her baby was a month old, and drinking tea made from wild geranium leaves.

Burdock, which we think of mostly because of its hooked, bristly burrs, was one of the most used herbal medicines among the Indians. A burdock tea was used as a tonic and a diuretic. It also soothed the aches of rheumatic joints, of sciatica and gout. Burdock crushed made a salve for wounds and eased skin irritations and burns. It was mixed with bean pods to make a medication for erysipelas. Only year-old roots were used, and these had to be dug in early spring or late fall.

JUNE 19

This was one of those beautiful June days that some people don't like at all.

It began with heavy fog, through which the sun shone like a floodlight behind heavy gauze, dazzling everything. It was warm, in the seventies, but the air must have been saturated. Every leaf and twig and blade of grass was soaking wet, dripping, and when the fog began to clear away around ten the whole world was dazzling, the sun sparkling on all those water drops. There had been quite a chorus of birdsong while the fog persisted, giving the scene an even more eerie quality. I wondered if the birds were calling to each other, to know where they all were, or singing just for the fun of it. Anyway, their calls echoed as in a vast auditorium.

Then the fog lifted and we had a hot, humid late morning. The temperature rose into the eighties. No wind. Just that hot lid of humidity. It was a day to sit and do nothing, but I tried to do some work in the garden. Five minutes with a hoe and I was soaked to the skin with sweat. So I gave that up, got out the riding mower and mowed the lawn and the borders of the garden. And even on the mower I sweated. But it still was a beautiful day.

By two it had begun to murk over. All that morning fog, or moisture from somewhere, gathered in vast clouds that surged like watercolor clouds. Thunder boomed in the distance. Lightning flashed. We were bombarded briefly. Then it rained, a first slash and then gentle rain that brought down the humidity and cooled everything. It rained for the better part of an hour, never really dousing things after that first downpour, and tapering off to a cool, misty drizzle. By four it was all over, the sky was almost clear, and the sun was shining. The sky actually was a cleaner, clearer blue than it had been for a week, and everything was washed, clean and refreshed.

We went out to the garden and found everything thriving and, in its own way, grateful. We picked heads of the most beautiful lettuce you ever saw, and we cut asparagus. Then we came in and washed the asparagus, steamed it, and had a feast of asparagus and lettuce not half an hour out of the garden, asparagus with melted butter, lettuce with oil and vinegar.

We took it out on the front porch and ate in the cool of evening, and we lingered almost an hour listening to the brown thrashers, the robins, the grosbeaks, the tanagers, and, last of the songsters, the wood thrushes. Then the whippoorwills began to call, up on the mountainside, and we knew it was eight-thirty. They seldom miss the mark by more than five minutes. We came inside and went to the sleeping porch at the back of the house and lay for another hour listening to the whippoorwills and being a part of that beautiful summer day.

JUNE 20

I had forgotten, until I ran across mention of it today, that the asparagus we ate with such relish yesterday—and will eat again today, and until the first of July—is a traditional remedy for gout. A nineteenth-century doctor asserted that asparagus boiled in white wine was the best cure he knew. We never boil ours in wine, but I have been singularly free from gout, now that I look back, in every asparagus season.

It is now authoritatively known that gout is not a consequence of rich food and vinous beverages. My doctor says, and the reference books back him, that organic meats and beer, of all things, will kick up latent gout. I happen to be one of those persons who live poised on the edge of gout, according to my blood tests, so I drink beer only occasionally and eat liver and sweetbreads only now and then. And, as I just said, I never have a flare-up, no matter what I eat or drink, during asparagus season.

The Indians had gout, though they had no alcoholic beverages until after the white man came. They did, however, eat quantities of organic meats, particularly liver. To combat the gout they used decoctions of elderberries and mullein, pennyroyal, skunk cabbage, plantain, burdock, and yarrow. In most instances, skunk cabbage excepted, they used both leaves and blossoms when they made their gout medicine. You can judge the prevalence of a malady or a disease among the Indians by the number of plants used to treat it. Incidentally, more plants were used to treat the common cold than any other ailment, so all that fresh air and sunshine didn't immunize the Indians from what we get leading a "sheltered life."

JUNE 21

The summer solstice occurs today. So does summer, according to the almanac, though some of us realists keep insisting that solstices and equinoxes, while priceless as mileposts in earth's journey around the sun, really are false markers when used to bound the seasons. Today certainly does not mark the beginning of summer—not summer on the land, where the seasons have their being. Nor will summer necessarily continue until the autumn equinox, except in the almanacs.

For that matter, though this is the day of the solstice it does not mark the earliest sunrise, the latest sunset, or the longest span of daylight, contrary to tradition and everyday belief. The earliest sunrise, discounting a few seconds variation, began on the 11th of June and continued through the 19th. The latest sunset begins today and, again with only a few seconds variation, continues through July 1. And the longest span of daylight, once more ignoring variations of a few seconds, though it does begin today continues through the 24th . . . So much for the statistics.

Summer, as a season, really begins around the end of May and continues through August. Actually, it is rather absurd to think of summer beginning just when the days start shrinking toward the cold minimum of winter, which is what they do now. Summer is growth and blossoming and ripening, and the approach of maturity and harvest. And growth certainly doesn't wait for the end of the third week in June. It varies, of course, with where you live, north or south, high or low. For a time I lived in the high mountain country of southwestern Colorado, and summer actually began there about the end of June. Then in six or seven weeks virtually all the growth of summer was completed, so that frost and autumn could arrive and start the crisp ripening by late August. Often there was snow by the first week in September, occasionally by late August. On the other hand, when I spent some time in North Carolina the summer growing season usually began in May and it usually extended well into September, occasionally right up till October.

Summer, then, is something earthy, in no sense celestial, and the occasion we call the summer solstice is one of those astronomical incidents that have no effect whatever on the growth of a corn crop or a carrot in the kitchen garden. Right around here, in this valley, we call it summer when the first hay is cut and stowed in barn or silo, and that happens nine years out of ten the first week in June, though sometimes it has happened the last week in May.

So a passing wave to the summer solstice while we go about our summer business, as we have been doing almost a month now.

JUNE 22

This is wasp time, and in the garden it is yellow-jacket time. Yellow jackets are wasps, of course, but of a particular species called *Vespulae*. Those in our garden live in the ground. Underground they have paper nests in which there are many cells, in each of which an egg is laid and hatches into a larva that goes through the pupa stage and becomes an adult wasp, a worker for the colony. Sometimes a single colony will contain several hundred or a thousand wasps.

We were wary of these yellow jackets in the garden at first, because Barbara is allergic to wasp stings. But we found that they leave us alone if we leave them alone, and they seemed to prefer bean beetle larva and other garden pests as food for their own nursery larvae. They soon cleaned the bean vines and went on to the squash plants. So we left them alone and mentally marked certain areas in the garden paths, those placed where they had their underground nests, as places to avoid. Thus far we have observed a truce.

Last year we had a couple of men here trimming shrubbery, and in the perennial border they scuffed up the entrance to a yellow-jacket nest.

The response was immediate and emphatic. The men ran, but not before they had been rather well stung. From their truck they brought a spray can and saturated the nest area with a wasp killer, then worked elsewhere the rest of the morning. By afternoon the colony seemed to be wiped out. But it was only quiescent. They sprayed it four times before they won the battle.

I was rather sorry to have the whole colony wiped out, but yellow jackets are testy creatures and once a war with them is started it must be carried to victory. Adult yellow jackets live largely on flower pollen, but their larvae are carnivorous. So the adults kill a great number of insects to feed them, and many of the insects they kill are injurious to trees or crops. I am quite sure the wasps are an important element in natural control of gypsy moths and other forest pests for which the pesticide makers have insisted that only chemicals, and particularly the wide-spectrum, long-lasting chlorinated hydrocarbons such as DDT, are truly effective. Actually, those pesticides kill these wasps and various other natural enemies of the gypsy moths and other leaf-eaters, so the net result is loss, not gain, in the war with the forest pests.

JUNE 23

At a quarter of eight this morning a young whitetail doe, probably a yearling, came over the fence from the home pasture into the back yard and began eating windfalls from the big early apple tree. One window of the sun porch on that side of the house was open and she was so close we could hear her crunch the apples. She was cautious but not skittish. After ten or fifteen minutes she went back into the pasture and back of the woodshed, where the grass is almost three feet tall and will be cut for hay next week.

Curious about what she would do, I slipped out the back door while she was behind the woodshed and stood there, motionless. I was dressed in khaki slacks and a white T-shirt and must have been totally visible against the red shingles of the house. But when the doe came past the woodshed she merely glanced at me, saw no motion, and went on a little way. Then she turned back, past the woodshed again. While she was back of the woodshed I quickly moved to the side yard just back of the sun porch and "froze" again. She came into sight, saw me, paused, stared, then went on a little way, to a big forsythia bush on the fence line, where she tasted a few leaves, evidently didn't like them, slobbered them out, and again went back to the woodshed. And again I darted past and stood motionless at the far side.

Once more she saw me there, seemed annoyed or puzzled but not frightened. She stared, looked away, then turned back once more, quite unable to make up her mind what to do. And once more I slipped around the woodshed and waited. She came into sight, as before, not more than twenty-five feet from me, and stared, flipping her ears for some sound, sniffing for some scent. But there was no air moving, apparently, no man-scent drifting her way. Her stare seemed to become a glare. She took two steps toward the fence and I wondered if she was going to come over it and challenge me literally face to face. She didn't. She snorted and stamped her forefeet. When that got no reaction from me, she barked, stamped again, barked once more, that hoarse, coughing sound that is so much like a dog's bark.

I have heard that deer-bark only a few times, and always before it was a doe's warning to her fawns, which immediately made for cover. This time it seemed to be sheer challenge. If she had been a buck I would have got out of the way, quickly, for a full-grown, angry buck can be more than merely annoying to an unarmed man. But this yearling doe amused me. I began to laugh at her, and must have made some sound, for she barked a third time, then turned and trotted back into the pasture a little way. There she stopped and looked back, flicking her tail nervously. I was still there. And with a final flip of that flashing white tail she loped on across the pasture and flowed up and over the fence—there is no other word than "flowed" for the way a deer clears a fence—and vanished in the underbrush at the foot of the mountain.

JUNE 24

Along with black-eyed Susans, and in some places preceding them, are the hawkweeds, both the yellow and the orange ones. Botanically they are called *Hieracium,* from the Greek for "hawk." The ancients believed that hawks strengthened their eyesight by drinking the juice of this plant. One of the common names for the yellow species is Canada hawkweed, but it as well as the orange species came from Europe originally. The European botanists who specialize in minute differences had a field day with the hawkweed. What we recognize as one species of about twenty listed in *Gray's Manual of Botany* is broken down by the European hair-splitters into 624 "subspecies."

JUNE 25

Over at the lake today we found the harebells in bloom. They are dainty and delicate-looking as plants, and marvelously blue as flowers, one of the most pleasant of summer blues I ever see. They look fragile, and the thin, wiry stems of the plants seem out of place in a rocky environment. But there they grow, seemingly right out of the rock ledges above the water, getting moisture from the night mists and sustenance from the bit of soil that has sifted into the crevices where they set down roots. They are tough and hardy enough to grow on New England's mountaintops, where both wind and cold can be extreme and where even the summers can be times of wide temperature variations. I have also seen them well up in the mountains of Colorado. And I have seen them in a New Jersey meadow. They are natives of Europe and those we have here, on the rocks at the lake, are identical with the bluebells of Scotland.

JUNE 26

Out in the vegetable garden this morning I wanted to do some cultivation, stir up the soil between the rows and discourage the weeds. I tried to start the garden tiller, and its engine flooded, refused to start, leaked gasoline, made a stench and a fire hazard. The carburetor float had stuck again. It has that habit. There was nothing to do but resign myself to a morning, or a good part of it, working as a mechanic. So I got the tool kit, took off the carburetor, dismantled it, readjusted the float, checked it for leaks, found none, reassembled the carburetor, and was about to put it back on when I decided to clean the carbon from the cylinder-head while I was about it.

So there went the morning. It was almost noon before I had the carbon cleaned, the cylinder-head back on, the carburetor in place, the controls all hooked up. I put gasoline in the tank, pulled the starter-cord, and it ran, smoothly and without a leak. I had done a satisfactory job. Another hour and I had done all the tilling I expected to get done before the heat of the day set in. And I was dirty, sweaty, vaguely triumphant at being master of that piece of machinery, and annoyed at the time it took.

But anyone who lives in the country has to be something of a mechanic, a carpenter, a plumber, an electrician, and a general handyman if he would live in any degree of comfort and privacy. There are people in the village who can do these things and do them better than I can, but it takes time to get them and they are underfoot while they are here. In a really troubled situation they are priceless, but for the little things even they thank me for doing them myself.

JUNE 27

We have been picking peas, our first picking of the season, and they are marvelously fine eating. We grow the bush peas and let them climb on low chicken-wire simply because they are easier to tend that way, and easier to pick. We have tried all ways, on brush and sprawling, and Barbara even sometimes lets the weeds grow and encourages the peas to climb on the weeds. The important thing is to keep them off the ground, keep their roots cool and covered, and not let the weather get too hot or too dry before they come to blossom. This last requirement is not always manageable, I must add. But I would forfeit half the remainder of the garden for the peas we grow. They are worth every minute and ounce of effort. Sometimes we have frozen them when we had more than we thought we could eat on a particular day. But two things have happened: Frozen peas, even home-frozen, are a substitute for the real thing, and we finally conceded that; and at the height of pea season one can eat incredible quantities of fresh garden peas. I can, anyway. So we now make whole meals of garden peas and bread and butter, and the freezer gets peas only now and then.

In the old days they were called "pease" or "peason." They were grown in English gardens, in colonial gardens here, even back in the pioneer woodlands. Hippocrates said that peas were much like beans, but "less windy." Galen said much the same thing but added that they "lack a cleansing facultie." I don't think the old Greeks really appreciated peas.

JUNE 28

Yesterday was a warm day and it ended in a warm evening. About six thirty, an hour or so before the sun would drop back of Tom's Mountain, we were sitting on the sun porch at the back of the house, looking out over the home pasture, which had just been mowed to clip all those tall tufts of grass the cows hadn't eaten. The air was sweet with the smell of cut grass. As we looked across the pasture, the air also was full of shimmer that danced and darted. "Dragonflies?" Barbara asked. I said yes, and I remembered the same thing a year ago, almost to the day.

There were hundreds, maybe several thousands, of dragonflies in the air over that sweet-smelling pasture, darting about like flycatchers, making the motions of pursuit. I went over to the edge of the pasture for a closer look, and there I saw thousands of other flecks of light, small as motes. They seemed to wink and vanish. At last I knew what they were—midges. Midges of all sizes were rising from the grass, for some reason probably connected with the fact that it was newly cut. And that was the reason for the dragonflies. They were hunting, feasting on those midges. They cup their legs into a kind of basket and seine the air, and they are so skillful they can outfly a midge. So there they were, all over that pasture, catching midges, and the long light glittered on their wings and on the midges.

I tried to catch one of the dragonflies to identify it, but it was no use without a net. They probably belonged to the *Celizhemis* family, which become adults in late June and are often seen in fields not far from water. Those there in the pasture probably were new adults, out of the molt either on the riverbank or the pasture brook only a few days. The midges probably were newly hatched too, in that remarkable coincidence of timing that one finds again and again in nature. The dragonflies emerge as adults just as there is plenty of food for them. The fact that the pasture was mowed yesterday is not a part of the scheme, but it fits into the pattern. Probably those midges swarmed out of the cut grass because they had lost some of their shelter.

That aerial dance of the dragonflies over the pasture in late June has baffled me for several years. Now I know the answer.

JUNE 29

If man is ever going to admit that he doesn't really own the earth, that he is dependent on the earth for his own life and well-being, it probably will be at this time of the year. Nature now surpasses man to such an extent that he can scarcely keep up with it. Life, green life, red-blooded life, even cold-blooded insect and reptile life, so far surpasses any achievement of man that it would be futile to attempt comparison. Even the farmer, on whose products we all depend for the food that sustains us, knows now that about all he can do is cooperate with the wind and the weather, the seed and the soil. The incredible energy of chlorophyll, the green leaf, dominates the earth, and the root in the soil is the inescapable fact. Man can't even legislate control of the roadside weeds.

Urgency is everywhere. The whole earth seems to be blanketed with grass, with green leaves reaching for the sunlight. The forests spread their canopies. The birds hatch their fledglings. Beetle and bee are busy at the grass root and the blossom. Butterfly eggs hatch and crawl and eat and pupate and become wings once more. Fish spawn. Meadow voles harvest the meadows, foxes and owls harvest the voles. Life throbs everywhere, over, on and under the surface of the earth.

And glib man talks of his power, his rights, his plans to remake a mountain or rechannel a river; and all his power is insignificant in the face of the leaf, the insect wing, the crawling worm. He doesn't own the earth. Why can't he admit it, for a few weeks at least?

JUNE 30

June closes out, the calendar year at its midpoint, the solar year just past its zenith. Summer, by the almanac, is barely begun, but all around me are the indisputable facts of summer. Trees now are a uniform green, settled down to photosynthetic work after the pastel spectrum that first appeared from their buds only a few weeks ago. The undergrowth is a green curtain in the woods, almost shoulder-high. In the meadow, on the hillside where the grass is short enough to let the sun reach them, tiny wild strawberries are ripe, blood-red, honeysweet. In the fencerow the wild roses bloom, a special soft pink that I find in no other flower.

Last night the fireflies were winking over the back lawn and the home pasture, more fireflies than I have seen for some years. I have a feeling that indiscriminate use of pesticides decimated the fireflies and that they are just beginning to come back. I also believe those pesticides sharply reduced the numbers of butterflies. Nobody stopped to think, when they were promoting those long-lasting chemicals, what they would do to the friendly, harmless insects. All they were interested in was killing a few noxious or destructive species. Finally the concerted work of the conservationists has achieved a national ban on DDT, the worst of the lot in general use.

A ruby-throated hummingbird was at the iris just before dark, last evening, feeding there, then hovering over the old bed of bee balm, which hasn't yet come to blossom. When it blooms, that is where they will feast, morning, noon, and evening. Watching that hummer, I thought again what a wonder it is that such a tiny bit of a bird can migrate all the way to Yucatán, and not by land, down through Mexico, but right across the Gulf, close to 500 miles nonstop. Where does it get all the energy? How does it pack sufficient energy in a body that weighs no more than a first-class letter, about half an ounce?

JULY

JULY 1

I find a patch of inconspicuous little wildflowers called beardtongue just down the road, where the crew had to blast away a part of the ledge rock twenty years ago when this road was rebuilt. This is the first year I have found beardtongue there. The nearest ones of their kind that I know are almost two miles away. But the ways of plant migration are sometimes mysterious, often surprising.

Pentstemon is the botanical name, beardtongue the common name. Both names came from the same feature of the flower, its fifth stamen. The plant belongs to the figwort family, the *Scrophularia*, and therefore is a cousin of the mulleins, the gerardias, and the betonies. A characteristic of all of them is the number five—five sepals, five petals, five stamens. But the beardtongue is a rogue. Only four of its stamens are fertile. The fifth, biggest and most conspicuous, produces no pollen. It is simply a big, hairy, tongue-shaped organ that seems to have no purpose. But the plant's names, both in English and Latin, come from that stamen —Pent-stamen, or fifth stamen, in Latin; hairy or bearded tongue in common English.

It is a small flower, pouch-shaped and grayish white or pale lavender. The flowers bloom in clusters at the tips of a branching main stem. But this new patch of beardtongue just down the road is made conspicuous to me by a dozen rough-fruited cinquefoils nearby, with their beautiful pale yellow flowers as contrast to the grayish beardtongues.

JULY 2

This has been a snake day, a rare day around here. We see few snakes. There is an occasional water snake on the riverbank, looking for frogs, and now and then I see a blacksnake at the far edge of the middle pasture. For a time there was a grass snake that seemed to live under or near the old milk barn we converted to a garage, but it has moved out or died. On the ledges up on the mountain there may be copperheads—this is copperhead country; but I have never seen one up there.

I am content to have it this way, for I am one of those who have an innate dislike for snakes. I grew up in rattler country, had caution drilled into me young, and never quite recovered from that early training. I know that most snakes are not only harmless but helpful, even essential in a healthy environment. But this is acquired knowledge, not instinctive. When I see a snake, my instincts shout, "Kill! Kill!" though I haven't killed a snake in many years, and the last one I killed was a copperhead, a good many miles from here. When I see a blacksnake or a water snake now, I grit my teeth and, unless it is on the front lawn or in the vegetable garden, I walk away and leave it alone. If it is in the garden or on the lawn, I take a stick and try to urge it to depart—and feel as absurd as a mouse-shy old granny.

Anyway, I saw five snakes today, two water snakes on the river-bank, a blacksnake back of the woodshed, and two garter snakes near the compost heap. And I feel very virtuous because I didn't harm any of them. Virtuous, and somewhat sheepish, too.

JULY 3

Yesterday's snakes sent my thoughts back about 300 million years, to the time when an amphibian found a way to hatch its eggs on land and eliminate the necessity of ever returning to the water. In our terms, that was the first reptile, and the event ushered in an age dominated by the dinosaurs, a word from the Greek terms for "terrible lizards." That age continued for perhaps 150 million years. During a considerable part of that time the reptiles, some of them the largest land animals of which we have any record, populated and ruled over the land. But somewhere along the way one of those reptiles, probably a relatively small one, grew a membrane between its legs, learned first to glide and then to fly. Another, which already had found it expedient to hatch its eggs inside its own body, enlarged an oil gland and began excreting from it a fluid with which to feed its young. Thus came about the beginnings of birds and mammals. Thus approached the twilight of the Age of Reptiles and the dawn of the Age of Mammals.

It wasn't quite as simple as it sounds. Nothing in nature is as simple as it sometimes seems when reduced to words. Evolution is not a straight-line process, like industrial manufacturing. If it were, the old models would be discontinued entirely and only the newest ones would be made. If that were true in nature, creatures without backbones would have vanished when vertebrates evolved, fish would have vanished when reptiles came along, and reptiles would have vanished when birds and mammals appeared. But nature doesn't work that way. Life diverges, but many of the old forms persist.

JULY 4

This, in our history and calendar of national events for special remembering, is Independence Day, and I am thinking about the Declaration and the way it came into being.

The Continental Congress, in June of 1776, passed a resolution that the colonies be considered free and independent, and a committee of five was named to draft a declaration to that effect. Of those five men, Thomas Jefferson, Roger Sherman, and John Adams were close enough to the land to call themselves farmers of one degree or another. Jefferson, who was chosen to write the text, was a muddy-boots farmer who knew soil and crops and who even had invented a new and better plow.

It was mid-June when the committee got down to work, and the land Jefferson knew so well was burgeoning. By the end of June any provident Virginia farmer has fryers ready for the pan, new potatoes ready for the pot, and fresh garden peas on the table. By July the land itself challenges a man to stand up and proclaim his manhood. The materials of his independence are all around him, if he is a countryman. Thomas Jefferson was a countryman, a farmer, a man still in his thirty-fourth year.

So he sat in a stuffy Philadelphia room, hungry for his acres while the solstice passed, and drafted a document that begins, "When, in the course of human events," and closes, "with a firm reliance on the protection of Divine Providence, we mutually pledge our Lives, our Fortunes and our Sacred Honor." Revised and completed, the Declaration was finally passed and approved by the Continental Congress on July 4. Jefferson, by the way, bought a thermometer that day and noted that the Philadelphia temperature at 9:00 P.M. was 73.5 degrees. The Declaration was printed in the Philadelphia newspapers on July 6 and first read in public on July 8. That day Jefferson bought a barometer to take with the thermometer back to Monticello and make systematic weather observations.

I suppose the Declaration could have been written in December or January, but I am sure it would have been a somewhat different document even if Jefferson had written it. In winter a man hugs the fire, thinks of comfort and security, and wonders if his supply of meat and hay will last out the season. By the time June is merging with July, his world is big as all outdoors and a man asks only uninterrupted time for his harvest.

As it stands, the Declaration cuts through to fundamental matters. In effect, it asks only that the big problems be solved so that a man can take care of the little ones for himself. It isn't a demand for three meals a day and a roof overhead; it is a plea for a man's right to provide such things for himself and be free and secure in them. I suspect that Jefferson knew that details of ideology were less important than a man's freedom to walk the fields and the right to stand on the hilltops proud of his independence.

JULY 5

Thinking about the Age of Reptiles a few days ago, I was discussing the way life diverges and how many of the old forms persist long after new forms have evolved. No one can say with certainty how many forms of life there have been or how or why some of them vanished. Our best reference file of the past is in the fossil beds, but even that is sketchy and incomplete. It is more like the contents of a few wastebaskets than a library of chronological data. There are gaps in the record that we can bridge only by guesswork and deduction. We constantly fall back on living antiques—reptiles, for instance—for confirmation of our guesswork. Out of fossils and living antiques and informed guesswork we have built whatever knowledge we have of the way life on this planet evolved and developed.

Change, as far back as we can see or envision, has been continuous. But nowhere along the line did basic life forms vanish completely. They elaborated, or they varied, or they diverged, but while nature was creating countless variants and multiplying life endlessly, some of the old forms persisted. So, although they are mere remnants of a kind that dominated the world for millions of years before they were superseded, snakes, lizards, alligators, and turtles still persist. The reptilian way of life was successful enough, in a few forms, to outlive the eons.

I could do without some of today's reptiles, but nature couldn't. They still fill a niche in nature's economy, and they represent a stage of evolution that apparently was indispensable in the long history of life. Moreover, they may be, like other forms of life that we consider antique, kept here on the reserve shelf of nature just in case they ever are needed again for some evolutionary purpose man cannot imagine.

Man thinks of himself as the peak of evolution, and from the human point of view he is—up to now. But that doesn't mean that the whole evolutionary urge, the driving compulsion of change, has come to a halt. It may mean just the opposite. The whole process of evolutionary change seems to have speeded up over the past hundred million years or so. And in some ways nature's economy is economical beyond belief; nature seems always to have the parts and materials at hand when they are needed for some job of rebuilding or remodeling. I am confident that if it should become necessary to revert a few eons and start evolving life all over again, somewhere in the infinity of nature would be the materials with which to do it. I am not fond of the reptiles, but there might be a less promising place to start than with them. Theirs was a tremendously exciting age with a wealth of possibilities.

JULY 6

It was not a peaceful age, that Age of Reptiles. Last summer I saw a primitive battle that, in a very minor way, reflected some of the violence of that ancient time.

It was a struggle to the death between a big snapping turtle and a five-foot water snake, and it was fought in a marshy flat at the mouth of one of the nearby brooks. How the snapper got a hold on the snake in the first place I do not know, but when I first saw them the snake was caught in those wire-cutter jaws, only the front two thirds of its body free.

It was a hopeless fight. The snake had no weapons but its constricting coils and the battering but fangless blows it could deal with its head. The snapper was not only armed, mouth and claw, but it was armored with its heavy shell. The snake hammered at the snapper's head and neck, striking repeatedly with no effect. It threw a coil of its body around the snapper's shell, tightened till its muscles corded, and the snapper merely braced its feet. With a twist, the snake flipped the turtle onto its back. The turtle's hind feet reached and raked with vicious claws and the snake's hold loosened. The turtle scrambled to its feet again.

Half a dozen times the snake looped and squeezed, with no effect at all. The turtle kept shifting its hold, each new bite taking more of the snake's vitality. Finally the snake swung a body coil toward the turtle's neck, its one chance of victory. Had it been able to catch the neck, the battle would have been over, probably a Pyrrhic victory, for the snake was crucially hurt. But it failed. The turtle, snapping with amazing speed, caught the snake just behind the head. That settled it, though the snake flipped the turtle over twice more in its desperate thrashing. At last it began to relax, the relaxation of defeat and death.

While I watched, there in the reedy marsh, I knew I was seeing, in modern miniature, even to the setting, the kind of battle to death that must have occurred constantly 100 million years ago. And such battles were always fought between reptiles, because there were no other major combatants on the land anywhere.

JULY 7

This has been a wet year, a very rainy May especially, and all the shrubs and bushes have been loaded with blossoms. I never saw so much bloom on the bush dogwoods—the tree dogwoods, too, for that matter—and all the viburnums. The wild raspberries we know as black-caps were white with blossoms and now are loaded with green berries turning red. Somehow, in all those rainy days, the bees evidently found enough dry hours to gather a great deal of pollen and distribute enough of it from flower to flower to fertilize more potential fruit than usual.

And now the elderberries are in bloom, an abundance of blossom, following the precedent of all the other bushes. With their big, flat-topped clusters of white flowers, they are doubly conspicuous. I see elderberry bushes in every moist hollow and on almost every hillside, places where I never was aware of them before.

With all this fruit there undoubtedly will be a rich autumn, for the oaks are full of young acorns and the hazelnut bushes seem to be loaded. And we probably will hear from the volunteer seers that it is going to be a very hard winter ahead. They always seem to reason backward—instead of saying there is a big crop of fruit and nuts because there was a favorable spring and summer, they say that the big crop means a hard winter is coming, that nature is providing plenty of food for bird and beast in what will be a trying time.

It may be a hard winter, but not because there is plenty of food on bush and vine and tree. That, I state firmly.

JULY 8

The number and variety of the reptiles during the thousands of centuries they dominated land life was amazing. It was as though animal life had exploded into a multitude of forms. We don't know why this happened, but it was during a geologic time when most of the land was low-lying and wet, when the climate was mild and humid, and when vegetation was so lush as to be extravagant. The jungles of tree ferns apparently were dying out, but other plants came spreading after them in profusion. It was after extensive glaciation of the southern hemisphere and before the massed glaciers moved down from the north. It must have been a fertile time for life, all life. Toward the end of the period the great mountain chains were rising and vast deserts came into being; but by then the big lizards had reached their peak in size and the first small mammals were beginning to get a foothold.

The smallest of the reptilian creatures were not much bigger than sparrows, but the biggest of them were almost ninety feet long, stood close to twenty-five feet high, and must have weighed about thirty tons. Some were lizards much like those we know today. Some were like today's alligators and crocodiles. Some were armored in huge scaly plates and armed with three long horns in a row on their snouts. Some were like huge, grotesque kangaroos with scaly legs and three-toed chicken-feet and ponderous tails fifteen feet long. There were even fishlike ichthyo-saurs with bodies somewhat like whales and legs reduced to paddles. There were water-dwelling plesiosaurs fifty feet long, with necks and heads like snakes and legs like oars. These had reverted to the earlier element, water, which their ancestors had deserted; but they, too, were reptilian and had the basic characteristics of their land-dwelling kin.

There were light-boned pterodactyls, with heads like alligators, bodies like bats, tails like long whips with tufted ends. They grew membranes that they could spread like wings. Some of them had a twenty-four-foot wingspread; some were smaller than robins.

But there was a basic flaw in most of these reptiles, especially the giants. Their bodies grew to enormous size but their brains remained almost rudimentary. The triceratops, a rhinoceros-like creature that weighed at least ten tons, had a brain that weighed no more than two pounds. And the stegosaurus, a thirty-foot lizard with a row of big vertical scales like a dorsal fin, had a brain estimated at two and a half ounces, about the size and weight of one of the small dry-cell batteries that power my flashlight. Some kangaroo-like lizards that stood twenty feet high had nerve centers over their hips larger than the brains in their skulls.

JULY 9

It was a fantastic world, an unbelievable age, the Age of Reptiles. Reconstructing it now, it seems astonishing that with all its possibilities for life, the forms of that life should have been largely limited to reptiles. Plant life was overrunning the land. Insects were swarming. But among the animals apparently the cold-blooded, egg-laying tribe dominated for centuries. Yet basic change must have been in the very air, especially during the later years of this age, for out of it came the vast variety of life we know today.

There is a temptation to say that this intense fecundity and the persistent trend toward giantism in the lizards was a result of what we think of as a favorable climate for growth. But that does not explain everything. Plentiful food encourages both size and numbers. But why did the bodies of so many of those swarming giants outrace their brains? An abundance of food made life easy, but a corresponding abundance of animal life created competitive conditions of life. Brain power would not have been wasted even in that environment so favorable to physical prosperity.

Life was a struggle, even in that Eden, a battle for existence. An eighty-foot-long plant-eater might easily find its necessary quarter of a ton of green food every day, but if it hadn't the wit to avoid attack by a twenty-foot, sharp-toothed carnivorous neighbor the plenitude of food was of no importance. It died in the midst of plenty, and even more quickly than it would have starved to death in a desert. And the carnivores ate each other. The world must have roared continuously with the battles of the titans.

But both the giant vegetarians and the giant flesh-eaters eventually vanished. It was the lesser members of the tribe that persisted; and the remnants of those lesser ones still survive. The largest of them are the alligators and crocodiles and the big turtles, all of them pygmies compared with the masters of the Age of Lizards.

JULY 10

While I have been poking around in the steamy savannahs of the remote past, trying to understand the Age of Reptiles, the often absurd present and the unpredictable future have been staring at me from the open door. And all around me the simple facts of summer and July have been proclaiming that this is midyear of a time when a man can find peace and comfort on his own acres.

July is abundance on the land. Its long days seem specially shaped for a man to tend and reap, to prepare for his own tomorrow, to enjoy what he has today. We have had magnificent lettuce from our own garden for a month. We had the finest of garden peas from our own vines, now supplanted by cabbage plants that will be heading before August is a week old. We had the first green beans almost three weeks ago, and will continue to have them from successive sowings until we can't face another bean. We have had new onions and baby beets and finger-size carrots, sweet as honey. In the fields the corn is almost waist-high. First-cutting hay is in the barns and second-cutting hay will be ready for the mower before mid-month.

Wild raspberries ripen, sweet and tanged. Acorns begin to fatten on the oaks. Sumac is rank wherever it catches a roothold along the riverbank. Wild mint abounds in every fencerow. Bee balm comes to bloom, to the delight of bumblebee and hummingbird. Poison ivy thrives, and nearby is the light green leaf and translucent stem of jewelweed, whose juice is one of the better wild cures for ivy poisoning. Daisies whiten roadsides. July proclaims itself wherever I look.

JULY 11

Why did the dinosaurs and most of their reptile relatives die out and end the Age of Reptiles almost 100 million years ago? Over the years scientists have offered a dozen or more explanations, and they are still "explaining." The most recent explanation I have heard came from Heinrich K. Erben of Bonn University's Institute of Paleontology. It is at least a variation from the ones we have had.

Near Aix-le-Provence in southern France a great many fossilized dinosaur egg fragments have been found, so many that Erben believes the dinosaurs used that site as a "nesting place" for thousands of years. By examining the egg fragments layer by layer and measuring the shells with an electron microscope, he has found that those in the lower, older layers were twice as thick as those in the upper layers. In other words, the later eggs were so fragile they were easily broken and the embryos killed. This is substantially what has happened to the eggs of the bald eagle and the osprey today as a consequence of DDT spraying. Research indicates that the DDT severely interferes with the production of hormones essential to making normal eggshells. There obviously was no DDT being used 100 million years ago, but the Erben theory is that overcrowding could cause a similar hormone imbalance and interfere with the creation of normal eggshells. Geological evidence, says Erben, indicates that the late Cretaceous Age in France was a time of drought which left a desertlike area with only a relatively few shrinking areas of normal vegetation. The big lizards crowded those areas, and one of the crowd syndromes is severe disturbance of the hormonal balance. So Erben believes the big lizards simply failed to produce hatchable eggs because they were caught up in the nervous effects of the crowd syndrome.

I should like to go further into this crowd syndrome matter, but not today. It has been a factor in animal populations in recent times, and it may even be a factor in human populations and human reactions today. Not enough is yet known about it to make hard-and-fast statements about its effects, but enough is known to call for further examination.

First, however, I should like to say a little more about the Age of Reptiles.

JULY 12

The most commonly held theories about the disappearance of the dinosaur tribe are based on climatic changes. It is generally believed that the climate underwent rather sharp changes about that time. It cooled off and became so much drier that many of the vast marshlands all over the earth began to dry up. If the big reptiles were to survive these changes they had to make adaptations, and the theory is that they failed to do this. This supposes that they had little adaptability, which is thought always to be true of animals with scant brain capacity. Yet how much brain, even relatively, has an ant or a bee or a wasp or a dragonfly? They were here before the big lizards, and they are still here. They have survived countless climatic and geological changes.

Some theorists believe the early mammals, creatures perhaps the size of today's rats, ate the reptiles' eggs. This, too, has an air of plausibility, since most of the big lizards were egg-layers. But there were a great many lizards, and there must have been a great many eggs. This theory presupposes a vast population of egg-eating mammals, each with a huge appetite.

Some believe the big lizards were simply outdated, that change was overdue, that the lizards, particularly the giants, had already outstayed their time. This has overtones of belief in cyclic change, but it is not in itself persuasive. It takes little account of the basic weaknesses of the species, which appear to have increased rather than diminished over the centuries.

Whatever the theory, the fact is that the big lizards did vanish, and they vanished rather quickly, in terms of geologic time, after they reached their physical peak. With our customary excellence of hindsight, we can say that as a species they had fundamental shortcomings or that they abandoned certain fundamental necessities for survival.

First, they outgrew their own brains. No creature with more brainpower in its hind legs than it has in its head has the wit to survive in a competitive world.

Second, their reproductive system was inadequate. We have no means of knowing how many eggs a prehistoric lizard laid, but it seems unlikely that a dinosaur ever laid as many eggs as a sunfish or a frog. To survive, an egg-layer must give enough hostages to the hazardous conditions of the hatch to insure at least two adult and reproducing offspring. And there probably was little parental care, if any. Reptiles seldom care for their young even as casually as some fish. The surviving reptile species give their young almost no care after hatching. Most of them, however, even the turtles and alligators, lay many eggs at one time. Perhaps that is one reason they survived. They gave their kind at least a mathematical chance.

Third, the big lizards probably were what we call cold-blooded. One modern theorist, Robert T. Bakker of Harvard's Museum of Comparative Zoology, thinks that unlike other reptiles the dinosaur tribe probably were warm-blooded. That, he thinks, is the only way they could muster the energy to travel as far and as fast as they did. But he thinks they succumbed to the cold because of their hairless skin. That agrees with the cold-blood theorists, who also believe they were wiped out by the cold. My theory is that they were cold-blooded, vulnerable to the cold weather, and most of them were too big to burrow into the mud and hibernate, as snakes, lizards, and turtles do today. One winter such as we have in New England would have killed them by the tens of thousands. There is some evidence that toward the close of the era, some of the pterodactyls, the pre-birds, did begin to warm their own blood, move over toward the warm-blooded species of today. But I have seen little evidence that the dinosaurs themselves ever achieved the warm-blooded status that Dr. Bakker credits them with.

And finally, although they branched out in all directions—or perhaps because of that—they specialized fatally. They were physically unable to accept change, even such minor change as the alteration of a few types of vegetation. This is obvious from their fossil remains. And, like most specialized animals of today, they may have been unusually susceptible to disease. Disease seems often to take violent and fatal toll when any creatures crowd their environment. And this leads directly to the Erben theory, at least to the crowded-oasis part if not to the thin-eggshell conclusion.

JULY 13

We recently had a series of sunspot flare-ups with bursts of radiation so intense that some scientists predicted they would affect our electric power systems. As far as I know, there were no serious effects. But who knows what effect that radiation may have had on plants and animals? We have little definite knowledge about such effects, but it is conceivable that intense bursts of solar radiation have played an important part in the mutation of species. It is even conceivable that intense radiation was a vital factor in the origin of the reptiles, particularly in the giantism that characterized their age and the fantastic forms that appeared. And it is possible that such radiation was a factor in their extinction. But that is at best speculative.

While they were here, however—and remember that the lizards large and small, and all the other ancient reptiles, dominated land life for about 150 million years—they developed certain characteristics that have had an enduring effect on most of the animal life that came after them. I am what I am at least in part because of what the ancient reptiles were.

So is my dog. So are the cows whose milk I drink and whose flesh I eat. So are the birds that make my mornings sing.

Basic to the change from amphibian to reptile was the development of a dry skin that protects the body from excessive evaporation. Amphibians died if their skin became dry. The skin of reptiles conserved the body's moisture. My skin conserves my inner moisture, releasing just enough to cool the skin by evaporation in intense heat. The reptile's skin usually was covered with some form of horny scales or plates, but in later stages some of those scales began evolving toward feathers, others toward hair. But in all of them there was freedom, at last, from the porous, naked skin that kept amphibians close to water.

The amphibians had developed legs strong enough to support their bodies without the help of surrounding water. The reptiles developed those legs into sturdy limbs for running, leaping, and fighting. They were usually four-legged, with claws on their feet, but some of them traveled on two legs. Others developed the toes and legs into wing frames for flight.

Reptiles produced eggs that would hatch on land. These eggs were larger than those of fish and amphibians, they contained a generous supply of food for the hatching fetus, and they had inner membranes and protective outer shells. Some of them, undoubtedly the smaller, physically lesser ones, developed a system of live birth, the mother retaining the fertilized eggs inside her until they hatched.

This was a transition stage—an experiment, perhaps—which some fish and amphibians already had achieved. But it was a fundamental step in the change toward placental birth, which is typical of the mammal. And in all reptiles, whether they laid eggs or had some transitional form of live birth, the eggs were fertilized inside the female by the injection of sperm by the male. The haphazard fertilization of eggs externally, common in fish and amphibians, was being superseded.

JULY 14

Change goes on all the time, day after day, year after year. But the big changes are so gradual we are seldom aware of them. No doubt the gigantic lizards died off gradually, though in geologic terms it may have been quite sudden. The geological clock deals in millions of years, not even in the centuries that we think of as long spans of time.

Even so, the lines of change, from geological age to age, are not really clear, and we have no readily comprehensible calendar for the changes in animal life. We speak of the process as evolution, which literally means a rolling out, or an unrolling. The scope of life at the time we have been discussing was broadening and becoming more complex. We think of ourselves as the apex of that process of evolution, which is understandable since we are the ones who pass the judgment. But I am not prepared to say the whole course of evolution was aimed at the eventual development of *Homo sapiens*. It may have been. Or man's appearance may have been sheer accident, one of those freakish happenings that occur in all forms of evolving life.

Man does have a degree of awareness and a capacity for life that apparently are unmatched. He has a phenomenal brain. But why did vestiges of all stages of evolution that we can trace persist? Why do single-celled organisms persist? Or primitive multicelled organisms, both plant and animal, even those so ambiguous that we cannot say of certainty which they are, plant or animal. Fish persist, even very primitive ones, and so do salamanders and lizards. So do insects, which are a source of knotty questions every time one wanders down this road of speculation.

If the whole evolutionary process was devoted to the creation of man, where do all these other forms of life fit in? I cannot say they were created only for man's use or to make this a more habitable, a prettier, or a more enjoyable place to live. I keep wondering if they haven't their own place and purpose in the order of life, and if they wouldn't have had that place even if I had never been here to be aware of them.

The reptiles dominated the world for about 150 million years. Most of them vanished when the mammals and birds became numerous. The mammals have dominated the scene about 100 million years, and man has been here only two or three million years. Perhaps we should wait a few thousand more years before we speak of the giant lizards as an experiment in evolution that turned out to be a failure.

The blacksnake on my mountain and the turtle in my river do not speak a language I can understand. They have nowhere near the brain capacity I have. I cannot grant them much intelligence, nor any imagination, love, or compassion. I am sure their powers of memory are limited. But they are here today, and their presence proves that the reptile, for all its cold blood, its oviparous birth, and its limited brain power, is a persistent and successful form of life. In its own way, that life has adapted to far more change than man has ever known. I can only hope that my own kind has as much persistence, as a species, as these reptilian neighbors of mine.

JULY 15

Now we have come to our time of summer heat, when even here in the hill country we have a blazing sun, scorching afternoons, and warm nights. We are fortunate in having a house situated at the foot of a mountain, for at sundown the cool air begins to flow down the mountainside and into the valley. The cool air is heavier than the warm air, so it flows somewhat like water, down the slope; and we open the windows at the back of the house, let that cool evening air come in and push out the afternoon's accumulated heat. This makes our evenings cool and our nights comfortable. It is a kind of natural air-conditioning arrangement, which I can recommend.

Most people who come to the country from the city and build a house choose a hillside site, or even a hilltop, for the view. They forget, if they ever knew, that the hilltop is where the winter gales whoop and roar, and where the summer sun sears and simmers. The valley can be a trap, of course, particularly if it has a stream, for streams rise in flood at times. But a site just up the hillside from the flood-plain is still in the valley, sheltered from winter blasts and summer searing. And it is blessed with those evening tides of cool air flowing down the hillside.

That is where I find many of the old cellar holes of vanished houses built by pioneers in this area, just above the flood-plain, at the edge of the valley. Those early settlers cleared and farmed the hillsides, but they snugged their homes under the lee of those hills, sheltered in winter, cooled in summer.

JULY 16

I mentioned that bee balm is in bloom, as though it were something routine. In a sense it is, for it blooms about this time each year. But there is something special about this plant, which some old-timers called Oswego tea and used in brewing a pick-me-up. It is a member of the big mint family, and in many places it grows wild. But not here. We had to get the roots from a friend and plant them. The wild species here is the one with a light lavender flower. Bee balm has bright vermilion blossoms. Both are bergamots, and both are patronized by insects with long tongues and birds with long beaks, primarily night moths, bumblebees, and hummingbirds.

The names of these plants fascinate me. Bergamot comes, ultimately, from the Turkish, *beg-armudi*, literally "a prince's pear," actually a species of pear. From there it was transferred to a pear-shaped orange, *Citrus bergamia*, whose rind yields an oil used in perfumery. And from there it was taken for the plant, which has an oil with a fragrance much like that of the pear-shaped orange. Brush against a bergamot plant and your clothes will have that fragrance for hours.

Botanically the bergamots are called *Monarda*, a name that honors Nicolas Monardes, a Spanish botanist of the sixteenth century who wrote tracts about medicinal herbs, especially those of the New World. The red species is *Monarda didyma; didyma* refers to the twin stamens. The lavender species is *Monarda fistulosa; fistulosa* refers to the tubular shape of the individual florets.

JULY 17

No doubt about it, it is summer now. The field daisies have been in bloom since mid-June, and now come the black-eyed Susans, whose color smacks you in the eye. I find in *Gray's Manual of Botany* that color is given simply as orange-yellow. To me it is a special brassy golden color, full of sunlight, a color that no artist I can remember except Van Gogh ever used.

Botanically it is *Rudbeckia hirta*, honoring two professors, father and son, both named Olaf Rudbeck, who were predecessors of Linnaeus at Uppsala. The *hirta* simply means "rough" and refers to the rough, mildly prickly texture of the stem and leaves. The plant is one of the composites, each flower a community of florets grouped in the center and surrounded by those brassy golden petals. The center florets really are not black at all. They are a purplish brown, and as they mature they appear almost as yellow as the outer petals, for they produce yellow pollen.

These brilliant flowers, originally native only to the open grasslands of the West, are now almost as widespread as the sunflower, another native of the western plains.

JULY 18

The movement of plant life about the earth makes me think of both the striking similarities between plant and animal life and the fundamental differences.

The structure of both plants and animals has at its core the basic protoplasm, the substance of the cell. Both have systems of utilizing food, creating new protoplasm and other cell materials, and developing the energy needed for the life processes. Both reproduce by some form of self-division, usually in the form of the seed. The seed in the plant is the equivalent of the egg in the animal. In it are contained all the elements for producing offspring from the parent, plus the mysterious agents which make that offspring substantially the same as the parent. And both plants and animals have the capacity for adapting themselves to their environment.

Plants, however, are not endowed with the means of movement that enable animals to move about their environment. Because plants can find their necessary food in one place, they remain in one place. They have roots, which anchor them and which draw from the earth many of their essential food elements. They have leaves, which capture both light and moisture from the surrounding air. Although they seem to have nothing like a nervous system, thay do respond to certain sense stimuli. Some are notably sensitive to touch.

The most notable characteristic of plants is that they not only gather their own food but manufacture it into usable form. And they store both food and energy. The chief agent in this manufacture is chlorophyll. Endowed with chlorophyll, the plant can convert inorganic materials—carbon, hydrogen, oxygen, nitrogen, and various minerals in small quantities—into sugars, and it can store these sugars in the form of starch. It can also store solar energy for use during the night and during heavily clouded days. In the process of manufacture, the plant absorbs water and carbon dioxide, and it gives off water vapor and oxygen. It is this capacity for manufacturing and storing food that makes the plants so vital to the whole animal world. Animals can eat only organic matter, and the greater part of the world's animal population lives on plant life directly. The flesh-eating animals live on plant-eating animals, so there is total dependence on plants.

JULY 19

A little while ago I mentioned the crowd syndrome in speculating about the fate of the giant lizards. I am reminded of this today by a newspaper report on the number of patients with glandular disturbances in the New York hospitals, and the fact that it is twice as high as it was ten years ago.

Some years ago researchers were studying the effects of overcrowding the environment with squirrels, rabbits, deer, and other game animals. The research was a part of a game management program, but it turned up something at that time brand-new, "shock disease," also called a crowd syndrome. It was found that at a certain point of population density physical changes occurred in the animals. Most of the changes were in the glandular system, particularly the pituitary and the adrenals, glands more directly affected by such emotions as fear, anger, and pain. When an area became crowded, many of the animals showed a shortage of blood sugar, enlargement of the adrenals, reduction of sugar storage in the liver, degeneration of the liver, and definite changes in the chemistry of the blood. These changes made the animals susceptible to diseases they normally would have easily thrown off. Instead, many of them died of those diseases.

But others did not die. They simply went mad. Not rabid mad, but frenzy mad. They ran in circles as though blind. They bumped into objects, injured themselves, and seemed to be unaware of the injury. Sometimes, even with food at hand, they failed to eat and starved to death. Sometimes they went into a lethargic state and lay down and died. Sometimes they went into a frenzy, thrashed about, and then died. When they were examined after such death their bodies showed no fatal disease except a disintegration of the nervous system. They died of "shock disease." They couldn't stand living in a crowd any longer.

The condition was found among fox squirrels in Michigan. Then, also in Michigan, similar symptoms were found among crowded skunks. They acted crazy and some died in their dens. Examination showed that their nervous systems had gone to pieces and they had a variety of encephalitis. Then it was found among snowshoe hares, who went mad, refused to eat, refused to come in out of the cold, and died. They, too, had enlarged glands, bad livers, the whole range of "shock disease." And finally someone remembered a report of the Kaibab deer when they were so seriously overcrowded, back in 1926–27. The action of the deer tallied with all the others. They evidently had "shock disease," the crowd syndrome.

And then, only a few years ago, a researcher in Iowa found that crayfish go quietly mad when they have to live in too much of a crowd of their own kind. They get jumpy and tense. Their nervous systems begin to go to pieces. They have all the symptoms of "shock disease."

Not too long after that, another researcher in the Midwest found that hogs get duodenal ulcers when they are penned too closely, when they have to live in too much of a crowd. They didn't go mad—they were converted to chops and bacon before that, apparently; but they had made a start.

Draw your own parallels, if you wish.

JULY 20

I have been out picking black-caps, which are sometimes called thimbleberries. They are wild raspberries, of course, which turn glossy black when they are ripe and have a seedy sweetness like no other berry I know. They are native to America, and I have known them in the Midwest and the West, where the fruit grew almost twice as big as it does here in New England, big as the big, sweet wild blackberries, but without the blackberries' core.

The black-cap vines are harmless-looking, where they grow more or less individually. They pluck at my clothes and they can scratch my arms but not very deeply if I use normal care. But up on the mountainside they grow in tangles that are like barbed-wire barriers, and when their canes die they become vicious. The thorns on those dead canes are doubly sharp and stiff as steel, and if I try to force my way through them I come out with torn clothing and with thorns in my flesh, for those dry thorns are easily broken from the stems when they have embedded themselves.

I haven't tangled with those raspberry thickets up there for some years, not since I stopped hunting partridges. The partridges—ruffed grouse, actually, which we more often simply call "birds"—love those briary tangles. I nearly always could put up a bird or two if I steeled myself and thrust my way into the briars. But now they live there undisturbed, in an unofficial sanctuary. And I pick black-caps here along the river, as I did today.

JULY 21

We have been having a series of those perfect summer days, with relatively calm air, moderate temperature that didn't exceed the low eighties, and the kind of blue sky and magnificent cumulus clouds that take me back to my boyhood on the High Plains. Those huge galleon-clouds drifted across that boundless sky and blotted out the sun briefly, and I, wandering the plains on foot, a young savage who in imagination was at least half Indian, followed the shadow of such a cloud, where it was cool even on a blistering day. Leisurely cumulus clouds that cast a shadow a boy could keep up with at a leisurely trot.

To have such days here, in these eastern hills, is a rare privilege. Too often the air is faintly misted with humidity from the seacoast a hundred miles away, or it is tinged with thin but recognizable fumes from power plants and factories forty or fifty miles away.

And when I say this it makes me think of the unthinkable crime that has murked and sooted and smogged the air of the High Country of the Four Corners area in the West, where Colorado, Utah, New Mexico, and Arizona meet—the vast coal-fired power plants that have been built there to supply electricity for teeming California's night-glare. And I wonder how much longer there will be blue sky anywhere.

JULY 22

We like to think of plant life as peaceful existence, properly removed from the bitterness of competition and the violence of war and murder. The meadowful of daisies, the woodland of oaks and maples and pines, the bogland of cattails and skunk cabbage and purple-headed ironweed, seem ideally arranged in a quiet pattern of peaceful coexistence. But the truth is not quite so idyllic. The battle for existence, the struggle for living space and livelihood, goes on in the plant kingdom just as ruthlessly, if not so noisily, as it does elsewhere. And the winners thrive and proliferate, the losers fade and vanish.

There are no idealists in the plant world, and there is no compassion. The rose and the morning glory know no mercy. Bindweed, the wild morning glory, will quietly choke its competitors to death, and the fencerow rose will just as quietly crowd out any other plant that tries to share its roothold. Idealism and mercy are human terms and human concepts. Nature doesn't seem to be concerned with them.

Plant competition, like animal competition, is for the necessities of life. Plants need water, air, sunlight, and root space. And it is not always the vigorous giant that wins this battle of the plants. Trees can starve grass to death, but a vine that unassisted cannot lift its leaves a foot off the ground can choke a tree to death.

In the corner of my study stands a length of white birch that is gnarled and twisted and grooved. I cut it from a birch tree twenty feet tall. That tree had the misfortune, in its sapling days, to have a bird plant a bittersweet seed in its droppings beside the tree. The seed sprouted and grew, and the vine, reaching for support, touched the young birch, twined around it, and began to climb. As the vine spiraled upward, lifting its leaves toward the sun, it clasped the sapling in its coils. As the tree grew, it ridged itself against the clasp of the vine, grew into the shape dictated by its embracing guest. Eventually the birch died, not hugged to death but robbed of sunlight and subtly weakened so it could not survive. When I found it, the tree was dead but the vine was thriving.

The Virginia creeper can do the same thing. Each fall I watch the flame of this plant's leaves across the river, a tower of crimson on the dead trunk of a poplar that was weakened and died. Perhaps it would have died without the presence of the vine, but the vine probably hastened its death. Wild grapes can do the same thing. So can poison ivy. And it all happens without a cry or a visible struggle.

JULY 23

This matter of plant competition can be seen almost anywhere, if one looks for it, but it is specially evident in arid areas. On the High Plains of my boyhood there were areas where the yucca, or Spanish bayonette, grew profusely. Yet those yucca plants seldom massed in a single spiny tangle; they usually grew as individual plants some distance apart. Later I knew that this spacing was dictated in part by the moisture available, thus minimizing competition. But it also was a result of a toxic agent many desert plants produce which inhibits the sprouting of competitors nearby. Given a few wet years, those desert plants multiply and begin to fill in the vacant spaces. But when the normal dry conditions return, the weaklings, some old but many young, die out and the original spacing is restored.

Here on my own lawn and garden I take a hand in the competition. If I were to leave this patch of bluegrass to the natural struggle, in a very few years the grass would be largely replaced by dandelions, plantain, and chickweed, which are forever trying to get the upper hand. And without my work in the garden with hoe and cultivator, the vegetable patch would be the scene of war to death among quack grass, pigweed, purslane, and German weed. Even the vigorous asparagus needs my help to maintain anything approaching dominance in its small area.

It is a fundamental struggle as old as life itself, and it is exemplified in every cultivated field and tended woodland. Man chooses the plants, whether they are forage crops or grain or trees, that he wishes to assist, and he gives them all the help he can. It has been thus ever since the first hunter gathered a handful of wild rye seeds and strewed them in a bare spot and scuffed a bit of soil over them—ever since man made the first gesture of the farmer.

But this constant competition, this war between the plants marked by the green of chlorophyll, is even less important in the plant world than the war between all green, self-supporting plants and the parasitic plants that have no chlorophyll.

JULY 24

My comment about the fungi, those plants that have no chlorophyll and live on the labors of others, was made just after I had gone outdoors and found a fairy ring of mushrooms on the side lawn. We had an all-day, slow, warm rain a few days ago and since then have had overcast, warm, humid days, ideal weather for mildew and mushrooms. They pop up overnight, flourish briefly, and droop and fade with a day or two of dry sunshine. But they strew spores even in that brief life, and that is one of the secrets of their persistence.

They are fungi, members of a huge family that learned millions of years ago to live on the labor of others and are a constant, inconspicuous threat to everything green upon this earth. And their threat is growing, not diminishing. Today there is at least one fungus species for every species of flowering plant that works for a living. The fungi make others gather their food. They live on organic matter, and their choice hosts are green plants. In discussing them, even briefly, I find it best to begin with the least of them.

All fungi spread by means of spores, one of the most venerable of all means of reproduction. Each spore is a single cell endowed with an intense urge to grow. Most fungus spores are too small to be seen by the naked eye. They ride the breeze, millions of them, and they are constantly falling on the leaves and stems of green plants. Most of the spores find no lodging place and soon lose their brief spark of life. But the fungi produce vast numbers of spores. By the simple law of averages, they persist and multiply. Of what consequence is the loss of a million spores if one finds a place to grow, mature, and produce two million new spores?

All plant stems and all leaves have minute pores through which they breathe. If a spore finds such a pore and worms its way inside, the fungus has a foothold. As soon as the spore achieves contact with living plant tissue it begins to grow. It grows into a mycelium, a kind of minute mass of filaments that reach out in all directions. The mycelium fibers thrust their way between cells of the plant and occasionally burst the cell walls. Once inside the cell, the fiber of this parasitic intruder begins to feed on the protoplasm. This parasite, the plant grown from that fungus spore, has tapped a source of food and energy. All it has to do is feed and grow. So it grows, extends its filaments to other cells, begins to take over the food and substance of the hard-working plant.

One such parasitic fungus can starve a healthy plant to death. It can eat out the substance of the plant's leaves or choke the plant's stem. It can destroy the host plant's flowers and make seeding impossible. But—and this is a grim truth that merely points up the insidious cycle— the invading fungus usually does not kill its host until the fungus itself has matured and is ready to produce spores. It comes to its own ripeness, scatters its millions of spores which seek other green plants, and then proceeds to finish the murder of its host, for which it no longer has any need.

JULY 25

Man is most aware of these insidious fungi when they attack plants he wants or needs. Smut that attacks corn is such a fungus, and it will soon appear here and there in the rows of sweet corn, by all the probabilities, and certainly in the field corn. On corn this fungus attacks only the maturing kernels on the ear, but it does widespread damage.

The rusts are another destructive form of fungus, and one of their principal targets is the cereal grains. There are about a thousand species of rust fungi in the United States alone. They are distantly related to the mushrooms on my lawn, though most of the rusts are microscopic in size. Some of the most destructive of them go through two stages, one of which requires a host plant quite different from that on which it does the most damage. Stem rust, for instance, particularly injurious to wheat, passes its intermediate stage in the wild barberry, where it forms yellowish patches on the leaves. These patches produce spores that attack wheat, or rye, or barley. By getting rid of barberry bushes near the grain fields, much of the stem rust damage has been stopped. Other forms of rust use the wild currant as an intermediate host. In my area all the wild currant bushes have been cleaned out for this reason.

The smuts are particularly insidious because the spores invade the grain itself. A single grain of wheat, for example, may carry 200,000 smut spores. These spores can survive several seasons, latent in the soil, so one crop of smut-infested seed can infect a field for years.

The chestnut blight that has killed virtually all the chestnut trees in America is a form of fungus. Its spores invade the trees through wounds in the bark and spread their hungry mycelium as a fibrous, cottony mass. If it starts on the trunk of the tree it eventually girdles the tree, destroys the cambium tissue through which sap and food are circulated, and the tree dies. If the attack is on a branch, the branch is girdled and killed and the fungus continues to spread.

The Dutch elm disease, which has killed so many New England elms over the past fifty years, is a similar fungus. It acts in much the same way, eventually girdling the tree and, in effect, choking it to death.

Not all invading fungi are so ruthless. Some of them merely form galls or tumors, knobby growths on a plant or a tree, or even on a leaf, where the fungi live and draw sustenance from the host plant but do not proceed to outright murder. Such galls are common on the goldenrod here in my valley. And the leaf-galls are easily found in almost any growth of oaks. They are occasionally found on poplar leaves, too, in my area. Perhaps one could liken these plant galls to nonmalignant tumors in the human body, whereas the smuts and the chestnut and elm blights could well be likened to cancer.

JULY 26

There are still other fungi that live with hosts and contribute an essential element to the host's life. I can look out of my study window and see examples on the roof of the woodshed, where there are patches of a tan-and-green lichen big as my hand. If I start up the mountainside I see similar lichens on the tree trunks, sometimes but not always on the north side; and I see them on the big rocks up there, just as I have seen them on mountaintops 14,000 feet high.

Lichens are dual entities, consisting of algae and fungi living in a cooperative arrangement in situations where neither one could live alone. This mutual dependence is called symbiosis, from the Greek meaning "living together."

Lichens live on rocks, for example, where no other plants can survive. In their symbiosis, however, the algae provide the food and the fungi store the necessary water and secrete acids that eat into the rocks and assure the symbiotic plant a foothold. The algae have chlorophyll and use air and moisture to manufacture food. The fungi are colorless, manufacture no food, and are wholly dependent on the algae for sustenance. But together they make out very well.

Other forms of this symbiotic life of algae and fungi are the reindeer moss of the Arctic regions and the trailing, pale-green streamers of old-man's beard on spruce and fir trees of the North. The Spanish moss so common on the live oaks of the South is not such a symbiotic plant, however. It is an herb, an incredible member of the pineapple family, the *Bromeliaceae*.

JULY 27

The largest of the fungi are the mushrooms, whose overnight fairy ring started me on this discussion of parasitic plants. They, too, need organic matter to live on, but many of them live on dead vegetable matter and only a relatively few invade living trees. Most mushrooms are scavengers, actually, rather than parasites, for they live on the remains of living things, not the living things themselves.

Those of us who live in wooded areas have but to step into the woodland to find some form of mushroom, since dead wood is the chosen food for many of them. They are common on old stumps and fallen trees, and if one finds a damp, well-shaded spot with a litter of rotting wood one is sure to find mushrooms. They cannot live long in sunlight. They are plentiful in many meadows after a rainy spell, and I find edible morels in my dooryard after a few days of rain in any May. But within twelve hours after the rain ends, if the sun comes out clear and blazing hot, they shrivel and die.

There are more than two hundred species of wild mushrooms, and in this group are found a good many poisonous ones. And mushroom poisoning is not to be laughed at. At the least, it causes painful intestinal upset and nausea. At the worst, it causes death. The deadly amanitas are among the most poisonous of all plants and are especially dangerous because the poison has already done its major damage before the symptoms of poisoning appear.

On living trees as well as dead ones are the bracket fungi, many of them looking like big oyster shells, some of them a foot or more across. These "brackets" are the outward indication of what is happening inside the tree. If it happens to be a dead tree, the fungus is eating away the lifeless but still organic wood. If the tree is still alive, the fungus is eating into it and spreading its mycelium, which will eventually kill that tree.

All these forms of fungal life spread themselves and propagate new fungi by means of spores. Just how old they are, in the long history of life, nobody knows. They probably are very old, but there are few evidences of such insubstantial plants in the fossil records.

They are important not only economically—in man's terms as well as in nature's—but probably in terms of evolution. The parasitic fungi, which are vastly in the majority, learned long ago the same basic habit that dominates all animal life. Fungi eat food that some other form of life manufactured.

In human terms, this may not be a pretty picture. But nature has no knowledge of such terms, no awareness of or respect for them. Nature is life, and life makes its own way with no sense of morality. Man, when he is tempted to make judgments in these matters, might well remember that he is essentially an animal and should reserve such judgment of his own kind. He, too, lives on other living things. Without the chlorophyll in the living leaf, man would perish. It happens that man eats not only the chlorophyll-manufactured sugars and starches but the flesh of other animals that live on the same thing. Man is, by definition, a parasite.

JULY 28

We are having a spell of hot, humid weather, ideal fungus weather.

The ability to live on the labor of other plants is typical of the fungi. How they learned it, or evolved it, is unknown. But they have this attribute, this ability, in common with animals. And when one follows the biological trail only a little farther one comes to strange, perverse organisms that are almost impossible to classify as plant or animal. There are water-dwelling animals that look and act like plants. There is a green alga that swims about like an animal and yet is a plant. And there are the slime molds which are typical of neither plants nor animals yet are close relatives, as such relationships go, of the fungi.

Slime molds have no chlorophyll and are unable to manufacture their own food. Yet they are not, strictly speaking, parasites. They live on decaying vegetable matter, chiefly on rotting wood. And slime mold has no clearly defined form, as does a mushroom or even the mycelium of wheat rust or the parasitic chestnut blight. Slime mold consists of a mass of naked protoplasm, the basic substance of all living cells. But this slime mold's protoplasm has no confining walls and no specialized organs of any kind. It is a gray or yellowish color and it has the consistency of the albumen of an egg. From time to time I pick up a piece of rotting log in a damp part of my woods and feel the slime mold, greasy and unpleasant to the touch.

This formless slime mold spreads slowly over whatever it touches. It seems almost to flow, and it does have a capacity for movement. As it goes, it sucks in, or at least surrounds and absorbs, organic food, bits of wood, bacteria, anything edible to slime mold. It absorbs this food and flows on, digesting what it can use and leaving waste material behind. It has no entity except this greasy, formless being, this slimy coating that is the total of slime mold. But now and then it thrusts up from its surface small warts or knobs that grow into spore cases. The spores ripen and drift away on the wind, and if they find a suitable piece of damp, rotting wood they flow toward similar spores and create a new patch of slime mold, another naked film of protoplasmic jelly, a new generation.

So there is the slime mold, technically a plant yet endowed with movement and having other vaguely animal characteristics. Its spores even have flagella, microscopic hairs which enable them to move about when they have been wind-borne to a suitable place for growth. There, near the very bottom of the vast heap of life patterns, endowed with what seems to be the very minimum of equipment for successful living, they persist and no doubt have persisted for millions of years. They are successful. They even have a purpose, as far as we can evaluate purpose, for they are scavengers of a kind. They help to reduce dead plant life to a form that can be used again by other, self-supporting plants.

JULY 29

It is difficult, if not impossible, to assess value for any form of life. Man persists in evaluating, and nearly always in terms of his own wants and needs; but nature has a different scale of values of which I am not at all sure we are aware except in the most general outlines. Life seems to be a purpose in itself, the fact of living and growing and perpetuating. Perhaps there is also the purpose of perfection, though I am wary of that term. Perfection in this sense would have to mean maximum possible development of a life form in a particular environment.

If one agrees with that, then competition among life forms becomes inevitable, and even on this limited, natural basis man has a responsibility to his own kind, to his own particular form of life. For some reason, man is endowed with ethical and moral values. It is his responsibility to use them to the utmost. He came along at a propitious time in the history of life on earth and he filled a niche that was unoccupied. There must have been a purpose for him, since nature seems to be organized on what man calls a purposive plan. This statement, of course, is made by a man, who again is drawing his own humanly biased conclusions.

But here is this world of life, teeming with different forms, plant and animal and forms not easily distinguishable as either. Here is this green world, this plant world, which seems at a glance to be so peaceful, so well ordered, so quiet and self-contained. And beneath that calm surface is the constant and unremitting struggle, this competition that makes less noise than the fall of a leaf. The balance in that world is so precarious that the shift of an ocean current or a prevailing wind can upset it. A cold air mass moves a hundred miles south and settles down for a few days, and whole states are swept with snow, crops are frozen, man's own economics are upset.

Animal life is somewhat less at the mercy of such changes. Animals can move about, migrate to a more favorable climate. Yet the whole animal population of the world is at the mercy of the rooted, green-leafed plants that cannot readily move. A changing climate can displace even the insect life of an area. And since insects often carry bacteria, the displacement of a swarm of mosquitoes could conceivably change the whole plant and animal life of a considerable area. For a time. Eventually a new balance would be struck, a new truce of sorts, and plants and animals would assume their proper places. This has happened countless times in the past, and no doubt it will happen again.

The war goes on. It has been going on for many millions of years. Out of it have come adaptations of old species to new conditions and the evolution of new species. Somewhere in the vast storehouse of nature there seems always to be a strain of life ready to creep into any opening, to occupy it, to proliferate, to fill the vacuum. If there is any inevitability in nature as we know it, it is life itself, growth and change. But the basis of it all, today at least, is the green world, the leaf with its chlorophyll and its ability to manufacture food. All other forms of life depend on that green leaf.

JULY 30

Here it is only the end of July and I see the first goldenrod in bloom, two species of it. One is commonly called early goldenrod, *Solidago juncea,* and the other is Canada goldenrod, *Solidago canadensis.* The Canada species has long, slender, sharply toothed leaves, the early one has broader, toothless upper leaves and small leaflets in the axils. Both bear their flowers in spreading, plumelike clusters.

I habitually think of goldenrod as a fall flower, though I know perfectly well that I can always find it in bloom by late July. I suppose this is because I didn't grow up with it. It does grow on the High Plains of Colorado, in favored places, and the same Canada goldenrod I find just down the road blooms there in late July. But out on the dry flats there is no goldenrod, or was none when I was a boy. Our autumn flowers were asters, and not many of them, and an occasional sunflower that persisted through September.

Goldenrod actually is an August-September flower, and usually has faded before the asters reach their peak of beauty and abundance. It has a habit of taking over abandoned fields and making them glow soon after Labor Day. The goldenrod holds those fields for three or four years, and then the brush begins to crowd them out, seedling birches and shrub dogwood and sumac, and then ash and box elder. And, if there are pines not too far away, the white pines will begin to creep in. But first comes the goldenrod, whose pepper-fine seed rides the wind on tiny tufts of gray fuzz.

JULY 31

Bouncing Bet is in flower, great clouds of it, along all our roads. A wild pink, *Saponaria officinalis,* it is also sometimes called soapwort, because its roots have a saponaceous quality, make a suds in which dainty garments can be washed, I have heard it said, and in which women sometimes washed their hair back in frontier days. Hence another common name, now largely forgotten—my lady's washbowl.

If bouncing Bet were only a little less abundant and a bit more difficult to grow, it probably would be a treasured garden flower. Instead, it is too often considered a weed. It grows madly almost anywhere, at any roadside, in any sandy back street, on any town dump. And it blooms profusely from July until hard frost. It even has a pleasant, faintly perfumed odor, as most pinks do, but that seems to please only the bees and butterflies. Nobody picks it for bouquets for the house, except small children from the city.

I still admire it, and I wonder how it manages to thrive under so many disadvantages. It spreads primarily from the roots, though it does produce seed that will grow. But road men mow it, spray it, salt it with the winter ice's runoff. Gardeners want none of it in their gardens. Farmers think it as much of a hayfield pest as daisies. Yet it does persist. And every summer I think how drab the roadsides would be without it. I also wonder whether there are several strains or whether it is a matter of soil that varies the color of those blossoms from snowy white through shades of pink to an almost wild-rose shade in occasional patches.

AUGUST

Queen Anne's lace is everywhere, particularly at the roadsides, and I bless our town's selectmen for sticking to their policy of mowing rather than spraying those roadsides with a weed-killer. It makes sense, in terms of economics as well as aesthetics, for when a roadside is stripped of its vegetation it quickly gullies and is undermined by rain and runoff. Grass and wildflowers form a protective mat that is strengthened rather than weakened by mowing. And we have the bonus of the flowers.

Queen Anne's lace, of course, is the wild carrot. Its fine-cut, bright green foliage is almost the same color as that of the tame carrots in the garden, though the root is very different, tough and bitter. The common name pays tribute to the flat-topped heads of blossom, dainty as fine lace and pretty enough to deck a queen. Actually, that head is an umbel, or a group of umbels, as botanists call them, of tiny florets.

Curious, I once counted the individual florets in one such head, and found 2,450 of them. Beyond that were the mathematics, which fascinated me. Each individual floret has five tiny petals. There were fourteen sepals, or leaflike green "spears" at the base of the whole head. There were seventy clusters of florets, each averaging thirty-five florets.

Now start with the basic 5, the number of petals. Multiply that by the number of sepals, 14, and you get 70, the number of individual clusters that made up the whole flower head. Arbitrarily divide 14 by 2 and multiply the 7 you get by 5 and you get 35, the number of florets in each small cluster. And there were twice as many clusters as there were florets in each cluster, 70 and 35, both multiples of the basic 5.

In the plant world there are persistent basic numbers. Five is one of them, five-petaled flowers being very common. Seven is less common, though it is occasionally found in stamens. All of which merely points to the habitual order in plant life, a way of organization that persists through all the members of each plant family. There is almost nothing random in any form of life, for that matter, though not even the philosophers can explain why. Nature has her own reasons, and somehow they add up to a system of order.

AUGUST 2

As I drive along the road to the village now I smell the corn pollen, a faintly tanged, vaguely spiced odor that I call a fragrance but that annoys some people. They say it is a "dusty" smell. Lucky for them that they do not live in Illinois or Iowa, where the whole countryside has that pollen odor from late July till September. Our valley here, a dairy valley, has its full share of corn, but by no means as much as the Midwest, where you sometimes can drive half a day and never be out of sight of a cornfield.

This corn pollen fragrance pleases me, in part because it means agricultural plenty, and hence national plenty, and in part because it proves that the American Indian had a streak of genius in his background. Corn, or maize, as Europeans have called it for generations to distinguish it from the wheat and barley they call corn, is a botanical achievement that modern man has never been able to duplicate. Somewhere far back in the mists the Indians of Central America created it from a native grass, by selective breeding and cross-breeding. We find cobs and miniature ears in ancient caves in our own Southwest, and archaeologists have traced the grain far back among the Aztecs and their forerunners. But no one has ever succeeded in breeding anything like even the primitive corn in the ancient caves from the known plants of the world. The best our modern plant men have been able to do is improve the yield or increase the size of the ears or alter the flavor of the kernels.

And I hope they never break that long-standing secret of those "primitive" Indians who first created an ear of corn.

AUGUST 3

The flowering plants are often spoken of as the most advanced form of plant life, with the blossom itself as the evidence. In this sense, the flowering plant is the plant world's equivalent of the mammal in the animal world.

I am not sure that I agree with this unless the word "advanced" is taken in a rather restricted sense. Man has a habit of calling any complex form of life or life process "advanced," with the clear implication that it is better or more admirable than its predecessors. From man's point of view, the highest achievement of evolving life is man, with his intricate arrangement of cells, specialized organs and members, elaborately complex nervous system, and remarkable brain. But the very simplest forms of life persist. They may never have "advanced" very far, but they proved long ago that simplicity can endure and that it long, long ago solved the basic problems of life. Man, endowed with intelligence and strong emotions, has other ideas about the purpose of his own life, but we have yet to verify any purpose in nature beyond life's own persistence.

And in that sense the blossom on a buttercup or an orchid is no more than a complex means of continuing life from one generation to the next. This should not lessen man's aesthetic or intelligent interest in a flower, but it does mean that man, not nature, invented aesthetics.

Since the original division of primitive life into the two branches, plant and animal, there has been relatively little change in the basic processes of living, maintaining life. To repeat, plants manufacture their food from inorganic substances, using the sun's energy to convert air and water into sugars and starches; and animals maintain their life processes by consuming organic matter, plants and other animals. These are fundamental processes that have been elaborated but not basically changed over hundreds of millions of years.

But the process of reproduction, though based on a common fundamental, has diverged in many directions. This has been particularly true in the plant world, with the most complex reproductive mechanism of all in the blossom.

AUGUST 4

Stripped of detail, the fundamental of reproduction is a division of the original life form. At its simplest, the single-celled plant or animal divides itself, nucleus and all, into two parts, both of which grow and in turn reproduce, always by self-division. As one moves down the eons of life history this self-division becomes more and more complex. In both plant and animal the parent individual, itself an elaborate organization of cells, achieves the power of creating special reproductive cells that are separated from the parent and grow new reproductive units. Essentially, this still is a form of self-division. In animals this special reproductive cell is the egg. In plants it is the spore or seed.

In most instances, the egg or the seed must be fertilized before it can grow. Fertilization is accomplished by the union of two dissimilar cells, the egg and the sperm. This necessity and this differentiation of cells and parents constitutes sex. The word "sex" comes from the Latin and seems originally to have meant to cut, to divide. It really means that there is a difference between the two parent organisms, the male and the female, which the French celebrate in that exclamation, *"Vive la différence!"*

In animals and in most insects the male and female cells are produced by separate individuals. In some plants this is also true, but in many plants the male and female cells are produced in the same flower or in different flowers on the same plant. If a flower produces both kinds of cells it always has both the female and the male organs. In a sense, the flower which produces both kinds of reproductive cells is one of nature's economies, a simplification of the basic means of reproduction. The simplification, of course, is in the method, not the means, since any flower is a complex of specialized organs.

We call the fertilization of the female cells in a flower pollination. This process calls for an ovary, or female organ, and a stamen, or male organ. The pollen, equivalent to the sperm of an animal, joins and fertilizes the ovule, equivalent of the egg in the animal. Together they produce fertile seed. Pollination is achieved in various ways, but always by some transport of pollen to ovule. Insects are the transporting agent in many cases. Birds sometimes do the job, particularly hummingbirds. Wind carries much pollen. Water carries pollen to some aquatic plants. And gravity is at least a contributing agent in such plants as field corn, which just now is dusting the air of my valley with pollen and which set me off on this discussion of flowers, seeds, and pollination.

AUGUST 5

Friends who think that if you only listen right the birds, beasts, and insects can tell you what the weather is going to be six months ahead stopped in this afternoon. "What kind of winter," they demanded, "are we going to have?"

"Somewhat cold," I said, "with snow from time to time, and ice."

"Oh, come now," they insisted. "What do the signs say?"

"Most of them say it was a good summer."

"Stop kidding," they insisted. "You've got it practically at your fingertips. All the goose-bone prophet stuff. Corn husks, woolly bears, feathers on the birds."

"I just told you," I said. "All the signs tell me that it was a good summer. They don't say a thing about the winter ahead. A good summer means plenty to eat for birds and beasts. The animals put on warm coats and the birds have good feathers simply because they are in good health and well fed. They will store lots of nuts and acorns simply because there will be plenty of nuts and acorns. Let's keep the horse in front of the cart, not the other way around."

"But what about the woolly-bear caterpillars? Don't tell me that caterpillars don't sense things. Who was it, some scientist, said the other day that worms can tell north from south."

"Some worms," I said, "are sensitive to the earth's magnetic currents. I don't know why, but a number of creatures are sensitive to such currents. But that doesn't make them fortune-tellers or weather forecasters. Not in my book, it doesn't. Anyway, why should a woolly bear try to guess about the winter ahead? What does it matter to him whether January will be mild or bitterly cold, or how much snow we will get in February? He will be in a deep coma, hibernating, frozen solid."

They laughed. "Then you're not going to tell us any secrets?"

"I don't know any such secrets. I've told you all I know."

But they left still believing there must be something arcane, something magic about geese and rabbits and woolly-bear caterpillars and the weather. I didn't bother to tell them how birds know when the barometer is falling and when to expect a storm. That would only have confused them still more.

AUGUST 6

There is a scientific explanation of that seed-egg process I have been talking about that is important to the specialist and perhaps interesting to the layman. This interpretation is called "the alternation of generations." It points up the idea that life is continuous even though it passes through a variety of forms in the same species. It applies to all forms of life except the very lowest, the single-celled. Perhaps the most graphic is in the life of a butterfly, which proceeds through the form of egg, larva or worm, pupa, butterfly, then egg again. Each of these forms constitutes a "generation," and each is quite different from the others. Yet all are necessary in the life history of a butterfly.

In a flowering plant there are equivalent steps. The common field mustard, a weed in the pastures of my valley, is a green and leafy plant that forms a cluster of buds at its tip and comes to blossom in May. The mustard flower has four small yellow petals and is bisexual, with one pistil, the female organ, surrounded by six stamens, the male organs. In the ovary at the base of the pistil are produced special reproductive cells or ovules. In the anthers at the tip of the stamens is produced the pollen, the male reproductive cells.

According to the alternation-of-generations interpretation, the individual grains of pollen, the male cells, are short-lived individual plants, though they are unable to reproduce alone. And the ovules, the female cells in the ovary, are also shortlived individual plants unable to reproduce alone. They constitute a "hidden generation" in the plant's life.

When these minute male and female plants, pollen and ovules, meet and fuse, they produce a fertile entity, the seed. The seed in turn will grow into a leafy, budding mustard plant, and when its yellow blossoms open, the whole process will be repeated. In this sense there is an unending continuation of life which passes through alternate forms, generation by generation. And the flower, the blossom, is no more than a mechanism for producing those minute "plants," the pollen and the ovule, which join to form the seed.

To the paleobotanist this interpretation explains, at least in part, the basic process of evolution. Plants, all life, apparently originated in single-celled ancients. In even the most complex plants and animals of today life still goes through that primitive form where minute flecks of parent life divide and unite in the creation of the seed or the egg. Male sperm and female ovules are created by the parent. These two basic units, the male and the female, must unite to create a more complex unit, the fertile seed or egg. Unless they meet and fuse, they cannot duplicate the parent and carry on the life process, including reproduction.

Broadly speaking, the female cells, the ovules, are quiet but hungrily receptive bits of life. They remain in the flower's ovary awaiting the arrival of the pollen, the male element. The ovule's whole purpose, as far as we can comprehend purpose, is to be fertilized. The male pollen is vigorous and active. In one sense, it is a spore. Its purpose is to find and fertilize an ovule. This impulse of necessity in both ovule and pollen is one of the most urgent yet one of the most persistently hidden of all the life processes.

AUGUST 7

An excellent example of this ovule-pollen urgency can be found in any cornfield, though only a minor part of it can be seen with the naked eye. Like most instances, the greater part of it occurs at the microscopic level.

Corn produces its pollen, its male cells, in the tassel at the tip of the plant. The ovules, the female cells, are on the young ear, farther down the stalk. The ovules are ranked on the cob, hidden beneath several layers of husk; but each ovule, each potential kernel of corn, has a long "silk," a hollow strand of soft vegetable fiber that reaches out into the open at the tip of the ear.

At a proper time, the pollen is mature and the ovules are ready for fertilization. The pollen, dust-fine, begins to fall from the brown stamens on the tassel. Gravity urges it downward and the wind distributes it from plant to plant. One grain of that male pollen, one spore, falls on the tip of one strand of silk. It is held there by a kind of adhesive secreted by the silk. The tip of that silk is an ideal place for the growth of that particular kind of spore. It grows into a male plant too small to be seen by the naked eye, a plant that thrusts a fine thread down that hollow silken strand toward the waiting ovule. That pollen grain, that almost microscopic spore, is endowed with enough energy and urgency to thrust that thread eight inches or a foot down that silken tube to reach the ovule. The ovule is reached, male and female cells fuse, fertilization occurs, and a kernel of corn begins to take form beneath the protective husks. The female ovule extended its silken invitation. The male pollen found that particular silk. In a matter of hours pollination, fertilization, had been accomplished. A fertile seed, from which another corn plant can grow, had been created.

This elaborate process has been evolved over millions of years. It began with the first plants that crept or were washed by the waves onto land. They were spore-bearers. The spore itself was a result of long evolution, a means of dividing the parent plant without destroying or greatly impairing its strength.

The spore is microscopic, and it is not always distinguished by sex. In the simplest form of spore plants an indeterminate form of plant grows from the spore, a bisexual plant, and from that plant is reproduced still another plant substantially like the original spore-bearing parent. Mushrooms are among the most prolific spore-bearers, a single mushroom often producing two or three billion spores. Mushroom spores are sexed, but they can scarcely be called male and female because there are four "sexes" among them and they will pair off only in certain groupings, say number 1 and number 3, or number 2 and number 4. In a favorable environment these spores grow into minute filaments, and if two filaments of the proper "sexes" meet, they fuse and grow into a mushroom capable of bearing more spores. But the unmated filaments that grow directly from spores are plants, intermediate forms and an essential part of the whole reproductive process. They are broadly equivalent to the searching pollen grain and the receptive ovule.

AUGUST 8

Rain yesterday, the slow rain we like to get at this time of year. And it continued into the night. But today dawned clear and cool, with a brilliant sun, and as the morning got underway a few of those huge, galleon-like cumulus clouds came slowly sailing across the sky. They were there most of the day, those first few and others like them, and they made me think of my boyhood and the High Plains of the West, where such clouds were so often seen on summer days. We would have preferred rain clouds in that dry land, but we got that incredibly blue sky and those huge, whipped-cream cumulus which were so big and had so much depth that they had blue shadows within themselves.

So we had a High Country day, when the heat was tempered in the shade because the humidity was very low.

This afternoon I picked chokecherries and we simmered them and set them to drain in a jelly bag on the back porch. Three years ago I found a chokecherry seedling beside the small gate to the barnyard, and I trimmed the sprouts and encouraged the main stem. It shot up to ten feet tall last year, and last spring it was covered with those tiny pussy-tails of white blossoms that attract bees by the hundred. The bees did their job, and now it was loaded with fruit. The birds made such a to-do, the robins and the jays, that I went to see what was going on, found the ripe cherries, and picked most of them. The birds can go elsewhere for their cherries. We shall have jelly.

AUGUST 9

The rain of day before yesterday, with the usual August warmth, has brought up a crop of small white mushrooms that I tentatively identify as *Agaricus campestris,* an edible species. But I am no mycologist, so we refrain from experimenting with them, though we have friends who laugh at such caution. I once had a friend who laughed at my caution in the presence of a rattlesnake, too. As they used to say in the back-country, he made a very handsome corpse.

Even though we eat only a few species of mushroom, all of them interest me, as I said somewhat earlier when discussing fungi at some length. They interest me at this moment as examples of reproduction by spores, the forerunners of seeds.

Many plants still reproduce by spores. Most of them are water-dwellers, but ferns, horsetails, and fungi are among the land-dwellers that cling to the spore system. Spores of most water-dwelling plants have hairlike means of movement, but the spores of most land-dwelling plants have no means of movement and usually are distributed by the wind. And most of them go through an intermediate state of individual growth before they re-create a plant like the parent. The fern spore, to take one example, is more direct in its process than that of the mushroom. The fern spore grows into a tiny, inconspicuous plant called a prothallium— from the Greek words meaning "before" and "young shoot"—and the prothallium has both male and female organs from which a plant like the parent is eventually produced.

No one knows why or when the primitive spore-bearing plants moved over toward the process of reproducing by means of a fertilized seed, but by the Carboniferous period, some 300 million years ago, there were trees that had begun to produce seeds. Apparently a plant of the fern type condensed the intermediate generation, the growth of the spore into a bisexual prothallium, and created a cone in which the essentials of this process could take place. Out of this evolved the fertile seed.

But here again, the old process, the spore system, was successful enough to persist. In some ways it is even more successful than the seed system, or at times it seems to be so. When those mushrooms in my dooryard come popping up within twenty-four hours after a warm summer rain, they certainly prove that their system is more efficient in some ways than the newer seed system. In any case, the spores persist, and they make me suspicious of all claims that new is necessarily better. New is different, and sometimes it is more effective, but it is not always better.

AUGUST 10

We heard the season's first katydids last night. The old belief is that first frost will come six weeks after the first katydid rasps his announcement, and it is seldom far wrong. That will bring first frost here soon after the autumnal equinox, and that is about what we expect, year after year. I expect frost with the late September full moon.

In any case, the clock of the season now points toward autumn. We have passed the midpoint of summer, which I always think of as coming around the first week of August, and though we still probably will have midsummer heat, even into September, the days now have changed their pattern. We have only a few minutes more than fourteen hours of daylight, an hour and a quarter less than we had two months ago, and the nights grow longer week by week.

We went to a special place on the lower mountainside today, to see the look of the land, to look across the valley at Canaan Mountain, to see if the ladies'-tresses, those lovely little orchids, were in bloom. We found the first of them, spiraling up their flower stalks. And we found the first great lobelias, of the showy blue flowers. We were especially pleased, for this is a date we observe for personal reasons, and when we find those little orchids we feel particularly favored.

Six more weeks till frost, the katydids said. Well, that gives six more weeks to enjoy summer.

AUGUST 11

Dawn comes later now. Sunup occurs about five thirty, daylight time, actually four thirty by standard time. And when I got up this morning and went outdoors to look around I was aware of a strange silence. No birds were singing. Not a robin was uttering a note, and even the cardinals were silent.

For years I have been told that birds sing for only two reasons, to lure a mate or to declare ownership of territory. And I seriously doubt that statement. If that were true, why would so many birds continue singing, from time to time, after the nesting was done, even after the fledglings were out and on their own? Robins do that, and so do brown thrashers, and so do a number of other species. Wood thrushes do; I hear them at evening several weeks after their young have grown up and left the nest.

I insist that many, perhaps most, birds sing not only to lure mates and claim territory but simply because they feel like singing. Did you ever listen to a house wren spilling over with song in mid-August, even on a hot day, when his mate has done her maternal stint and the youngsters are out rustling their own living? I hear a couple of those wrens every day now, and they aren't challenging anyone or luring anyone. They are simply voicing their high-tension exuberance, their love of life.

But even the wrens are sleeping later. Maybe they are no longer so full of summer celebration.

AUGUST 12

I recently said in public print that "nature's purpose, so far as we understand purpose at all, is to perpetuate life, not destroy it; to strengthen life, not weaken it; to garland and fructify the earth, not to blight and devastate it."

Now comes a querulous letter from a man who says, "Please explain the purpose of nature's floods, famines, plagues, earthquakes, hurricanes, tornadoes, etc." And he goes on to say, "If man did not protect himself against nature, he would soon be wiped out."

We obviously live in different worlds, this man and I. To him, life means mankind, nothing else. All the teeming life around him, plant and animal, is beyond the boundaries he recognizes. Nature, the whole world and even the universe, according to his lights, is or should be designed and dedicated for the welfare of man. He even blames nature for floods and famines as well as plagues. He, I am sure, believes that only the Corps of Army Engineers stands between him and a repetition of Noah's flood, and that DDT is the answer to every overpopulated land's food shortage. Nature, in his cosmos, is the enemy. It must be dammed, drained, paved over, timbered off, bulldozed, smothered and overwhelmed by man's machines and his sprays and biocides.

How can you tell such a man that life is more than his own egocentric self? How can you explain to him that man is a minority species in this world, that he is here on sufferance, and that nature could do very well without him, that it did very well indeed before man appeared?

AUGUST 13

Discussing plant reproduction a few days ago, I spoke of the evolution from the spore to the seed, which was accomplished by the flowering plants. As I said then, what this did was condense the intermediate processes and create a blossom within which the seed could be formed.

The blossom of a plant is really quite simple. It has only a few essentials. There is the pistil, the female organ, equivalent to the uterus and ovaries of the female mammal. In it are the female cells, the ovules, awaiting fertilization. And there are the stamens, the male organs, equivalent to the penis and the testes of the male mammal. They produce the sperm cells, the pollen, full of urgency to find and fertilize the ovules.

Those are the essentials. They can be found in notable simplicity in the inconspicuous flowers of most grasses, many of which consist of little more than an ovary and three stamens. The grasses have achieved this simplicity because they are pollinated by the wind and need no assistance from insects or birds. More complex blossoms, especially those depending on insects for help in pollination, have elaborate sepals and petals. The sepals are the leaflike coverings of the flower, often the bud sheath, and in some ways resemble leaves. They may have evolved from leaves. Usually the sepals are green and have chlorophyll in them, just as do leaves. The petals are the divisions of the corolla, the cup that usually surrounds the pistil and the stamens.

Some flowers have no sepals, some no petals, but the great elaboration and variety of floral forms have been in petals and sepals, in their shapes and colors. Some flowers have nectar to lure insects. Some have deep pockets in which pollen or nectar or both are hidden so that the visiting insect must invade to reach inside and get the treasure, and thus unwittingly leave pollen from another flower to fertilize the ovules. Some have their stamens and pistil so arranged that the insect visitor simply releases the pollen for self-fertilization. Whatever the arrangement, the blossom's design seems dictated by a need to insure pollination of the ovules.

AUGUST 14

The whole architecture of a flower, whatever its shape, has only one basic purpose—production of fertile seed. This urgency toward reproduction is characteristic of all flowering plants. Typical of it is the profusion of pollen. The sperm cells, the male pollen, vastly outnumber the egg cells, the ovules.

I am struck by this prodigality each spring when a big Norway spruce beside my house comes into flower. There are hundreds of catkinlike clusters of male flowers, but only a relative few female flowers, or potential cones. When the pollen begins to fall, it comes in a golden mist. At that time we must keep the windows closed on that side of the house or floors and furniture would be filmed with golden-tan spruce pollen. The floor of the open porch is covered with it so thick that I sweep it into windrows for the dustpan. All this from one big tree, and all waste pollen, pollen that failed to find a female ovule to fertilize. It is that one spruce tree's extravagant outpouring of male sperm to insure that perhaps five hundred cones shall be fertilized.

Every flowering plant does this, to some degree, from ragweed to columbine, from tulip to apple tree. Wind-pollinated species, such as conifers and grasses—and ragweed, so poisonous to everyone with a pollen allergy—are most lavish with their pollen, but in all flowering plants there is an unbelievable prodigality of pollen production, a tremendous excess of male cells over female cells.

AUGUST 15

It is usually taken for granted that the petals of a flower were evolved to serve as landing platforms for the insects that pollinate it. This may be correct, but the reasoning is not necessarily absolute. It is also taken for granted that the petals are colored to attract insects. This too may be subject to challenge. Some researchers say the insect eye cannot distinguish color. Others, with perhaps more persuasive evidence, say that bees and certain other insects are aware of color, particularly in the red end of the spectrum.

When we speak of color we think of it in terms of our own vision. But color is a matter of wavelength, and the human eye has a limited range of perception for such wavelengths. The color spectrum was devised as a gauge of man's visual scope, but we know there are color waves beyond that rather limited range, just as there are sounds beyond the range of our hearing. It is conceivable that an insect eye—or the eye of some birds and some animals—would be unable to see color as we see it, yet capable of distinguishing not only colors we can see but those we cannot see. We know, from experiment, that many birds and some animals react visually to color much as human beings do. They have some degree of color vision in the same sense that we do. But it is possible that insects are sensitive to colors in other ways than through their eyes. They may "hear" colors, or "smell" them. If locusts and grasshoppers are aware of sounds through sensors in their legs, why shouldn't other insects be aware of color though some other kind of sensors, perhaps on the top of their heads or even under their bellies?

When we say a flower's petals are colored to attract insects, then we are merely speculating on cause and effect. The colors we see may be incidental to some other emanation of which we are unaware but to which insects are acutely sensitive. Or it may be that color has still another purpose that we know nothing about. Or it may be that color has no purpose at all.

I am not even convinced that everything in nature *has* a purpose. Maybe some things just are. What, for instance, is the purpose of the infinite variations in the patterns of snowflakes? Wouldn't an ordinary six-pointed star suffice, if there is some reason that snow must come in a hexagonal pattern?

AUGUST 16

The whole matter of color in flowers is shot through with fascinating questions. But the blossom itself is really not at all mysterious. It is a rather complex arrangement of specialized organs designed to do a particular job—to produce male and female cells, to bring them together, and to create fertile seeds from which plants substantially like the parent will grow.

This is a process typical of all life. In one form or another it is found throughout the plant and animal kingdoms. I see it going on all around me each year, from the time the first coltsfoot comes to blossom in a sheltered hollow till the last aster fades and the witch hazel comes to bloom. I see it in the drift of "cotton" from the poplars and the blow of milkweed floss, in the pollen haze over the cornfields and the swarming of bees in the apple trees in May. I smell it when the lilacs bloom and the basswood drips its honey, when the clover whitens the meadow and when goldenrod makes September golden.

It may be that the blossom is the highest achievement of the whole plant world. I find it fascinatingly complex. And it may be that members of the composite family—sunflowers, asters, goldenrods, thistles, and all their kind—are the most advanced of all the flowering plants. I have already registered my reservations about that word "advanced." I would add only that to me the composite flowers, with their tightly packed dozens of individual florets, have merely achieved a kind of community system, a "social organization" something like that of the ants. Perhaps this is advancement, of a kind. Perhaps it is an example of social efficiency. But each season I still celebrate the fact that there are individuals, the wild lilies, the wild roses, the anemones, the columbines, who thus far have resisted such evolution. The flower is not only an efficient achievement; it is beautiful, and it is entitled to be as much an individual as I am.

AUGUST 17

This morning, about six forty-five, a young doe that looked like a yearling came down from the woods on the mountain, across the home pasture and to the apple trees in the back yard. She paused there a few minutes, looked all around, then arched herself over the pasture fence into the yard, came to the early apple tree and began eating windfalls. She was so close that we, standing in the sun porch at the back of the house, could clearly hear the crunch of the small green apples as she ate them. She stayed there almost fifteen minutes, wary but not skittish. Then, evidently having had all the apples she wanted, she turned and went back over the fence into the pasture and back to the woods.

We are always glad to see the deer come down to the yard, to know that they are not so afraid of this house that they dare appear only in the deep darkness of night. And yet, for their own good, I would never want them to become tame enough to come and eat from the hand. I want them to continue wary and distrustful of man, all men including me. That is their only protection.

Deer come in many colors, or at least many shades, some gray as wolves, some golden blond, and all degrees between. This young doe was a beautiful blonde, just about the color of fresh new buckskin. A honey-blonde. I was amazed at the way such a striking color could fade into the background of tree trunks, bushes, and green leaves, but the moment she reached the woods she seemed to disappear.

AUGUST 18

Joe-pye weed is in bloom, has been for about ten days. For some reason, there is more of it this year than I have ever seen. It appears in every odd corner of a pasture, a neglected field, a woodlot, even down along the riverbank.

I am always baffled by the way the upper leaves of joe-pye weed turn purple even before the flowers appear. It makes me think of the way lilac leaves show purple when they first come out of the bud along with the tightly closed flower buds, just as though the whole packet were suffused with that rich violet color. I wonder if there is some tendency of the leaves, particularly on the joe-pye, to merge with the blossoms. Color, as I was saying a few days ago, offers many questions that we have no ready answers for. This makes me wonder if the joe-pye weed's leaves once were all purple and faded into green, or if the blossoms once were all green and slowly turned to that strange pinkish purple for some obscure reason. Or if the plant simply grew this way, with those purplish upper leaves and those pinkish purple flowers. There are about twenty-five species of *Eupatorium,* and only the two or three commonly called joe-pye weed show this purpling of the upper leaves. Most of the others, including thoroughwort, boneset, and snakeroot, have white flowers, occasionally pink.

AUGUST 19

For the past ten days I have seen a strange plant coming to bloom in an old fencerow a couple of miles down the road. Today, driving that way, I stopped the car and had a closer look. It was goat's-beard, botanically an *Aruncus,* a tall plant with long, spikelike branches upright at the top, each ending in a cluster of very small white flowers. Each cluster looked like a bottle brush tapered to a point. It had a faint, pleasantly sweet fragrance.

This goat's-beard belongs to the rose family and is a cousin of meadowsweet, hardhack, and the cultivated spirea. Cousin, too, of the apple, but at some distance. The rose family has so many members I always lose track. Most of them produce some form of fruit, but this *Aruncus* doesn't produce anything worth more than passing notice by anyone but hungry birds. Birds probably planted this plant in the fence-row, excreting the seeds as they perched there. This is the first time I have seen that flower in that fencerow in the twenty-odd years I have known it.

Strange, how one becomes so well acquainted with a road or a place that one is no longer aware of its details, yet when something new or different appears there the eye sees it almost at once. The ordinary, the known and expected, no longer seems to register. But if something strange is there, no matter whether it is big or little, conspicuous or commonplace, one sees it.

AUGUST 20

In the late afternoon sunlight now I often see hordes of tiny, gleaming insects, like swarms of midges, in the air. A good many of these are what are known as microlepidoptera, very small moths, and probably these I see are of the family called *Blastobasidae*. These are miniature moths, gray in color and with a peculiar sheen to the front wings. Their larvae bore their way into seeds and nuts and even into galls on plants. Most acorns you find on the ground in the winter contain at least one, often several, of these larvae.

These microlepidoptera include a variety of miniature moths that add to the shimmer of insects wings in the slanting sunlight. We usually think of all those insects merely as "gnats," but they even include moths whose larvae are leaf miners, so tiny they actually eat their way into the fabric of a leaf and eat out the material between the two "skins" of a tree leaf. Look now and you will see these "mines," which appear on the leaves as either transparent markings or, as in the leaves of columbines, as white tracings. The extremely small moths whose eggs hatch into these leaf miners are of special beauty, when seen under a 10-power glass, more brilliant than any of the big moths and butterflies, some think. The problem is catching them to look at. They dance in the air like motes in a sunbeam, and they are too small to be caught by any of the ordinary nets.

AUGUST 21

The differences between butterflies and moths are not particularly important. Moths generally have larger, heavier bodies, and they usually have more elaborate antennae—the antennae of many male moths are feathery. Nearly all butterflies have club-shaped antennae, smooth with a knob at the end. A few tropical moths, however, have club-shaped antennae, almost exactly like those of our more common butterflies.

Butterflies also are primarily diurnal, flying only in the daytime. Most moths are nocturnal. I never see the big ones, the sphinx moths for example, except at dusk, when they come to the flower garden and gather food where the hummingbirds were busy all afternoon.

The larvae of both butterflies and moths eat leaves and other vegetable matter, but the moth larvae have earned a reputation for being very destructive, while those of butterflies are seldom spoken of as pests. Probably the tree defoliation by gypsy moths and the various loopers is a factor in this. But the common cabbage butterfly can do heavy damage in a garden or on a truck farm if not kept in check. I find that even in the dictionary one of the primary distinctions made between moths and butterflies is that the caterpillars of moths are "plant-eating," implying that butterfly caterpillars are not plant-eaters. Which, of course, is untrue.

AUGUST 22

I saw my first purple asters today, the species called *Novae Angliae,* commonly called the same thing in English, New England aster. It seems early, but the asters always come "early." I don't expect them till September, for some reason that makes no sense. Asters to me are autumn flowers, and autumn doesn't start until September—maybe that is it. Actually, of course, a good many of the asters begin to blossom here in August. But, if I may rally a dubious excuse for myself, the big purples are not among the very early asters.

Anyway, the clump in our fencerow just down the road from the house was in bloom this morning, and what a magnificent color that is. The rich purple of the petals is set off, of course, by the deep, rich brassy yellow of the flower's center. And these are big flowers, fully an inch across. They will grow even bigger under cultivation. I once saw a clump of them transplanted to a corner of a vegetable garden, tended, fertilized, and practically coddled, that had a tremendous bloom of flowers a good inch and a half across.

There is another purple aster, somewhat later, called the New York aster, and again the botanical name follows the common one, *Novi-Belgii*, for New Netherlands, the early name of New York. But its color is not so rich and it varies a great deal, from pale violet to a kind of blue violet.

There are dozens of native asters—most of our wild ones are native —but to me the New England aster is queen of them all.

AUGUST 23

The goldfinches have been feasting on thistle seeds, and in doing so they have shimmered the air over our home pasture.

Several big bull thistles, as we used to call them, grow in the edge of the pasture. Botanically they are *Cirsium vulgaris,* or "common thistles." They are very prickly, gray-green plants with fat tufts of deep purple blossom that ripen into heads of silvery white floss. At the bottom of each strand of that fine floss is a tiny black seed. The goldfinches are very fond of these seeds. They come to the thistles as soon as one of the flowers is "ripe" and begin to tear out that floss, nip off the seeds, and let the wind have the glistening, silky floss. I have seen a goldfinch work at one thistle head for half an hour, tear it almost wholly to pieces. The sight is not only fascinating—it is spectacularly beautiful, the glistening white thistle floss, the bright yellow and black of the male goldfinch, and the blue of the late August sky. The thistledown streams away like gleaming smoke, and the goldfinch fairly hops up and down with excitement as he plucks out tuft after tuft from the ripe head. He snatches at the tiny black seeds but never gets them all. So he has a hand in planting those thistles all down the valley.

If it weren't for the goldfinches they attract I would declare war on all those thistles and probably clean them out of the pastures. And, thanks to goldfinches and wind up and down the valley, I probably would have thistles every year just the same.

AUGUST 24

It has been raining all day. It began in the night, a consequence of a tropical storm that came up the coast but didn't swing inland. It swung eastward instead, but we have been getting the outflung effects, with a gusty wind that didn't do any damage. But the rain has come down in sheets, at times.

Those tropical storms have tremendous breadth. They set the air to swirling and create an atmospheric turbulence several hundred miles in diameter. When they come up the coast they have a tendency to veer inland. We have to watch them when they reach Cape Hatteras, for that is where they usually "recurve" inland or swerve the other direction, out to sea. But even if one of them keeps out to sea and misses Cape Cod, we get the effects, primarily in the form of heavy rain. Only occasionally does one sweep into our part of New England. The latest one was in 1955, and some of the scars of that one are still in sight.

Today we got only the gusty wind, which did no damage, and rain. I went out to the gauge at the far corner of the garden about ten this morning and found that we had then received just over two inches. By midafternoon it was almost three and a quarter inches. I haven't been out since, but by nightfall the total may be four inches or more. That will mean flooding downstream, in the lowlands. By morning the river here will probably have risen at least five or six feet. But we have at least ten feet of leeway, so we probably will not get any floodwater even on the road.

AUGUST 25

The rain ended just before midnight. But the brooks were roaring all night long; I heard them every time I wakened. Two brooks come down off the mountain and wander across the pastures to the river, and both of them have rapids and minor falls at the foot of the mountain. Under a normal head of water they gurgle and burble, a pleasantly drowsy sound; but when they have as much water as they had last night they rumble and roar and can be heard half a mile away. It is a wet, rumbling sound, with just a hint of thunder in it. But we know it for what it is and go to sleep comfortably with it in our ears. In daytime we are scarcely aware of it. I have to listen this morning to hear it.

The world looks over-drenched, something like a long-haired dog just out of a bath. If it could shake, it probably would create another rainstorm. Even a light breeze brings down a shower from the maples. They could stand a toweling.

Down the road a field of alfalfa, almost ready for cutting a third crop of hay this summer, has been badly wind-blown and lodged, as farm folk say. The wet plants become top-heavy and the wind puts them down in swales like troughs between ocean waves. When the farmer tries to mow that field he will have trouble with that lodged hay, probably will lose it.

The river has risen a good six feet and is still rising, as the runoff upstream swells all the brooks. My gauge shows that we got a little over three and a half inches of rain.

AUGUST 26

Thinking about that storm and all that rain, I think about how large a part water plays in my daily life. In the spring I wait for the frost— frozen water—to go out of the ground so I can plow and plant. I plant when the moisture content of the soil is favorable to the sprouting of seeds—and, of course, when the temperature has risen to a favorable point for germination. I trust to rain to water the fields and garden, to provide them with a sufficient amount of soluble minerals to make the plants grow properly. In the heat of summer I hope for enough clouds— water vapor—to temper the strength of the sun for me and the growing things around me. If it is too wet, the plants may drown. If there is too much rain in too brief a time, the river will rise in flood. If there is not enough rain, the crops will wither and my spring and my well will fail me; I shall be without water my body needs each day. And in winter my life and my mobility are eased or hampered by the amount of snow and ice in this valley. The valley itself—its size and contours and fertility—is a consequence of flowing water that has been at work here ever since this land was lifted above the ocean bed. Water, which simply flows down-hill.

As long as there is life here, there must be water. Remove the water and you put an end to life. Life, which as we know it must have originated in the water. As it evolved, the plant and animal life of which we are closest kin emerged from the water onto the land, a dubious escape into another element. We are still here, living on the land, terrestrial creatures and terrestrial plants. But we never really escaped. We still carry the ocean in our veins, and we perish without water.

AUGUST 27

A whole field of goldenrod is in bloom down the road, one of those abandoned farm fields that has simply gone back to natural growth. It was farmed until five years ago, but not only hasn't been plowed but hasn't even been mowed since then. Now it is a vast patch of goldenrod with a scattering of gray birch seedlings. There are at least five species of goldenrod, early, sweet, large-leafed, showy, and rough-stemmed. The colors are so nearly identical that you have to examine leaves and stems to identify them by species.

There are about twenty-five species found in the Northeast, but perhaps ten are common. Most of them have the typical plume of blossom, several of them multiple plumes. Sweet goldenrod is easily recognizable by its strong odor of anise. Most of the others have only a rather pungent, slightly resiny odor.

The standard botany manuals list seventy-five species of goldenrod in the United States, all of them native. We tend to think of goldenrod as an autumn flower—I do, at least—along with asters; but some species bloom in late July. And it is nearly always through blooming by the third week in September.

AUGUST 28

A phone call came this afternoon from someone who wanted to know why she can't find sweet-fern listed in her fern books. She wants to get some, from a nursery, for her wild garden. Where can she find its name?

I had to tell her to look in a book on shrubs. Sweet-fern is not a fern. It is a shrub belonging to the same family as the bayberry, the sweet gale family, botanically *Myricaceae*. It is a small family, with only half a dozen members.

Sweet-fern grows here, just up the road from my house and along paths over the hills in all directions. The plant is a foot or two high with dull red or brown stems and long, narrow leaves with deeply indented edges. The leaves faintly resemble several species of ferns and brackens. But the leaves are aromatic on the sweet-fern, and not on the ferns and bracken. It is a faintly sweet, strongly spiced fragrance that reminds me of the fragrance of bayberries. It has blossoms, rather inconspicuous, the male a drooping catkin less than an inch long. The female blossom, usually born on a separate bush, matures into a tiny nut in a burrlike cluster of bracts, all rather rusty green. This nutlet and its bracts are also aromatic when crushed.

New England farm wives once gathered sweet-fern to put among their bed linens. It left the linens sweet-smelling and it kept away musty odors.

AUGUST 29

This was a beautiful day, from start to finish, or at least till sundown and into the evening. I am writing this just after dinner, before we go out and sit in the cool of the evening.

It was clear and bright this morning, with just a bit of mist over the river and a trace of ground haze over the pastures along the river. The temperature was a comfortable fifty-two degrees. The haze burned off by nine o'clock and the sky was almost High Country blue, my highest praise. We have too many dirty blue days, or washed-out blue days, from a touch of distant smoke high in the air, probably, or a tinge of humidity from the seacoast seventy-five miles away. But today was clean, clear blue, exactly the color it should have been. And the temperature didn't top eighty degrees all afternoon. Bright sun, clear sky, and just enough of a breeze to keep the air moving, to rustle the leaves of the maples very softly, a mere whisper.

The afternoon was a lazy afternoon, not hot-lazy when you don't want to move, but leisurely-lazy, when you did only what you wanted to and took your time about it. I puttered in the vegetable garden for an hour or so, doing nothing very important but appreciating the way every-thing has grown and come to proper harvest. We have had all the garden produce we wanted with enough to freeze for next winter. Now we are eating some of the best tomatoes ever grown—every year, it seems, they are the best—and within another week or so we shall begin to can tomatoes, the only vegetables we can.

And this evening is comfortably cool. It probably will be another night in the fifties.

AUGUST 30

The milkweed pods are big and fat, and very green. Soon now they will begin to take on that silvery look of approaching ripeness. Then the leaves will turn to that beautiful coppery tan. And finally the pods, big as a goose head, will split open and that silvery white floss will begin to spill out on every wind, each tuft of it carrying a seed.

The milkweed is a strangely contrary plant, in some way. Its floss should have some commercial use as a fiber or a fluff, yet nobody has ever succeeded in using it except to stuff a cushion or two. The juice of the plant has some of the properties of raw rubber, and once, many years ago, chemists tried to make commercial rubber from it. I believe Thomas Edison was interested in the experiment. But it failed.

The plant does have fibers in its stem that are useful. They look something like monofilament nylon fish line. They lie just under the outer skin of dead stalks from last year's plants, and orioles in my valley use those fibers in building their nests. They seem to be a good substitute for horsehair, for the orioles at least. Break a last-year's milkweed stalk and you can find these fibers, about a dozen running the length of each stalk.

Curious, a few years ago I took a couple of milkweed pods into the house to count the number of seeds in them. The number ran to just about 225 to each pod, not half as many as I had expected. But enough to litter the whole house. I should have done it outdoors.

AUGUST 31

The sun and I rose almost together this morning, just a few minutes after five. I set the coffee to perk and went outside to look at the morning, and I knew this was the end of summer. I can't say why, in one simple statement. I just knew by the look, the smell, the feel of the air.

The temperature was in the forties, but that alone wasn't the answer. I couldn't see anything particularly different from what it was a week ago, and yet I knew that by tomorrow's sunup it was going to be autumn. And it had nothing to do with the calendar.

Summer ends when the ripeness sets in, when the work of the hot season is finished. You can see it in the leaves, if you look closely, in the way they hang, the dullness of their green. You can see it in those early asters already in bloom. They have a look of—well, triumph is the only word that expresses it. Daisies are gone, black-eyed Susans are gone, Queen Anne's lace heads are past their prime, joe-pye weed is in bloom, and now come the asters. They will own things from now till hard frost, with a short break in attention for the gentians.

And you can hear it among the birds. No bird-song, but a kind of restless twittering, the harsh, questioning call of the robins, the sharp cries of the flickers. They will be gone soon, the robins first, then the flickers. And I will be hearing the soft chittering of the chickadee, the harsh laughter of the jay, the triumphant caw of the crow. This morning I heard a querulous robin, and an answer from another robin up the road. Then I heard, back in the woods, the restless hammering of a pileated woodpecker on a dead limb. It was like a tattoo summoning the troops before taps for another summer.

SEPTEMBER

SEPTEMBER 1

Almost every year September brings us a flock of robins, obviously getting ready for a long trip. They are here today, out in the home pasture, quietly talking among themselves, restless but never going far. They will be around maybe a week. Then we will wake up some morning and not see a robin. They will have taken off for the South for the winter.

Actually, of course, not all the robins go down to Georgia and Florida and the other Gulf States. We have robins here every winter. Apparently we have had them a long time. I used to think they were lazy louts that didn't want to make that long trip down and back, maybe even a hardy strain that had evolved over the years. Then I learned that a good many robins spend the summer in Labrador, and that some of them, at least, come down to New England for the winter. That would make them migrants, too, because in the spring they would go back up north to Labrador to nest. We don't miss them because the migrants from the South take their places.

In any case, there is a flock of twenty-five or thirty robins out in the pasture right now, chattering like winter cruise passengers eager to get aboard. They won't be around here much longer. And within a week after they depart I will be seeing a few robins again, in the bogland down the road. I will see them off and on all winter, and next February they will be coming into our dooryard to poke into the grass where the snow has melted over the septic tank. They will go to the village, and people will report "the first robin" and insist we will have an early spring.

SEPTEMBER 2

We have been making jelly. Apple jelly, and mint jelly.

We made the apple juice several weeks ago, from a big crop of windfalls that were too good to waste. I gathered them, sorted them, we cut them up, simmered them, and set them to drain in jelly bags. We got several quarts of thick, rich apple juice, put it in jars, and stowed it in the refrigerator for a cool jelly-making day. Today was it.

Once you have that juice, that essence, the final step to jelly isn't particularly hard. It does warm things up in the kitchen, but today was one of those fine fall days when a little extra warmth didn't matter. It felt good, in fact.

We started with regular apple jelly, made two batches of it, poured it into jelly glasses, paraffined it, set it to cool. Then for the mint jelly, which has an apple base around this house. But first you must have the essence of mint. So I went out into the home pasture, up Millstone Brook a little way, and gathered wild mint, which grows there profusely. Some say this is our only native mint. "Wild mint" is its only common name, and the botanical name is *Mentha arvensis*. I gathered a half a peck of leaves and branch tips, brought them home, and "bruised" them, as the recipe-writers say. I gave them quite a beating, in fact. Then we covered them with vinegar and simmered them, strained them, and had a capful of good, strong essence of mint in vinegar.

We added this to the apple juice and were ready to make mint jelly. Almost ready. When we measured the sugar, we were a cup short. I would have to get out the car and go to the village and buy sugar. But Barbara said no: "I'll bet we can make it right here."

She went to her purse and found two of those small packets of sugar they serve in restaurants. In a dress pocket she found three more. I looked in my jacket pocket and found a few more. Then she turned up a real trove of them in the small case she had with her when she was in the hospital for a minor operation last May. There must have been two dozen of those little packets that she had moused away.

I looked in the cupboard, found a sugar bowl we hadn't used in six months. It had six or eight spoonfuls in it. Barbara looked in a tea set and found a bowl with ten lumps of sugar. One way and another, we managed it.

In went the last cupful of sugar, up went the heat, and the mint jelly was on its way. This evening there are a dozen glasses of beautiful green mint jelly cooling on the big table in the enclosed back porch, along with two dozen rosy pink glasses of apple jelly. The mint jelly, I admit, is green only thanks to a small vial of vegetable coloring, from which several drops were added during the cooking. Essence of mint leaves isn't green; it is a kind of late September brown. But it has a fine green fragrance and a fine green taste, and with a little help from the chemists it comes out a rich emerald color.

SEPTEMBER 3

The great lobelias are in bloom with a warm blue-violet color. I was looking for ladies'-tresses, the little autumn orchids, on the lower slope of the mountain, and there were the lobelias, several plants of them. Ladies'-tresses and grass-of-Parnassus bloom now and often close together; but you have to look for them. No one can overlook the great lobelias. They stand three feet tall, single spikes with the blue-and-white striped flowers on the upper third of the stalk. The flowers are shaped like fat tubes with the lips split into three parts below, two parts above, a perfect invitation to the bees.

The lobelia family was named for a Flemish herbalist, Matthias de l'Obel, and it includes another September surprise, the cardinal flower, which looks a good deal like the great lobelia done over in cardinal red and the "petals" more loose and ragged. The family also includes a weedy little plant called Indian-tobacco, the most common of all the lobelias, found at almost any roadside. It is a small plant with a single, only occasionally branched stem, at most two feet tall, with tiny pale blue flowers tucked into the axils of the upper leaves. The base of the flower is swollen and becomes a fat little fruit capsule. The leaves of the plant are almost stemless, hug the main stalk, and are very acrid in taste. They were used by some of the old herbalists in medicine, probably to give it that bitter, dark-brown taste. They are not a good substitute for tobacco. If the Indians ever smoked them, they had tougher tongues than I have. The memory alone makes my mouth pucker.

SEPTEMBER 4

It was a chilly morning, down to thirty, with a touch of frost here and there. Early frost, from a minor cold wave that passed through in the night. We probably will have another two frost-free weeks. But when I went out to look at the garden I saw a big bumblebee crawling out of a ragged zinnia blossom, where he must have spent the night. He was stiff and slow and he crawled out into the sun and just sat there, waiting for the sunlight to put life into his cold-blooded body again.

I went on to look at the late beans. They had escaped the frost blight. But near them were two big black ants trying to go somewhere and walking like very old, very arthritic men, barely able to climb over the smallest pebbles in their path. They, like the bumblebee, were at the mercy of the air temperature.

Insects are cold-blooded creatures. Chill them and you slow down all their body processes. Their blood must be molasses-thick on such a morning. But by ten o'clock, when the sun had brought the air temperature up to sixty degrees, the bumblebees were flying normally and the ants were scurrying about as usual.

Insects are prodigal with energy. Theoretically the bumblebee is too big and heavy to fly on its inadequate wings, but by beating those wings 240 strokes per second it accomplishes the seemingly impossible. Such activity burns energy fast and can be sustained only by constant feeding and a highly efficient digestive and circulatory system. But there is no energy left over to warm the body or the blood. Without the warmth of the sun their blood thickens and their whole system slows down. They are at the mercy of the outer air.

The insects apparently achieved their form of efficiency long ago. They evolved into a form that was perfect for their own needs, and they have not noticeably diverged from that form over the eons. Some fossil cockroaches have longer antennae than those of today, but how much energy was needed to shorten a pair of needlessly long antennae? The whole life-force of the insects apparently was directed toward survival, and in that sense the insects have been more successful than any other kind of life we know except the unicellular creatures, which also reached early perfection of their own kind. Certainly the insects are the only greatly diversified form of life that has persisted so long without material change.

Is this a virtue or high achievement? I have my doubts. It seems to me that change is a basic law of nature, change, diversity, possibly improvement. Of course, I may be speaking thus as a kind of animal that is himself a result of continuing, persistent, and possibly explosive change. Therefore I may be unduly biased But when I see a cold-numbed bumblebee or ant, I do wonder why their kind hasn't changed more over the centuries.

SEPTEMBER 5

Thinking again about those cold-blooded creatures I was discussing yesterday, I wonder now if their very resistance to change hasn't made the insects the most successful of all the living creatures we see around us.

That, of course, would depend on what we mean by success, and I cannot concede that mere survival is enough or that resistance to change is necessarily evidence of victory over anything except change itself. We are dealing here with life, and life is—or should be—more than mere existence. To me it is. Otherwise, why should there be life at all? Such a concession would reduce all life to a meaningless level.

I can conceive of an insect colony as a kind of unit of life, a composite of many motile cells which are individuals. I, too, am a kind of composite unit composed of many individual cells, some of which have limited mobility, but always within the confines of my own body. But even if I grant such identity for the whole colony, say, of an ant community or a hive of bees, there still remains the question of the community purpose. Complex and efficient as it is, its total achievement is nothing more than a mass of instincts and reflexes all directed toward survival, toward perpetuation. A whole community of ants cannot achieve even thought enough to create anything more imaginative than the ant colony that has been typical of their kind for eons. Even as a community, a kind of composite unit of life, no society of ants has ever evolved anything comparable to even the simplest of primitive man's arts. And there is no evidence of thought, either concrete or abstract, in even the best organized of the social insects, beyond a dubious 1 percent of thought which one researcher grants to an ant. And the researcher himself terms that a trifling fraction, most difficult to discover.

Yet the insects did achieve many skills, and the social insects long, long ago did achieve an organized form of life that has a superficial resemblance to the kind of life man eventually adopted. That cannot be dismissed out of hand. Somewhere that instinct toward shared work and a common purpose must have originated. We can rationalize it in the ant and the bee as a remarkable means of race survival, but we cannot ignore it. We have the same impulse. We have enlarged and expanded it, and we have refined it with thought and conscious purpose, but something of it is there in the human background. To that extent we must recognize our link with those very old, almost totally different, and mysteriously originated creatures, the insects.

SEPTEMBER 6

After that light, spotty frost a few nights ago the weather turned warm, as I expected, and this was a hot, humid day that felt more like July than September. We even had a brief but very loud thunderstorm this afternoon. Less than a quarter of an inch of rain fell, but the air was cooled off and this evening it is comfortable again.

After the thunderstorm had passed, we canned tomatoes. The other vegetables we store for winter use are blanched and frozen. But canned tomatoes are a delicacy, in my lexicon, perhaps because they were the primary source of vitamins for which we had a deep springtime hunger in my boyhood. We bought canned tomatoes at the store, sat on the front step, knifed open the cans, and ate those tomatoes as though we were starving.

So today we can them ourselves, in glass jars. And it really isn't much of a chore, spread out the way we do it. We pick the tomatoes as they ripen, and those less than perfect are simmered and juiced every few days. The juice is stowed in the refrigerator till canning day. Then we warm the juice, choose the prime tomatoes for the jars, scald and skin them, put them in the jars, cover them with the warm juice, put on the lids and pack them into the pressure canner. Over the heat they go, the pressure builds up, is maintained five minutes or ten minutes, depending. Off the heat they come. And when the canner has cooled, out come the jars to cool, be tested for seal and stowed in the root cellar.

Tonight we have eighteen quarts of newly canned tomatoes.

SEPTEMBER 7

Out in the lower pasture today I found a surprising number of caterpillars on the milkweeds. Monarch caterpillars and tiger-moth caterpillars, as nearly as I could identify them. I know the monarchs, those unmistakable yellow-and-black striped fellows.

The strange thing about them was the timing. Those caterpillars should have pupated almost a month ago and they should be mature butterflies by now. Those monarchs will be in trouble, unless the autumn reverses its usual pattern. Those caterpillars certainly aren't going to walk all the way to the Gulf of Mexico.

Monarch butterflies have several broods, over the summer, but it is this late brood that goes south for the winter and returns in the spring to start the cycle all over again. They travel in great swarms, at times, and on other occasions in small groups. They seem to be flying somewhat at random, but they manage to make their way southward ahead of hard frost. Occasionally a swarm of them will be caught in a storm and blown far out to sea. It is believed that some have been blown clear across the

Atlantic this way. Individuals have landed on ships several hundred miles out to sea.

In the spring it is the females that return, pregnant females ready to lay eggs on milkweeds, which are their chosen food. The males seldom get all the way back, dying of fatigue or old age or being eaten by birds on the way. One researcher, by the way, reports that a monarch butterfly tastes a good deal like cold, dry toast.

SEPTEMBER 8

I haven't seen a flicker in two weeks. Before that they were gathering in flocks of a dozen or so, flying nervously about, chattering. That is the way they always do just before they migrate. All summer they are rugged individualists, almost never seen in groups. They march about the lawn, waddling in a way that is almost a strut, looking for insects, especially for ants. Ants are the bread, butter, meat, potatoes and pie for a flicker. They are good neighbors. I like to have them around, even though they do have one bad habit—they eat poison ivy berries and excrete the indigestible seeds, which take root and grow. I have to spray under their favorite roosts every year.

The flicker is one of the few eastern birds I knew as a boy on the Colorado plains. One summer there a strange bird appeared, spent much time feasting at the big anthills, and seemed to resent the presence of the meadowlarks. I had no idea what it was and one day I shot it, the way the old-time ornithologists shot birds, to have a close look and identify it. I took it to a friend who knew many things, and he told me it was a flicker, a kind of woodpecker that didn't have to have trees. He said it was rare out there on the flats, and it certainly was. I never saw another, except in the cottonwoods along the Platte River thirty miles north. That one, of course, was the western flicker, with red shafts to its wing feathers. The eastern species has yellow shafts, a rich orangy-yellow.

SEPTEMBER 9

I heard a peeper this afternoon, a spring peeper, one of the little tree frogs that make such a welcome clamor in April. Now and then one of them calls in the autumn, but seldom more than one or two. I have no idea why they call, since this isn't mating time for them. But this yelping little peeper, which isn't much bigger than my thumbnail, reminded me of all my amphibian neighbors, particularly of the frogs that trill so pleasantly through the early summer. They will soon be digging into the river mud, settling in for the winter.

The frogs came from the water, lived most of their lives on land all summer, now return to the mud. They learned to breathe with lungs, shed their tadpole gills, though they also breathed somewhat through their skin as their remote ancestors did before the first fish evolved gills. Now they will retreat not only into the mud but into the remote past and breathe through their skin in hibernation.

SEPTEMBER 10

Rain in the night, and a thunderstorm with quite a bit of lightning. But it was largely clear this morning and turned out to be a cool fall day. It never quite reached 70 and had wind enough to make it feel even cooler.

One of our big maples is beginning to show color. This is early, but I see no sign of sickness in the tree. Several other maples just down the road are also showing yellow. And the high-bush cranberry shows the deep orange of near-ripeness. In another couple of weeks those berries will be cherry red, ready for picking and for their eventual appearance as jelly at the holiday feasts of the months to come.

The whole feel of autumn is with us now. All but the frost. And if we can skip frost for another couple of weeks, we will have more ripe tomatoes. After the frost we will be through with the garden for this season. After that will come the annual clean-up, preparing for winter.

SEPTEMBER 11

I was watching for nighthawks today, but I saw none. I watch every September. But now I begin to think I was specially blessed that one year, and that once is considered enough for me.

They were starting their migration, as they always do in late August. I was not surprised when I saw the first few, four or five, coming down the valley, circling as they came, each circuit reaching a hundred yards or so farther south. I was out in the home pasture and I stood and watched. After a moment I saw a whole cloud of nighthawks behind those first few. As they came closer, it was apparent that there were hundreds of them. That circling stream of scimitar-winged gray birds must have been a mile long.

They were flying low enough to permit me to see the white bar across the wings and the white streak across the tail. And all were circling, as those first few were, wheeling slowly in a counter-clockwise pattern and moving gradually down the valley. They were silent as owls.

I came to the house and called Barbara and we stood in the dooryard and watched for a long half hour. Then they were gone. I never saw them again.

I knew nighthawks when I was a boy on the Colorado plains, and it pleased me to find them here. But there normally are only a few. We seldom see one more than a few times each summer. And their migration routes apparently don't normally include this valley. But I keep hoping, watching, as I did today.

SEPTEMBER 12

This has been a dull, vaguely menacing day, overcast but with interludes of bright sun. There is another tropical storm off the Virginia capes and threatening to come on up the coast. We have that storm's outriders, clouds that break in big rifts now and then and let the glow of blue sky come pouring through.

These tropical storms, by the time they get to Hatteras, are tremendous wheels of "weather" that spin out these vast streamers that go trailing after the inner wheel of the storm center. We get those outflung clouds. If the storm veers out to sea from Hatteras, we will have clearing weather within a day or two. If it comes on up the coast we can expect rain and wind, probably a great deal of both. If it turns inland, as such a storm does once in a long time, we can expect trouble, big trouble. Floods, roads and bridges washed out, power lines down, houses swept away, and an aftermath of suffering, sickness, even death.

This evening is dour and drizzly. The forecasters haven't yet decided what the storm is going to do.

SEPTEMBER 13

A rainy night and another drizzly day, with that storm still hovering off the Carolina coast. Now it has bred wind as well as rain for us, though the wind is mostly in gusts. And the rain has been fitful. At noon when I went out and looked, my rain gauge showed just a trace over an inch had fallen since yesterday morning.

I sometimes think the worst of these storms is the waiting, the uncertainty, the "Will it?" and the "Won't it?" Something like the crises in our lives. I can face trouble when I know what it is and where it is coming from. It becomes difficult to handle when it is a mere uncertainty, a vagueness, something I can't get my hands on. If we are going to get a storm, let's have it and get it over with. If it is coming this way, tell me it is coming. I'll brace myself, make sure the house is tight, the barns and outbuildings as secure as they can be made. But when I am merely told, "The storm is still off the Carolina coast, and we can't be sure which way it will turn," I have nothing to go on.

I spent much of the morning checking doors and windows in the outbuildings, making sure they are secure. The house itself is as secure as it ever will be, and we have taken all precautions. We have spring water that comes to the house by gravity. There is enough food to last us a month or more. There is a Franklin stove for heat. In the basement is an old gas cook stove, fed by bottled gas, for the emergency. We could make out.

Now I wish that uncertainty were over, that this storm would either come or go away.

SEPTEMBER 14

This started as another day of glower and intermittent rain. We had hard rain in the night, well over an inch of it by my gauge. But by noon the uncertainty ended. The weather people announced, without equivocation, that the storm had turned out to sea. That means it is moving on up the coast but well offshore. Cape Cod probably will take a battering, and we may have another day of high, swirling clouds, but that seems to be all we are in for.

Now we can get back to other matters.

And that probably shows how superficial are the veneers of immediacy that coat most of our lives. In the face of a big storm we can drop all other concerns and think only of the weather and its effects. We can almost turn back the clock and calendar, to a time when men lived with and by the weather and the natural world. We have got so far away from such fundamentals that unless our lives or property are actually threatened we leave the weather to the forecasters and remain immersed in "matters of real consequence"—in politics, business, war, all the inter-human things that occupy so much of our daily lives.

I must add now that the rain stopped soon after noon, and by four o'clock the sun was shining as innocently as though there never had been a storm anywhere in sight. Tomorrow probably will be bright and shining.

SEPTEMBER 15

Before the storm I was discussing amphibians, and was about to say that frogs and toads were, in a way, among the most successful of them all. At least, they have survived, which is more than can be said for most of those early amphibians. Fossil frogs and toads have been found in rocks 50 or 60 million years old, and they seem to have been almost identical with those of today. Fossils of frogs with tails have been found in rocks 200 million years old, but except for the tails those frogs were not greatly different from those of later periods. In all that time, then, 150 million years or so, evolution did little to the frog except remove his tail, which must have been an invitation to his enemies and, from any logical standpoint, should have been sacrificed sooner than it was. But nature and the slow processes of evolution move at their own leisurely pace.

Generally, that is. But not always.

SEPTEMBER 16

It is frequently said that this is the Age of Mammals, that the mammals now dominate the earth. That is a fine, large statement, and we believe it—"Man is a mammal, isn't he? And he is in control of the earth, isn't he?" But what about the insects? Those small, cold-blooded, chitin-clad bits of life crop up to pose gnarly questions every time one makes a big generalization in this area. I suppose, however, that one can say with some certainty that mammals do now have a large degree of dominance. At least, we mammals have thus far kept the insects from overwhelming us. With the help of birds and small beasts, which we are too often reluctant to admit. So probably a man can call this the Age of Mammals and get away with it, though it is a dubious claim.

The mammal is a comparatively old form of life. The earliest fossil mammals date from the Triassic period, about 190 million years ago. Most of the mammal families of today have fossil ancestors dating back from 60 to 100 million years. The very early mammals were small, about the size of today's rats, and some were so tentatively mammalian that the paleontologists say they were reptilian in many characteristics. That would be inevitable, since the mammals presumably sprang from the reptilian stock.

What is a mammal? Briefly, a mammal is an animal that usually has fur or hair, is warm-blooded, has four limbs, bears its young alive, and feeds those young from mammary glands in the mother.

There are exceptions, as there are variants in almost all families of animals. In the Australia–New Zealand zoo of primitives, for instance, is the platypus, which hatches its young from eggs laid in a nest. Yet the platypus is a mammal, fur-bearing, warm-blooded, four-legged, and with mammary glands. There are no mammary teats, however; the milk oozes from pores in the skin and the young lick it off instead of suckling. Also in the Australian zoo is the echidna, the spiny anteater, which also lays eggs and has no teats on its mammary glands. And there are the marsupials—kangaroos and all the others whose young are born in a kind of larval stage and are nurtured in the mother's abdominal pouch at her mammary teats. In the United States we have only one example of the marsupial family, the slow-witted opossum.

With the exception of the strange variants characteristic of the Australia–New Zealand area, the world's mammals are relatively obedient to the broad rules of their kind. But they are vastly varied, from the tiny pygmy shrew to the whale, from the field mouse to the elephant. Some have horns on their heads. Many have hoofed feet. And all have teeth set in sockets in their jaws; among all the other animals, only crocodiles have such teeth. And all mammals have diaphragms, that sheet of muscle across the body cavity separating lungs and heart from digestive organs.

SEPTEMBER 17

In terms of physical equipment, the mammal is the most complex of all animals. Even the mammalian heart is complex, having four chambers to separate pure blood from impure blood and circulate only pure, aerated blood to the body's vital organs. And all mammals have comparatively large and complex brains, relatively much larger and more complex than the brains of insects, fish, amphibians, or reptiles. Only the birds come near the mammals in brain size relative to total body size.

Man speaks of the mammals as the highest achievement of evolution. By a stretch of the imagination I can conceive of the insects, if they ever were to consider such matters, believing that they, not the mammals, are the superior ones. In terms of brain power, however, there is little doubt that the mammal does stand at the top of the heap, with man at the very peak. But since we do not know the purpose of evolution, if indeed there is any purpose, such a classification may be somewhat arbitrary. If persistence of the species, for instance, were the criterion, the insects surely would be among the logical applicants for high honors. The insects have been here, in substantially their present form, at least 200 million years, perhaps 250 million. Mammals have been here at most about 190 million, so we still have a few million years to go to prove that we have the endurance, as a species, that the insects have already demonstrated.

SEPTEMBER 18

A small flock of Canada geese flew over today, heading south. We were in the house and heard them, that unmistakable sound of geese on the wing, which is to me much like the barking of small dogs in the distance. We went out, and there they were, flying only moderately high, heading down the river.

It is early. Geese don't normally migrate from our area in September. Perhaps these were merely flying from one local pond to another. But the sound of those geese was all autumn, all October and autumn wanderlust.

I have high respect for the Canada goose, which is a very bright bird, any way you look at it. All birds, of course, have a weather sense, since they are natural barometers—their bones are hollow, and react to atmospheric pressure. But geese seem to be particularly gifted in this regard. I have known a flock to pass up two or three of what appeared to me clearcut weather warnings in the autumn, then take off for the South just twelve hours before the season's first winter storm struck.

Geese are good mates, good parents. Whether they actually mate for life or not, I do not know, but they are supposed to, and I have known one to haunt the place where its mate was killed, refusing to leave for days. And they are among the best flyers of all our birds. One flock of geese is known to have traveled, nonstop, from James Bay, Canada, to Louisiana—about 1,700 miles—in sixty hours.

SEPTEMBER 19

The Virginia creeper has turned that magnificent crimson it does at its peak of color, and now it stands out vividly along the river. It climbs the dead elms and makes a fiery show all the way to their scraggly tips, giving them a brief, colorful look of life, a color they never achieved when alive.

Some people call it woodbine, and sometimes I do, too; but several other climbing plants are also called woodbine, here and there, and only this one is called Virginia creeper. It is a cousin of the grape, botanically, and its botanical name, *Parthenocissus,* comes directly from the Greek words for "virgin ivy." It has no relationship to poison ivy, for which it is sometimes mistaken. The creeper's leaves come compound, five or occasionally seven to a stem, and each leaf coarsely notched at the edges. Poison ivy leaves come three to the stem and are not notched; they have a smooth, almost oily look, which the creeper's leaves lack. And by now both species are in fruit, the poison ivy berries gray-green and in loose clusters, the Virginia creeper's berries definitely blue and in broad clusters, with red stems.

The leaves of the two plants readily distinguish them, and once recognized they will be long remembered. Virginia creeper turns that strong, clear red. Poison ivy turns red and orange and yellow, often all three on the same vine. Poison ivy, too, can be beautiful now; but leave it alone or be sorry.

SEPTEMBER 20

We are having almost perfect fall weather. Fall begins day after tomorrow, with the autumnal equinox.

That word, autumn, goes all the way back through Medieval English and Old French, *autumpne* and *autompne,* to the Latin *autumnus,* which is listed as "of uncertain origin." It simply means the third season of the year, that time between summer and winter, and apparently it always has. But my big dictionary adds, comfortingly, "the season known in America as *Fall."* Fall, of course, means many things—the fall of the leaves, the fall of temperature, the fall of man perhaps. Follow that word back and you come out at Old Dutch and Old German, *vallen* and *fallen,* meaning to go down, to descend, pretty much what we mean today when we use the word as a verb. It must have come to us as a season name through the Anglo-Saxon.

Whatever you choose to call it, it is a beautiful time of the year, a comfortable and comforting time. It brings some of the most beautiful days, with clear, blue skies and mild winds and comfortable temperatures. It is adorned with color in the woodlands. It is the end of summer, but it also is a thoroughly pleasant interval between summer and winter.

Today was a perfect autumn day. . . . And there I go, slipping out of fall into autumn. . . . All right, a perfect fall day, too.

SEPTEMBER 21

The northern lights were dancing last night. If they hadn't been putting on a minor display two weeks ago I would think they were ushering in the autumnal equinox. It seems early, to me, to be having this fantastic display in the northern sky; but then I remember that the aurora is most often seen early in the autumn, and now and then early in the spring. Grant my own belief that September is a part of autumn, and it all fits.

Last night the display was quite spectacular. It began with a whitish glow in the north which expanded into a huge arch and began to flicker, as though an enormous curtain were being raised and its folds were illuminated. Then a tinge of red appeared low down, and it rose and faded. Other curtains of light appeared in the distance, to wave and flicker and vanish. And blue and green as well as red and even a touch of yellow were there, almost like the tongues of an enormous bonfire on the northern horizon. And finally, after more than an hour of varying brilliance, the whole display began to fade.

The aurora—and it occurs at the South Pole as well as at the North—is believed to be a consequence of atomic or subatomic action. Protons and electrons from the sun appear to be trapped in the Van Allen belt, then funneled toward the earth's poles by the earth's magnetic currents. As they enter the atmosphere they collide with molecules of oxygen and nitrogen in the air and excite them to luminosity. An apparently clear relationship between the occurrence of sunspots and auroral appearances has been shown, indicating that the proton and electron showers do have a definite part in the creation of the aurora.

The first few minutes of watching the Northern Lights always gives me an almost primitive sense of awe and apprehension. Then I catch hold of reality and can appreciate the uncanny beauty of the whole display. But I know that if I were an Ice Age man I would be out there in the flickering auroral light dancing a fantastic ritual of either triumph or appeasement, I don't know which.

SEPTEMBER 22

This is the day of the autumnal equinox, which of course is only an astronomical incident, not an actual event in earthly terms. We use it as a milepost in time, to mark the beginning of the fourth quarter of the solar year. In terms of climate and weather, it has no particular meaning. Meteorologists insist that there is no such thing as an "equinoctial storm," because the equinox itself cannot create a storm. To me, such a statement is no more persuasive than to say we never have an Easter storm or a year-end blizzard.

Actually, we often have some kind of stormy weather about now, and it is common habit to call it "the equinoctial storm." I shall continue to do so. This year we are fortunate—no such storm. Today is bright and sunny, almost perfect fall weather. But by my reckoning we have had fall weather, the look and feel of fall, for almost three weeks now. And in my book September is an autumn month, no matter what the equinoctial factors may be. In my calendar year, autumn consists of September, October, and November. December is a part of winter.

However, from twelve fifteen today, when the sun passed the celestial equator moving south, until the winter solstice in late December, it will be almanac autumn. I don't particularly like that definition, but even meteorologists use it. It is the earth that moves, not the sun. But let's not get fouled up on that point. Theoretically, day and night are equal today, too; and actually they aren't. And I am not going to try to rationalize that today either.

SEPTEMBER 23

The chickadees have come down from their summer haunts on the mountain and whenever I go outdoors now they swoop from the trees or bushes in what appears to me to be a greeting. Evidently they haven't forgotten last winter, when I fed them sunflower seeds. They knew me by sight, came and perched on my hand, or on my hat or my shoulder while I filled the feeders. It may well be that they remember me only as a perambulating source of food, but at least they do remember. They have that power of memory. They can learn.

That is true of all birds. Some learn faster than others, of course. I never think of house wrens as particularly bright birds intellectually, though I do appreciate the fountain of song that bubbles from the male early and late. Last summer, though, a pair of wrens nested in the big Norway spruce beside the house, and one morning two of the three fledglings, more eager than able, fluttered out and down onto the grass. The parent birds raised an uproar. I went to see the cause and they threatened to attack me. Their noise attracted three robins and a catbird, all of whom were ready to pitch into me. So I left them to their own devices and watched while the fledglings hopped into the shade of a bed of evening primroses.

The parent birds spent the whole day fluttering from their one remaining chick in the nest to those two prodigals, watching for danger, burning up I don't know how much energy. The grounded chicks spent the night among the primroses and the next day the hysterical vigil was resumed. The third day the chicks were able to get into the air on brief, uncertain flights, and eventually the parents herded them to apparent safety in a patch of sumac on the riverbank. By then the fledglings could fly thirty or forty yards.

But this I noticed: When those fledglings first fluttered from the nest and I approached them, the parents were frantic. By the second day they were apprehensive but less than frantic at my approach. By the second evening I could crouch beside the fledglings without an uproar from the parents. They chattered apprehensively, but made no gesture of attack. They had learned that I was not a predatory enemy. They didn't come and perch on my shoulder and twitter a request that I shelter and protect their young ones, but they didn't try to drive me away either. They learned something. They had the brain capacity to learn from experience.

And that is what I mean about the chickadees and, to a degree, about all birds. They seem able to appraise a situation and act with something approaching reason rather than with unreasoning instinct. Wild birds seem to learn more quickly than domesticated fowl, probably because the domesticated one has little need to face the unexpected situation that calls for swift learning or quick, decisive action.

SEPTEMBER 24

Back of the bird's ability to learn and remember, of course, is its brain, which makes all the difference between reason and reflex. And that brain has the same origin as mine.

We go back to the time of the giant reptiles, when (I spoke of this earlier) the very first mammals were minor members of the teeming animal community. Before the mammals played any really important part in what was happening, the dinosaurs arose, had dominion, and declined. The giant reptiles vanished, and there was room for those early mammals to grow and prosper. They needed more energy, which was provided by a turn to warm-bloodedness. That called for changes in the heart. That, in turn, encouraged bigger and more active brains and sharper senses. In such a time, natural selection inevitably was a major factor—those with inferior brains perished before they could reproduce. Thus—perhaps—were these new, intelligent species created.

SEPTEMBER 25

Whatever the cause of the reptilian downfall—and we have examined various theories earlier—climatic change probably was one factor. The climate was cooling off. There was nothing like an Ice Age—the advance of the great ice sheets was still another 100 million years ahead—but I have only to watch the ants and beetles in my garden on a thirty-five-degree fall morning to imagine what such a chill in the air would have done to a cold-blooded dinosaur weighing fifty tons. And the factor of live birth and parental care must have been another.

The mammals seem early to have evolved a system of live birth, the eggs hatching inside a placental sac in the mother and being nourished and developed there, relatively safe from predators. This minimized outside danger to mammalian young in the egg and early growth stages. And with young that were fed from mammary glands in the mother, parental care became characteristic of mammalian life. The family came into being. With exception made for the insects, especially the social insects, only the birds and the mammals ever developed any great degree of family consciousness.

In birds and mammals, then, the family became the foundation for the flock, the herd, the pack, the tribe, which in turn created a sense of concerted effort toward a common purpose. If there were packs of sharp-witted, sharp-toothed mammals foraging together and raiding the rudimentary nests of the big lizards, and if the growing chill in the air made those lizards more and more sluggish, the result was foredoomed. The mammals eventually would dominate.

SEPTEMBER 26

So much for theories and speculation. Toward the end of the period, when the big lizards were definitely on their way out, the mammals began to take over the dry land of this earth. And by then they had begun to diverge in a hundred different directions, to break up into many specialized families.

How these divergences came about is not known. I suspect that cosmic radiation had its effect on the genes of heredity. There seems to be ample evidence of periods of intense radiation at about that time, and we know what profound effects such rays can have. Certainly mutations appeared, and then the mutations were subjected to the process of natural selection. Some of the variants were plant-eaters, some flesh-eaters, some omnivorous. Some burrowed into the ground for safety from their enemies. Some evolved long, agile legs and found safety in running away. Some grew fierce claws and fangs. Some took to the dry, arid wastelands. Some returned to the oceans. Some hid among the rocks. Some took to the treetops. And all of them used their wits, some more than others.

Conditions of climate and geography favored the mammals. Most of the modern continents were by then above water, most of the mountains we know today were already formed. Most of the modern plants were in existence. The alternate advance and retreat of the big glaciers of relatively modern times had not yet begun. The world, in brief, was a hospitable place for the mammalian form of animal life.

SEPTEMBER 27

The color has begun to show in our sugar maples, big patches of orange leaves up near the top. On the mountainside the birches are starting to turn, definitely yellow in places but not yet that vivid buttercup yellow that will come. The lower bushes have been in color the past week or ten days, reds and purples that have deepened day by day. And their berries have made a brilliant show. The high-bush cranberries, one of the maple-leafed viburnums, had a big berry crop and they began to turn yellow two weeks ago, then matured to a rich orange color, and now are turning that cranberry red which makes them unmistakable. The bush dogwoods have a big fruit crop this year, too, and the red osier dogwood glows with the red of its berry stems, though the berries themselves are a dull blue.

Wild grapes are still green but will ripen within another two weeks. The wild clematis, which was covered with small white bloom in early August, now has a tangle of wiry styles where each blossom matured. In bloom, it was called virgin's bower; now it is called, and calls for the name, old man's beard. Youth to old age in one summer. In the meadow where jack-in-the-pulpit stood high last May now I find a cluster of bright red berries surrounded by wisps of dry leaves—the jack gone to fruit. But not edible fruit; it is fiery hot, even as the root itself, which is sometimes called Indian turnip.

The sumac is flashing red almost everywhere.

SEPTEMBER 28

A dull, drizzly day, and uncomfortable-looking; but the temperature was in the low sixties. I went out for a walk and didn't mind the weather half as much as I had thought I might. Anyway, there is something attractive about a misty day. You can see things you quite overlook on a bright, sunny day. I like to go out and look at the color in the trees on a misty morning. Then I can see the individual trees, not have them lost in the big background of color. There wasn't enough today, however, to make that possible. Another week and we will be in finery fit for any holiday, and from then till the middle of the month will be the height of our color season. We say, as a general rule, that Columbus Day, October 12, is the peak-of-color day three years out of four.

I walked down the road, and in our lower pasture I saw three deer grazing. I suppose they had come down in the mist with a feeling of safety. They saw me, watched me, then went on grazing as long as I continued to walk. But when I stopped and looked at them more than a moment, they decided it was time to go. White tails flashed, they bounded to the far fence and flowed over it, graceful as a silk scarf flowing in the breeze.

I have rarely seen a deer make an ungraceful motion, but a few years ago I was driving down a back road when a young doe appeared out of the woods and started down the blacktop road ahead of me. I slowed down and she stayed there on the road in front of me for a good half mile, one of the most awkward sights I have ever seen. That hard surface did something to her gait, made her look almost like an old milk cow galloping down that road. Finally she came to another patch of woods and turned aside, onto the grassy shoulder, trotted there a little way, then flowed up and over the fence, her normal graceful self, and glided into the woods almost like a shadow.

SEPTEMBER 29

We heard a fox in the night, the first one we have heard this fall. It was barking quite close by, in the dooryard it seemed. From there it went up the road, still barking. A red fox, not a gray. We have both, but the gray fox's bark is hoarse, rough. The red fox's bark is sharp, higher pitched.

There's a fox den back in the rocks on the bank of the deep cut where the old railroad once ran. It was a part of the line from Hartford to Poughkeepsie originally, and it had been reduced to a stub only eight miles long, from Canaan to Lakeville, when we first came here. Then that stub of track was abandoned and torn up and we bought the old right-of-way across our land. With it we bought back an easement to and water rights in a spring up the mountainside, the spring that provides the water supply for our house most of the year. The railroad never had used that spring, as far as I can find, but there was its easement and claim to the water in the deed that came to us. As I remember, the easement was dated sometime in the 1880's.

The fox den was in use when we came here, twenty-odd years ago, and the stub line was still in use, with a short freight train over it twice a week. I used to wonder what those foxes thought of trains. Then one winter day I found tracks that showed one of those foxes had tried to walk a rail, had fallen off a couple of times, then had walked that rail a good half mile. Maybe the foxes liked to hear the trains pass, too.

SEPTEMBER 30

The color is really coming in the trees now. The poplars down the river are turning just enough that they look golden in full sun though they still are green. The soft maples in the lowlands are in full flame, all the shades of red from scarlet to deep crimson and even pink, the color of strawberry ice cream, here and there. The ashes always catch my eye, for they do strange color things. Last year was a special ash year, for some reason. They turned yellow as birches, a rich golden tan, an odd blue that is peculiar to them and never seen on any other tree, and a kind of bluish bronze. I have never seen anything quite like the display they made. I doubt if they will be so lavish this year, but I shall be satisfied if they give us a few days of their own special blue look before they turn bronze and then rusty yellow.

This has been an almost ideal fall for color. A couple of light frosts early in September, then just enough rain to keep things moist and no really hard frosts. We are due for one now, overdue, in fact. I shouldn't be surprised if we get a hard frost tonight or tomorrow night, for we have a full moon tomorrow. The harvest moon, and if it comes after mid-September it often is accompanied by frost. Hard frost now won't stop the color. Two weeks ago it would have hurt it. But now the natural withdrawal of sap has left the leaves ready for frost. A frost followed by a week of sunlight would give us spectacular color.

OCTOBER

OCTOBER 1

We grew a row of sunflowers again this year, at the far end of the vegetable garden, this time a species with smaller heads than the enormous ones we grew five or six years ago. Those big ones had stalks like young trees, three inches through at the base and some of them thirteen and fourteen feet tall, and the heads were bigger than dinner plates. I cut a few of the heads one year and hung them in the woodshed to dry, and within a week they had been stripped clean. Mice, I suppose.

Well, this year we grew these smaller ones, and about ten days ago I cut about a dozen of the ripe heads—before the jays cleaned them out—and put them in the woodshed to dry. I put them in a basket made of one-inch wire mesh, suspended from the rafters by long wires. I thought the mice couldn't get down those wires.

Today, after watching the jays make gluttons of themselves at the sunflower heads in the garden, I looked in the woodshed, just to make sure. What a mess! Every one of those heads I had stowed so carefully and so confidently in that wire basket was rifled, every seed gone, and all the chaff and hulls were there on the floor beneath, along with three or four empty heads that the mice, or whatever did the job, had heaved over the edge in their drunken revelry. They must have been drunk, on sunflower seeds, to have made such a thorough job of it and to have left such a clutter.

So we shall buy sunflower seed again this winter.

OCTOBER 2

We have been taking in what I hope is the final harvest from the garden. It's high time we had a hard frost and put an end to things out there. That's one of the primary benefits of living in this land of four seasons—

autumn puts an end to the vegetable garden. A man shouldn't have to be thinking about weeds and a hoe more than six months a year.

So we brought in the winter squashes and put them down cellar to dry out and harden off near the furnace before we stow them in the cool root cellar. We picked the last of the green beans. I am very fond of the first picking of beans, and I maintain my enthusiasm through most of August. By September I eat them grudgingly. By now I don't want another bean. So we will freeze these.

I dug the last row of beets. We will boil, peel, dice and freeze them, to be made into Harvard beets in the winter. I dug the last of the carrots. We will cut them into rounds and freeze them, for stews and for plain boiled carrots. I pulled the last row of onions, which will be used in the next couple of weeks. We don't try to store onions. When an onion goes bad there's only one thing I can think of that matches it—a lemon that has gone bad.

And Barbara picked tomatoes, every big tomato that showed a promise of color. She stowed them in cartons, between layers of newspaper, and put them on the glassed-in back porch. She will be plucking ripe tomatoes out of there for another month. Then we will throw everything that's left out on the compost.

OCTOBER 3

I was discussing mammals the other day, how they rose to dominance as the big lizards declined. Everything was right for those mammals. They proliferated. The vast tribe of grass-eaters, the deer, the bison, the ancestors of the horse, of the cow, of the sheep, began to specialize. The carnivorous beasts, particularly the cat and dog families, grew to large size and intense ferocity. The aquatic animals, whales, seals, walruses, and all their kind, occupied the waters of the earth and found in them vast quantities of food. And the lesser ones, the rodents, the whole tribe of gnawing creatures that may have come directly from the very earliest mammals, filled the chinks in the living space—the mice, the rats, the squirrels, the rabbits, the beavers, and all their kind.

Among themselves, the mammals multiplied tremendously and spread over the earth, from the tropics to the polar regions, from the waters and the marshlands to the woods, the plains, and the deserts. Today there are about 15,000 species and subspecies of mammals, grouped by zoologists into 118 families. No one can say with certainty how many species have vanished over the past 50 or 60 million years, but some of them certainly evolved down dead-end alleys and are known only by fossil specimens.

I shall not try to follow in detail the evolution of the mammals, but I shall summarize briefly the changes in one typical example, the horse.

Sixty million years ago the horse was only about a foot high, a doglike creature with five toes on each foot. It was common here in the Americas, on both continents. Nourished by lush green—it was a vegetarian from the start—it grew in size, became as big as a collie dog. Its feet changed, perhaps to increase its speed, since it was prey for the big meat-eaters; two of its toes shrank and disappeared, so it became a three-toed animal. Then the outer two toes shrank and became rudimentary, so that it walked on one toe. Thus the hoof of the modern horse evolved. And as the toes shrank and vanished, the body grew to the size of today's pony.

For some reason still unknown, the prehistoric horse vanished from America about 30,000 years ago, along with vast herds of other large animals. But the wild horses of central Asia persisted and became the direct ancestors of the horses we know today. The horse was tamed, it is now believed, only about 4,500 or 5,000 years ago, on the steppes of the Ukraine.

Of all the mammals we know today, the story of the horse's physical evolution is the most nearly complete in paleontological evidence.

OCTOBER 4

The story of the mammals is not so much the story of feet or hooves or ears or tails as it is the story of a brain, and it is not the story of any one family of animals. In all the creatures that preceded the mammal the brain was essentially a nerve center whose primary function was to run the relatively simple processes of the body. As vision and other senses improved, certain areas of the brain increased in size and efficiency to receive and transmit the messages these senses picked up. But most of the actions of the animal were a result of instinct and the brain's function was limited. I mentioned earlier that some of the giant lizards had brains smaller than the nerve centers that dictated the motions of the hind legs. Insects developed more brain power, proportionate to their bodies, than any of the early animals; yet the insects never advanced much beyond the stage of instinctive action.

In the mammals, however, the brain began to grow and increase in capacity. Perhaps most important of all, it developed a sense center that could take account of the messages delivered by eyes, ears, nose, and tactile organs. This was new. It enabled the mammal to receive a complex message from several sense sources at once. Out of it eventually came the mental capacity to appraise such a complex message, not merely to set instinctive actions into motion.

Paleontologists and biologists can point to a whole series of changes in the brain. They can show how one area developed, then another, all leading toward full development of the best brain we know, that of man. It is a long and complex story, best told by the specialists; but involved in it are the factors of memory, anticipation, and reason. All three of these faculties are vital to intelligence. Lacking any one of them, the animal is forced to fall back on primitive instincts.

OCTOBER 5

Why the brain should have grown and become more and more complex in the tribe of mammals that eventually led to man is one of those mysteries of evolution that may never be solved. Certain tree shrews, squirrel-like animals of Java, show a line of evolution toward man, particularly in their brains. The tree shrew's forebrain or cerebrum is developed beyond that of any other primitive animal. The forebrain is where the sense impressions are received and sorted out. It is also where orders originate for bodily response, especially what are called manipulative actions. Manipulative actions lead toward skill with the hands and fingers.

The tree shrews indicate a brain development that was carried still further in the lemurs, the marmosets, and the monkeys. Out of that phase of evolution, somewhere along the line, it is generally agreed that man's ancestors must have emerged. It is now largely accepted that the first men were not apes. They were variants in a common stock, and they evolved along their own path. There are some resemblances to man in the apes, but the ape tribe went their own way after the original division and apparently they never were even semihuman.

Much has been made, at one time and another, of man's anatomy in comparison with that of the ape, and especially of man's development of the opposed thumb. Many have insisted that the opposed thumb is responsible for man's evolution and his unique degree of dominance over his environment.

Perhaps so, but not even the opposed thumb could achieve a great deal in the way of skill without a brain to guide it. When I remember men who still had remarkable manual skills after the accidental loss of a thumb, or men who developed remarkable skills with two-fingered mechanical hands after they had lost their own hands, I am skeptical of such broad conclusions. I think of the ant and the bee, so instinctively skillful with no hands or fingers but only their mouths with which to work. And I think of the skill of the oriole, weaving a nest with only its beak for a tool.

OCTOBER 6

A couple of gray squirrels were busy out in the side yard this morning, looking for pears under the tree at the edge of the vegetable garden. I wondered whether they were after the pear seeds or the fermented juice from the windfalls.

Those windfall pears and their fermented juice seem to have a lure for a variety of creatures. Wasps like them. As soon as the pears begin to fall from the tree, the wasps gather, chiefly yellowjackets and those big "golden digger" wasps that live in the garden. They eat ripe pears, but when a ripe pear has begun to ferment they will fight anyone, or even each other, for possession. They seem to be unregenerate tipplers. I have found them, after an afternoon of sipping at one of those fermented pears, staggering about, too drunk to fly. And at that point they will sting anything in reach, so I leave them strictly alone. By the next morning they are pretty well sobered up, but they seldom go away. They are hooked on Five Star Old Bosc, or whatever these pears are.

Some woodchucks go for a pear binge, too. A couple of years ago a 'chuck wandered into the yard, found those pears, and sampled one. One led to another, and within an hour that chuck was loaded. When I went out with a gun he gave me one look, staggered a little way, toppled over, got to his feet, and ran headlong into a fence post. Shaking that off, he headed for the grape vines that make a big tangle on the garden fence and lost himself in there somewhere. I was laughing too much to take a shot at him, so he escaped. But he came back the next day and several days after that, and got pretty well potted each time. He never touched another thing, so I let him have his spree. He must have run into bad luck that winter, though, because I never saw him again. Could have had a bad liver.

After watching those squirrels a while today I decided they weren't looking for seeds. They, too, had their feet on the figurative brass rail, and they were there almost an hour. But they apparently can hold their liquor better than woodchucks. They seemed a bit tipsy when they left, but they didn't fall out of the big maple across the road when they climbed it. Probably old topers.

OCTOBER 7

This is a wild grape year, and a barberry year. I never saw the grape vines so loaded with fruit. Possums and coons will feast. We shall gather some and make wild grape jelly, which is rather special. But the barberries seem to have few customers except the ruffed grouse. Some people make jam or jelly from those bright red berries, but that is one we have never tried.

The barberry has an unsavory history because the American species is susceptible to wheat rust. It is a host, in fact, and the rust, which is a form of fungus, can live in the barberry for a long time, just waiting to get a chance at a field of wheat. Therefore, the American barberry is unwelcome in wheat areas, often is dug out and burned. The Japanese variety, however, is immune to this fungus. It is the one that usually is planted for decorative hedges, and it normally bears more and bigger berries. Thanks to the birds that eat its berries, it now has been spread throughout the Northeast and grows wild here, along with the American species.

The wild grapes are those small-fruited ones we call river grapes. They have a sharp tang and they are very seedy, but they do make good jelly. Now and then we find a vine that must have at least some of the old fox grape ancestry, for the grapes on it are big' as the end of my little finger and they have an almost sweet flavor. The true fox grape, which was the source of our Concords, is a good-sized grape, at least half an inch in diameter.

OCTOBER 8

We went out for a drive today to look at the color, which is almost at its peak. We drove maybe twenty miles, up the valley, over the mountain, down the far valley, around the lakes, back over the ridge and up the valley to our place, a big circle. It was beautiful. Not really at the peak—the sugar maples will be more brilliant in a few more days—but at a point where we kept saying, "See that!" and "Just look over there!" The ash trees have outdone themselves. They run from an almost golden yellow through a warm tan, a chocolate brown, and then a strange purplish green and a blue so subtle I can't place it. Normally we get only that subtle blue and the purplish green, which fade to a rusty brown. The birches are shimmering gold. The sumac is fire, pure fire. The swamp maples run from scarlet to maroon. And over on the other side of the mountain there is a stand of sassafras that is full of golden yellow and cherry pink. Not much sassafras in this area, though.

We went, and then we came back up the valley to our own place. And off there to the left, on the ridge, was that brilliant yellow maple we admire every year. The grove of white ashes around the falls from Springhouse Brook were all those fantastic ash colors I just mentioned. The soft maples low on the mountain were twice as red against the white pines just beyond. And that lone maple on the knoll, as we call it, was a beacon, brilliant scarlet from top to bottom. That is one tree I shall never forget.

We came home, I say, and we were silent until Barbara said, "This is best of all."

OCTOBER 9

I saw an opossum today, just down the road, and his whole face told me that he had spent most of the day eating wild grapes. Possums are the most untidy animals I know, and in many ways the most inept. They don't belong this far north. Every winter I see a possum picking its way through the snow with the most self-pitying look imaginable on its face. It takes two steps and sits back and shakes those pinkish forefeet, practically shivering, no matter what the temperature is. I don't know how many times I have stopped my car and got out and pushed a poor chilblained possum out of the wheel ruts in the snow, over to the roadside bushes, so I could get past without running over the stupid beast. They freeze their ears and even their tails, which almost cripples them—their tails are prehensile; they use them in climbing trees to get at those wild grapes, as well as bird nests. A possum will eat anything it can get down its throat.

Possums always remind me of what I was saying a few days ago about the human hand and the opposed thumb. The opossum and the raccoon are perfect examples of what a brain can do and what a hand cannot.

Both possums and raccoons are among my close neighbors. I see them often. They both are mammals, the opossum a marsupial, a mammal that bears very immature young and rears them in an abdominal pouch. The opossum has a foot like a human hand, even to the opposed thumb that is especially noticeable on the hind foot, which leaves a print much like that of a very small human baby. Yet the opossum is one of the most blundering, incompetent animals I know, slow-witted and so immature nervously that it literally falls into a faint, a kind of coma, at any sign of danger. Its brain is smaller, compared to its body size, than that of a field mouse. It survives as a species largely because it is so prolific and has so few natural enemies.

The raccoon also has five agile toes on each foot, but it lacks the opposed thumb. Its fingers are so adept, however, and its brain so clever, that it can open a cage latch with little hesitation, and it can even open simple padlocks after a few minutes of inspection and trial. The raccoon uses those adept forefeet with more skill than most six-year-old children use their hands. The essential difference between the opossum and the raccoon is in the brain. The raccoon is one of the most intelligent of all small animals, has the biggest brain and the best-developed coordination.

But there are only a few low-scale mammals, like the opossum. Most mammals evolved, over the millions of years, into creatures with some capacity for thought, brain power beyond that of any of their ancestors. And that, to me, is the distinction of the mammal, not the biological fact that the mammal bears its young alive and nurtures them with its own milk.

OCTOBER 10

Mammals have been evolving ever since the Triassic times, almost 200 million years ago. The mammalian brain has been growing all that time, in one direction or another, and the vagaries of nature and environment have somewhat shaped that brain's capacities. Why and how man evolved is still a mystery, but here he is, endowed with the best brain of all, the biggest capacity for reason, as far as we know, the most active memory and imagination. It is a long way back to the giant lizards and the lesser variants from which the first tentative mammals must have evolved but out of that variant in life form came the world we know to-day. You and I are the result of all those millennia of change, and I refuse to admit that the decisive factor was the opposed thumb or the ability to walk erect on two legs.

The factors of evolution are many and complex, but it seems un-likely that the course of life ever took a more decisive turn than the one that began enlarging a primitive nerve center into a brain, which began displacing instinct with the fundamental power of reason. There are several theories about what happened and why, all of them still theoreti-cal but worth looking at, when we get to it. But for now it suffices that it was at that point of change, when some mysterious variant in the genes prompted the first glimmering of thought, that man really began to be what he is today, good, bad, or a complex mixture of good and bad.

OCTOBER 11

The horizons begin to widen for us. The peak of the color has passed in the woodlands and some of the leaves have fallen. You would never know it to look at the trees, but under them is a crisp layer of new-fallen leaves still bright with their reds and golds. In the treetops there is a last burst of color, most of it some shade of tan or yellow, which makes the reds more emphatic.

I always think of this time, when the woods begin to open up, as the best time of the whole fall season. Now I can begin to see the hills in their own contours again. I can stand in my dooryard and see the sky without craning my neck. I can look up the valley and see next month coming, if I half close my eyes.

I can also go into the woods now and not see a partridge or a fox or a deer unless I sit on a stump for at least half an hour. Wherever I walk it is like walking through a vast bowl of cornflakes—*crunch, crackle, crunch.* Dry leaves everywhere. I can be heard coming half a mile away.

The bittersweet begins to open that outer husk and reveal the bright orange berry beneath, and there is a wealth of bittersweet fruit this year. Barberry bushes are loaded. High-bush cranberry, which really is a viburnum, has ripened its berries to a clean cranberry red—and a cranberry tartness, too.

OCTOBER 12

After talking about Triassic times, 150 to 200 million years ago, as we have been doing, it seems strange to think of Christopher Columbus and his voyage less than 500 years ago. But the whole history of the white man in this country has occurred since then, and the entire history of man in America probably doesn't reach back much more than 25,000 or 30,000 years, 50,000 at the very most. So we have to shift from millions to thousands to hundreds. From geologic time to calendar time.

On this day in 1492 Columbus was dealing with a crew that had rebelled a couple of days earlier and been put down and were still sullen. They had insisted that the ships would soon sail right off the rim of the world, into oblivion. Yesterday they had sighted the leafy branch of a tree, which helped quiet things down. Trees do not grow in midocean, nor do limbs with still-green leaves float there. So the ships kept to their course, and on this day they sighted land. Before nightfall they reached an island that Columbus called San Salvador. The native Indians called it Guanahani, and today it is known as Watling's Island, one of the Bahamas. It was land, under whatever name, and when they landed the sailors kissed the sand and blessed Columbus.

Columbus died fourteen years later, in poverty and largely forgotten. He never did reach the North American mainland, and he wasn't the first European to reach the Americas—the Norsemen were, about 500 years ahead of him—but his discoveries marked the beginning of the history of America as we know it today.

OCTOBER 13

It is ironic but true that man, the tireless questioner and investigator, knows almost all there is to know about the ancestry and evolution of the horse but does not know how or when man himself originated as a species. Man remains a mystery to man, though there are theories and speculations and probabilities, and there is a limited amount of recognizable evidence of man's origins.

It now seems certain that man and ape had a common ancestor somewhere back down that long, dim corridor of time. But no one has yet discovered that ancestor. Evolutionists believe that the common ancestor was the insect-eating, forest-dwelling shrew we have spoken of before and, from the tree shrew to the lemur, the marmoset, and the monkey, perhaps. Out of that phase of evolution, somewhere along the line, it is generally agreed that man's ancestors must have acquired the acute senses, the potential intelligence, and the higher-than-average manual dexterity that mark the species today. Eventually, according to this theory, these pre-men learned to walk on two legs and developed intelligence and reasoning powers that in some degree replaced the age-old animal reliance on instinct alone.

The time scale for such a process of evolution is too vague to specify, but those who hold this theory come down eventually to the Tertiary period, perhaps 40 million years ago, and base their further reasoning on geographic and climatic changes known to have taken place then.

OCTOBER 14

The reasoning back of the shrew-lemur-marmoset-monkey theory is drawn from known geologic facts. Major topographical changes occurred, particularly in Africa and central Asia, at about this time. Mountains, particularly the Himalayas, were thrust higher than ever before. North of the Himalayas, the climate changed from warm and humid to cold and dry. South of the mountains, the climate continued much as before. Until this vast geologic upheaval, the whole area had been one huge semitropical forest. After the change, the trees vanished from the area north of the mountains.

Throughout this whole area, according to this reasoning, there had been a thriving population of lemuroid animals. When the Himalayas became a barrier, these animals were divided into two groups. Those south of the mountains continued their forest life and eventually became apes. Those north of the mountains, caught in a cold, dry, inhospitable region without trees, were forced to adapt to rigorous new conditions or perish. They adapted, and became the ancestors of man.

Thus goes the theory. By no means all evolutionists accept it. Even as a layman I can find serious objections to it. The first point that comes to mind is the fact that the Himalayas did not become an impassable barrier overnight. The climatic change was gradual enough so that if these lemuroid animals had even the intelligence of rabbits, which isn't asking much, they would all have migrated south into that hospitable forest when living conditions began to deteriorate north of the mountains. A second point (this is getting ahead of our story, but must be mentioned here) is that most of the hominids, or manlike pre-men, found thus far were south of the Himalayas, not north of them—in East and Central Africa, in fact.

The theory, however, is based in part on the belief that difficult living conditions bring out the best potentialities in any species. Obviously, only the fittest survive. Without the readily available food of a lush woodland, say the proponents of this theory, those fittest survivors would broaden their diet and become omnivorous. The search for food on the vast, cold plains would force them to become nomads. Difficult living conditions would sharpen their wits and put a premium on intelligence. The dull-witted ones would die young and without offspring. The strong, clever, intelligent ones would survive and pass along their superior qualities to their progeny. With plant food scarce, they would become meat-eaters, and this would call for the hunt and the hunter's weapons. The cold climate would demand clothing. Without trees in which to hide, they would be forced to resort to a common defense against their enemies. Communal life, the tribe, would come into being. Because they were mammals and their young matured slowly, family life would be imposed upon them.

So much for this theory, which seems to me to start with preconceptions and reach back for causes.

OCTOBER 15

There is little doubt that some such species did appear and did survive, somewhere, that it did increase in intelligence and manual dexterity, and that it eventually achieved speech. Speech meant communication beyond the level of grunts and squeals. With speech this two-legged animal had the medium for exchange of ideas and experiences. It was becoming man. The earliest evidence of primitive man yet found gives evidence of brain capacity sufficient for intelligent speech.

Anthropologists are wary of specific dates, but until recently the earliest fossil evidence of recognizable man was conceded to be about a million years old. Examples of pre-man, called hominids, date much further back. But it is only since 1859, when Darwin's *The Origin of Species* was published, that there has been any real understanding of the meaning of fossil evidence available. Since then, a considerable mass of that evidence has been accumulated and evaluated, but many gaps remain and many factors still are speculative.

The story now can be traced back five to ten million years and covers a sequence of changes from the very early "Fire Apes" of South Africa—*Australopithecus prometheus*—down to more or less modern man.

The problem of dating is indicated by the fact that for years it was believed there was only one Ice Age during the Quaternary period, and that man dated from that time. Now it is known that there were at least four Ice Ages during that period. With each discovery of another authenticated Ice Age, man's history has been pushed back a few more thousand years. Now it seems likely there will be another revision of the dates of the ice, perhaps this time foreshortening the estimates of modern man's age.

OCTOBER 16

Now the oaks begin to come into their own. The maples have had their day and are largely stripped of their leaves, which lie beneath them but still are so brilliant they give a feeling of sunlight even on an overcast day, such as this one is. But for a few weeks more the oaks will make the woodland a colorful place.

Oak colors are what I think of as earth colors, deep reds, purples, browns, leathery tans. I have seen all these colors in the rocks of these eastern mountains. The oaks achieve them, however, not from pigments they absorb from those rocks but by chemical action. They are anthocyanins, chemically speaking, which turn red in the presence of acids, blue and purple if there is less acid and more sugar present. The dogwood leaves have anthocyanins, and so do swamp maples, sassafras, wild cherry, the gums, the sumac. When the sap is withdrawn from the leaves, residues are left, and the color that comes depends on whether more sugar or more acid is present in those residues.

Now the oaks display their colors at their best, like an exhibition of fine leathers for binding treasured books. For a few weeks they will be on display. Then they will fade to various shades of brown and the oaks will stand all winter with dry, rustling leaves the color of the earth beneath them.

OCTOBER 17

The ash-leaved maples, which most of us know as box elders, have a huge crop of seeds this year. Box-elder seeds are keys, or samara, like the seeds of all other maples. (I shy away from that word, "samara," which makes me think of Japanese swords, not maple seeds, though it comes from the Latin word for the seeds of the elm tree.)

Not all box elders bear seeds, since the male and female blossoms are borne on separate trees. The female trees, of course, bear the seeds. These are the only maples I know that are not bisexual. The only way you can tell the sexes apart in the box elders is by their blossoms in the spring and their seed tufts in the fall. The female trees bear the keys (or samara) in tufts, as many as a dozen in a bunch. They dangle on stems an inch or two long, like fat tan tassels in the October wind. Unless they are plucked off they remain on the tree all winter. They are good fare for birds and small beasts, however, and many of them are harvested before spring.

Box elders will yield sap in the spring, like sugar maples, which can be boiled down to syrup or sugar. The yield isn't as generous as that of sugar maples and box-elder sugar has an acid bite, but it was sometimes used by pioneers who had no sugar maples to tap. Box elders are also hosts, in the spring, to purplish brown and black soft-bodied beetles of the family *Lamiinae,* which made them unwelcome as dooryard trees in the small towns of the Midwest I knew as a small boy. Nobody seems to want them as dooryard trees today either, perhaps for the same reason.

OCTOBER 18

A misty morning, with the mist rising in great swirls from the river as the sun warmed the air and a breeze came down the valley. One of those beautiful sights we so often take for granted, dismissing it as fog and telling ourselves it masks "the view." As I stood and watched the mists slowly rising this morning I wondered what view was more beautiful than this. The mountains across the valley are always there, to be seen whenever one looks. They have their varied aspects, with the time of year and the time of day, but otherwise there is little variation. This morning mist, on the other hand, never is the same twice, not even within the same hour.

I think of mist as being a low-hung cloud, a cloud that has come down off the mountain and filled the valley. Fog is something else again, in my lexicon. Fog is blinding, stifling, somehow. It traps me, makes me feel a prisoner. It has no life, no movement, no beauty. Fog is merely wetness that hasn't yet settled on the grass. To me, fog settles and mist rises. The meteorologist has his definitions that probably don't match mine, but his are technical definitions and mine are really emotional.

OCTOBER 19

Acceptance of man's antiquity is relatively new. As recently as the 1860's many were saying that, on the evidence in the Bible, man's total history could not be much more than six thousand years. This seems absurd today, but it was not until the latter half of the nineteenth century that scientists and investigators began delving deeply into the past and accepting the idea that man was a much older creature than had generally been believed. Significantly, Biblical scholars as well as geologists and anthropologists had a hand in this revolution in thinking. For instance, they found that much of the time sequence in the Old Testament was symbolic rather than literal, and that some of the classic stories such as the account of the Flood were much older than the people who set them down in the Bible. Working together, archaeologists and Biblical scholars pushed back the story of man in the Near East many centuries.

Meanwhile, the geologists and anthropologists elsewhere were gathering data that pointed undeniably toward primitive man who groped toward civilization many thousands of years ago. By early in the present century the rough outlines of early man's picture had begun to take shape, though the dates for his emergence as a species were still inconclusive. Only in the past fifty or seventy-five years have those dates been pushed back as far as a million years. And now even those dates are being questioned.

There are two principal types of evidence of primitive man's existence. One is skeletal remains, all of which are fossilized. Skeletal remains of those remote days, at least as far as man is involved, are extremely rare. Primitive man seems seldom to have chosen for his deathbed a place where his bones would be readily preserved. For that matter, few fossil remains of primitive apes have been found, either. Apparently apes, too, had the wit to avoid quicksands, tar pits, and other fossil factories.

The other type of evidence is cultural records—tools, weapons, ornaments, anything that clearly shows man's handiwork. In some instances, charcoal from fire can be regarded as evidence, particularly if it is found in association with man-made tools or other artifacts.

OCTOBER 20

Two sounds of autumn are unmistakable, the hurrying rustle of crisp leaves blown along the street or road by a gusty wind, and the gabble of a flock of migrating geese. Both are warnings of chill days ahead, fireside and topcoat weather.

The geese now are on the wing, close to their usual schedule. Cold weather, seasonal weather, has begun to settle in up where most of the geese spend their summers. Quite a lot of them now spend their summers around here. This is relatively new. A quarter of a century ago the geese rarely nested this far south. But for the past ten years I have seen goslings on most of the local ponds almost every summer.

Most birds migrate in silence, but not the geese. Whether you are walking down a city street, standing in a suburban backyard, or working in a rural woodlot, you know when the geese fly over. First you hear that distant gabble, a faint clamor that seems to echo from the whole sky. You search the sky, and the gabble comes closer. Then you see them, flying high, marking a V almost like a pencil line of dots.

You listen and watch, and the flight is so high it seems almost leisurely. If it is a close V in formation, it is almost certainly Canada geese. If it is a looser V, rippling and waving, or if it is a long line like one leg of the V, it more likely is the less common snow geese. Whichever, the flock's gabbling is like the voice of restless autumn, and the flight never wavers. On and on, over the hills and the towns and the cities, to the far horizon and still beyond, southward. And only that restless echo, faint and haunting, remains.

They are footloose as the autumn wind, and they follow the sun. There is something both exhilarating and faintly sad in the echo of their going. Maybe it is the echo of another summer gone. Maybe it is the freedom song of the skies. Whatever, it haunts the earth-bound heart.

OCTOBER 21

The autumn days shorten, but even as they shorten they increase in height and breadth. It is as though there were a constant ratio that keeps the days in balance. If it seems strange to think of any day in such dimensions, I have only to look about me, now that the leaves have thinned out. My eyes can reach. New vistas are open. The horizon is there just beyond the row of maples from which the morning breeze shook a shower of gold and scarlet. The sun slants in the window where, only two weeks ago, the shadow of the elms lay deep.

The hills are no longer remote, and at night I can look up and see the constellations of Andromeda and Pegasus. Even in a land of trees, we no longer are canopied from the sky and walled in from the horizon. Our earth's distances invite the eye. And as the eyes reach, so must the mind stretch to meet those new horizons.

True, they are not new horizons. I have seen them in a long succession of other autumns, and they have been there through all the winters I have known here. But the fact that they now seem new, if only because newly seen, is human reason enough for the seasonal succession. We bind our lives and thoughts with too many walls and canopies, at best. It is good to have those barriers thin away, from time to time, and reveal the broader scope. It is good to be reminded that not only the day but life itself is a matter of more than one dimension.

Autumn is the eternal corrective. It is ripeness and color and a time of maturity; but it is also breadth, and depth, and distance. What man can stand with autumn on a hilltop and fail to see the span of his world and the meaning of the rolling hills that reach to the far horizon?

OCTOBER 22

These beautiful autumn days have brought a spell of Indian summer weather, with frosty nights and clear, warm days when the temperature gets up into the seventies. There has been a haze in the air, on the far horizon, and though I am not at all sure it isn't smoke and fumes from the inferno along the lower Hudson almost a hundred miles from here, it looks like Indian summer's traditional haze.

Some say that haze was smoke from fires set by the Indians, who drove deer out of the woodland and took their winter meat the easy way. Some say it was from fires set by the white men to clean out the underbrush and open the woods so there could be no easy surprise attack by the Indians. You can account for such haze in many ways, if you start from a reason such as that the Indians were lazy hunters or that they waited for late autumn to make raids on white settlers. From all my reading of the records, neither of these suppositions was true.

Forget such tales and simply enjoy such days. They are ideal for wandering, footloose and without obligations. On a day like this I could tuck a sandwich in my pocket and walk twenty miles—if I didn't have to walk back again. I am as lazy as those traditional Indian hunters. Instead, I probably shall climb halfway up the mountain this afternoon, sit on a rock for half an hour watching the squirrels, then come home. It is very easy to walk *down* that mountainside.

OCTOBER 23

I went up the mountain yesterday, a bit over halfway, up past the springhouse and to the old walled field that once was a hayfield and now is a grove of white pines eighteen inches through at the butt. The squirrels didn't welcome me. In fact, they must have been busy among the oaks farther down the mountain, for I saw only two while I was up there. But there was a pileated woodpecker that sounded a magnificent tattoo for me on a dead elm beyond the pines.

Those big woodpeckers leave me in awe. They are so big, big as a crow. And that cockade is so red, so startling. And that beak—when I have watched one of those big fellows chiseling slabs off a dead tree I have thought that beak could jackhammer a hole through a cement wall. The rattle of a pileated woodpecker's beak at work actually is almost as loud as a jackhammer in a city street.

One year one of those big fellows took a dislike to a big gray birch over at Twin Lakes, just around the mountain from here, and started work on it. First it cut a hole six inches long, three inches wide, and halfway through the trunk. Then it cut another that size a foot lower down. Then a third one just above the first. Then a fourth one. And after that we got a normal autumn wind, and the whole top of that tree snapped off. There wasn't a worm hole in it. No excuse for that pileated attack. No wonder this fellow is called Cock o' the Woods, Log Cock, and Lord-God-Almighty-bird. That last, with Good-God-bird, seems to me to be just about right.

OCTOBER 24

Our Indian summer is over. We had a hard frost last night and today is chill and overcast, with the feel of snow in the air. I hope the snow holds off. Snow in October just doesn't seem right. We needed this hard frost to close things up for the season, but it is still too early to blanket things with snow.

OCTOBER 25

No snow, but hard frost again last night. And now, at last, there is a quiet in the night that has not been there since the hylas began to yelp last April. The fiddlers and scratchers, the hummers and buzzers, have lived their lives, left their hostages to fortune in egg and pupa, and died of old age and the cold. Only an occasional indoor cricket will be heard from now on. The rhythm enters another beat. Winter comes, and after the equinox next March we will approach another spring, the quickening of life again. But there is no real ending now, any more than there is an ending with sunset. There are only varying aspects of the continuous, of nature.

The words that come so readily to the tongue, or the fingertip, are vague. We talk of "nature"—I did just now—and what we mean is life, the whole life principle. We too often think of nature, and even of life, as apart from ourselves. Biologically, we are animals, capable of procreation, needing food and drink, tolerant of a relatively narrow range of temperature and humidity, physical weaklings subject to injury and disease, organisms that will eventually wear out and hence of limited lifespan. That is what I have been talking about for weeks and months, and pages and pages of this book. And I still have more to say about it.

Yet we all talk of "the animals" as apart from ourselves, and of "nature" as apart from this environment where we live. Actually, nature is you and me and the air and water around us, wherever we are, and the soil underfoot. Nature is a mouse, a rat, a bear, an earthworm, a louse, a flock of geese, a child and its parents.

OCTOBER 26

I suspect that we set ourselves apart because nature is so unforgivably impartial—nature is no more concerned with the welfare of mankind than with that of rabbits or snapping turtles or periodic locusts. So far as dispassionate inquiry has yet determined, nature is a complexity of impersonal forces and materials whose only purpose is to sustain and perpetuate life on this planet. No one particular form of life, but the basic life-force, whether expressed in algae or slime mold or daffodils or buzzards or tigers. There are countless life-forms, from microscopic bacteria to elephants and whales and giant redwoods. And men. Man just happens to be one of those forms, a relatively minor one and a conspicuous physical weakling at that. Man is bigger than a fox, smaller than a cow, lacks fangs, claws, horns, and poisonous saliva, is so naked of skin that he sunburns in summer, is frostbitten in winter, and is an open feast for fleas, gnats, mosquitoes, and all manner of insects.

And man is a newcomer, an upstart. Nature got along without him a long time. It is quite possible that man is a sport or a biological accident. Even without his own ingenuity, he might be disposed of and dispensed with, as were countless other species that preceded him. There is evidence that other sports and biological accidents were destroyed when they proved intolerable in their environment or were a menace to the total life force.

Until man evolved, life was primarily a matter of survival, and change was largely limited to accident and evolution. Man has altered that somewhat, particularly with relation to his own kind and to those forms of life on which he is dependent or which he thinks threaten his comfort or security. But mostly man has changed himself and his immediate environment as he moved from the trees to the caves, from the caves to the river valleys, from the valleys out into the open plain, and thence across the whole of the land until every habitable part of the earth became known to him.

OCTOBER 27

Now we are getting frosty nights one after another. Most of the migrant birds have gone south. I saw a flock of black ducks on the river the other morning, but they were skittish and restless. They probably have moved out by now. The Canada geese on the lake just beyond the mountain probably will be there a while longer. They wait until a real snowstorm and biting cold are at hand before they start south.

The winter birds are just beginning to come down out of the woods, where they spent the summer. I see flocks of sparrows, mixed flocks of several species, along the roadsides now, feeding on the seeds of lesser plants that we call weeds. The goldfinches are still at the thistles, but now it is hard to tell them from the sparrows, for they have put on winter garb. Those eye-catching yellow-and-black males are as undistinguished now, in color at least, as their females have been all summer. But there is a special air about a goldfinch. If you see what looks like a sparrow strutting like a goldfinch, you can be sure it *is* a goldfinch.

The chickadees haven't been around since mid-September. They came down off the mountain then to get their share of seeds from the sunflowers we had growing at the lower end of the garden. How they knew they were there, or that the heads were ripe, I don't know. But they knew, and they came and stuffed themselves, probably getting even more than the jays did. But when the sunflower heads were empty the chicks went away again. They will soon be back, though, not begging but demanding a daily ration of store-bought sunflower seeds.

OCTOBER 28

The countryside has a ragged, unkempt look, as though things had been neglected. The fact is that nature isn't very neat in these matters. Rural roadsides are rustling and swirling with fallen leaves. Dried goldenrod stems strew seeds at random. Milkweed pods gape and spill fluff like goose feathers from a bed pillow with a tear in it. Wild grapevines and Virginia creeper dangle from trees and tall bushes and sprawl in treacherous loops among the riverside weeds. The withered grass needs combing and brushing. And the little backwater bog is a mucky tangle of broken reeds, sagging stems, and raveling cattails. The abandoned oriole nest in the wide-topped elm begins to fray.

Man is ridden by a neat conscience. He must rake leaves and clean up the summer's remnants, probably to proclaim his tenancy by making things neat and tidy. Nature doesn't bother. The tree thrives in its own trash and the seed sprouts in the parent plant's own midden heap. Tomorrow thrives in yesterday's litter. And each new season grows out of the leftovers from the past. That seems to be the essence of change, and change is the basic law of life.

Nature hasn't time to be neat and tidy.

OCTOBER 29

Wind and weather now hurry. The storm that was in Colorado day before yesterday will be here this afternoon. We are on a winter schedule, which means that we are in a five-day weather cycle. The summer cycle is a seven-day rhythm. Because summer winds are lighter, summer storm systems move more slowly across the country from west to east. Winter winds are literally heavier. Cold air weighs more than warm air, and cold air travels faster.

The days move more swiftly now, too, with late dawns and early dusks. The days march toward the winter solstice like a winter farmhand with the wind at his back. And the long nights become the sleep of the earth itself, the rest, the waiting.

The fox barks in the night, in the glitter of winter starlight. The deer shelter in the hemlock thickets on the mountain. The woodchuck sleeps, breathing only once in five minutes. And that hurrying wind whistles in the naked maples. November is at hand. This is the hurrying, impatient wind of winter that I hear in the night.

OCTOBER 30

The more we urbanize, the more we crowd out or destroy wildlife. The plow, the chainsaw, the bulldozer, and the automobile are the worst enemies of foxes, raccoons, opossums, skunks, rabbits, and deer. But over the years man has managed to rescue some birds and animals threatened with decimation or extinction.

For example, in 1900 beavers had been eliminated from all the eastern states except Maine, and from all the states in the Mississippi Valley, where once they had been prolific beyond count. Today, beavers are common in almost every state in the Union. In some places they are even considered a nuisance and have to be controlled by trapping.

In 1907, elk were common only in and around Yellowstone Park, and the total number of elk south of the Canadian border was estimated at 41,000. They were totally missing from their onetime eastern range, which in the eighteenth century included parts of New England. Today, there are about one million elk in sixteen states, though still none in New England.

As recently as 1930, wild turkeys were common only in a few southern states. Today, they are found in forty-three states, several of which are outside the original wild turkey area. And the turkey flocks, where they are properly protected, continue to grow and enlarge their range.

No doubt about it, man destroys wildlife. The record, on balance, is very bad. The list of exterminated species is long and, what is worse, still growing. But the record shows that when man feels it is important enough, he can protect and save wildlife, too.

OCTOBER 31

Nobody knows what happened to the big lizards except that they lost dominance and died. We say the mammals survived and multiplied and evolved into clever, adept creatures because competition, climate, and other factors encouraged such evolution. But why the same processes were not at work in the big lizards remains a puzzle nobody seems to have solved. We simply say the lizards became bigger and bigger in body, but their brains did not keep pace. So they outgrew their own limited intelligence. And toward the end of their era, according to some theories, the mammals, insignificant though they were in size, undermined the whole structure of lizard life. The egg-laying lizards apparently were almost totally lacking in the instincts of parental care of the young. So if the busy little mammals ate the eggs and the hatchlings of the big lizards, the end of the dinosaurs was inevitable.

Granting the plausibility of these theories, other factors were also very likely at work: The climate was changing. The food supply was diminishing for the big lizards. Many of them were vegetarians and needed several hundred pounds of food a day. As the food diminished, starvation threatened. The offspring of weakened parents must also have been weaklings. And as the vegetarians died off, the carnivorous lizards who fed on them ran out of food. This could have been a disastrously vicious circle. Perhaps it was.

NOVEMBER

The unknowns outnumber the knowns. We are dealing not with a jig-saw puzzle from which a few pieces are missing, but with a few pieces that probably are a part of a puzzle from which most of the pieces are missing. Somewhere along the way those early mammals became tree-climbing members of the lemur family, with better eyes, more adept paws, and bigger brains than those of the ratlike predecessors. They became monkeylike creatures, and their kind diverged in many directions. Millennia were passing, became millions of years. There were apes that walked on their hind legs, had eyes that provided binocular vision. Perhaps this is where those rising Himalayas thrust themselves into the picture—if they actually did. Such a theoretical barrier would have isolated one group of these creatures in an arid, treeless environment and forced them to sharpen their wits and improve their intelligence.

Perhaps. And out of this, perhaps, came the early hominids, from which eventually came man. But if one follows this supposition even a little way, one is promptly confronted by all kinds of challenging questions. Start with the theory that the hominids arose north of the Himalayas and the apes south of them. Then try to fit this with the fact that virtually all the evidence known today about those early pre-men comes from Africa, not from anyplace in Asia. The only plausible answer demands a degree of leap-frogging that I cannot easily accept.

Pass this puzzle for now. There may be other answers. To me, it is far more important that these hominids were divergent from the original line in ways that made them fundamentally different from the apes. They had bigger brains, but still not as big as those in the most primitive man we know. They had more adept hands, and they made and used tools. They were crude, poorly chipped stone tools, but tools, for all that. And in their later stages they learned to capture and use fire. That perhaps was their greatest accomplishment.

Some believe these hominids evolved as long as 15 million years ago. But the dating is vague. Artifacts and bones found in Africa do indicate that they were alive and active more than ten million years ago. And what evidence we have now would persuade any observer that they lived a rather full life, in the human sense rather than as animals. They had some kind of tribal organization, a family life, and plenty to eat. Apparently, also, they had evolved some means of communication, though not yet full speech. They were not scroungers. Wherever they went, they seem to have ruled their environment, for they had that overwhelming combination, fire and weapons.

NOVEMBER 2

When and how hominid became man is another of those questions still deeply shadowed. For a time the scientists were searching for what they called "the missing link," that creature which marked the crucial transition from ape to man. It must, they believed, be somewhere in the bones of the past. But now the thinking has changed. The high probability is that there were apes and there were pre-men from whom, in time, man evolved. The pre-man, or hominid, is now regarded as one of the most successful products of evolution; not as a missing link, but as an identity in itself.

But the change from hominid to human remains both a mystery and a problem in reasoning. On all counts, the hominid was a successful product of evolution. He lived a good life, particularly in comparison with the teeming animal life all around him. All the habitable parts of the earth were his to enjoy, and all that teeming animal life of the era was available for food and clothing. In organized groups, he could hunt down and kill almost any animal on earth, and he was so vastly outnumbered by food animals that there was never any threat of starvation.

But it was about this time that the Ice Ages began changing the whole landscape and climate, as well as the geography, of the northern hemisphere. Before the Ice Ages ended, everything alive in this hemisphere was going to be changed in some way.

The Ice Ages continued, with alternate advances and retreats of the massive ice sheets, for more millennia. And then, perhaps 30 thousand, perhaps 50 thousand, years ago there was a series of intense solar outbursts. A huge tongue of solar flame, undoubtedly rich in ultraviolet rays, flickered across the vastness of unprobed space. It was so intense that one flash of it melted rocks on Earth's moon. Earth itself had an atmosphere that somewhat tempered the blast as it swept across the land, but there was no shield against its invisible effects. We know now what a minor bombardment of that kind, created artificially, can do to the genes of almost any form of life. It can warp and twist and utterly transmute the transmissible core of being, whether the thing transmuted be a rabbit or a wild grass, a hairy mammoth, or a moth.

We can only guess at what it may have done to any hominids in its path. Perhaps—and this is sheer guesswork, by those who are professionally scornful of guesses—perhaps that flash of indescribable solar energy worked a change in the genes which control the growth of the brain. It is known only that about that time the first men, those with brains almost the size of those in men today, were here and beginning to affect the life around them. And perhaps other profound changes occurred as consequences of that solar flash. New plant life began to appear. Many of the big animals, the mastodon, the mammoth, the long-horned bison, the giant sloth, died off soon afterward. Some have speculated that pre-man killed them off, but that seems unlikely.

Whatever the cause, by the end of that great Ice Age, soon after the solar flame flicked across the land, the giant animals of the northern hemisphere were dying off. And man, the creature with a big, new brain, was on his way toward dominance.

NOVEMBER 3

One of the most disturbing elements in life today is man's tendency to drift or stray from the basic elements of his environment, the fundamental rhythms of life. As he has evolved complexities of living, which he calls civilization, he has repeatedly lost perspective of himself and his cosmos. Surrounded by institutions he evolved and structures he built, he too often believes he can ignore or repeal the most enduring fundamental of all—cause and effect. And he tends to minimize the importance of life itself—not only human life, which has been appallingly cheapened, but the great stream of life, the whole life principle of this earth. Man is a part of that life principle, but his tendency is to dominate. Domination leads to belief in omniscience and omnipotence, so he sets himself apart, almost beyond natural law.

We see this every day, hear about it every hour. A crew with bulldozers must move mountains because someone wants mountains moved to get at a bed of coal or a lode of ore, or valleys filled so a factory or a city can be built there. A crew with chain saws must cut down a forest because man wants more paper, more plywood, more timbers. A crew of dam-builders must dam a river because a city wants more electricity to run mechanical toothbrushes, can openers, artificial climate-makers, more water to wash automobiles, to flush more dirty streets.

It is of no consequence that a mountain is an entity, with its own place in the scheme of the land, or that a tree is a living thing that grows slowly, year by year, or that a river is not only water but fish and fowl and a whole spectrum of aquatic life that will be destroyed when the river is dammed or diverted. It is important only that the Plan be carried out, a plan made without knowledge of or accounting for the whole consequence.

NOVEMBER 4

We hear talk about protecting this element of the environment, or that element. And too much of the talk is as arrogant as the destruction itself. It assumes that man is the sole judge of what should be saved, that he can save what is the essential part and thus control nature. But what we are dealing with is really not at man's command. It is the life-force, the total which is nature itself. What we should be saying, and believing, is that we will respect life, all life. That is the essential, the respect that comes from understanding, the respect that leads to a sense of proportion and a proper sense of humility. Man is not a god. He cannot create new rhythms in nature or long disrupt the old, eternal rhythms. Man can conserve what he has, he can control his own actions, but the environment does not belong to him. It belongs to the whole of life, and there is little doubt that if man too long or too completely abuses that environment he will be eliminated from it. At the very least, he will be reduced to a minor element in the whole spectrum of life.

As I was saying, when the first hard frost had brought quiet to the night again, the stridulating insects had lived their lives, left their heritage for another summer, and perished. I live on, a sentient man in a shelter that protects me from the killing cold. I live here only because I have made my compromises with the life around me, with this environment, and I can continue to live here in relative comfort and safety only so long as I continue to make those compromises. I am both wiser and more adaptable than a field cricket or a katydid. Or am I, after all? They have been here at least a hundred times as long as my own kind. In terms of life, they are a success. Perhaps it is too soon to know about man.

"Oh," I hear a challenge, "but crickets and katydids cannot think! They cannot dream, and plan, and create, as man can."

Is that the difference, then? Is the dreaming and the planning and the creation important if it does not recognize the whole life-scheme? After all, I, too, am a part of that, a part of all the life we know, of the very fundamentals of life. If there are answers, that must be the one that endures, year after year after year.

NOVEMBER 5

The leaves are all down, at last, except those that persist on the oaks and the beeches. Even the weeping willow has finally conceded that summer is at an end.

The willows are a strangely individualistic species. They grow readily from their own stems—break off a branch, thrust it into damp soil, and it will take root and grow. Cut willow for fence posts and after a few years you will have a row of willow trees instead of a fence. And willows hybridize so wantonly that they often are hard to identify. In the spring they are early to bloom, early to leaf. In the fall, as now, they are among the latest of all trees to cast those leaves. Their withes are tough and flexible, though their wood is soft and brittle. They are much used in basketry and once were used instead of cordage to bind bales of rural products.

We have a huge old weeping willow out near the garage. It was a mere sapling when we came here, almost a quarter century ago, but its roots soon reached the shallow water table and it grew like a weed. Now it is close to 100 feet tall and has forked so widely that we've had to lace it together with steel cables to keep the winter wind from hurling it, limb by huge limb, onto the garage. Its rough old trunk now is more than five feet through, and it sheds enough twigs and leaves each fall to cover half an acre. In terms of strict economy, we should cut it down and be rid of it; but we love that old wastrel of a tree and it can stay as long as it has one big limb reaching toward the sun and the stars.

NOVEMBER 6

The tamaracks are like bronze flames now. Deciduous conifers, the tamaracks shed all their needles in the fall and stand naked through the winter. But before the needles fall they turn the most beautiful bronze-tan color imaginable. Next spring the tamaracks will come to blossom; the female flowers with scarlet scales and the male flowers bright yellow, tiny blossoms with delicate colors that seem almost out of place. A few weeks later they will shimmer with light-green new needles, soft as kitten fur.

Such spring delicacy could be achieved only by a tree as tough and sturdy as the tamarack, which grows farther north than any other tree in North America. It also grows right here, in southern New England. But it is essentially a northern tree and its finest groves are to be found north of the Great Lakes. In the North it thrives in the boglands, but in the northern Rockies it grows on rocky ridges too. And here in New England I find it on hilltops, now and then, though it prefers lower slopes and old beaver meadows.

It is also known as hackmatack and larch, and up in the panhandle of Idaho, where it used to grow in thickets so dense a man couldn't penetrate them on horseback, it was called buckskin, probably because of the bright tan color of its bark. Both hackmatack and tamarack probably stem from Indian words, but nobody seems to have traced them to their source. In Maine the tree is often called a juniper, though it is only a distant cousin of the true juniper, as those State-of-Mainers would soon enough find out if they ever tried to make gin with tamarack cones for flavoring.

NOVEMBER 7

I said earlier that we know almost all there is to know about the evolution of the horse, but relatively little about the evolution of man. I didn't pause then to tell why. Now I shall try to.

The Tertiary period, during which pre-man and man evolved, continued something like 60 to 80 million years. The horse also evolved during that time, and the paleontologists have literally thousands of fossil bones of horses at all stages to study. But not only do we lack even one complete monkey skeleton of that period; all we have with which to reconstruct the story of the evolution of the primates is a few handfuls of broken bones and teeth. Most of these fossils, moreover, are from places far apart, scattered over the whole area of the Old World. For literally millions of years, there are gaps with no evidence whatever, not even a tooth, not even one fragment of bone.

The marvel is that the archaeologists have accomplished as much as they have, reconstructed as much of the story as we know today from such fragmentary evidence.

Until the past fifty years or so, bones and artifacts could be dated only in geological terms, with reference to known strata of rocks. This was a crude and only roughly approximate system of dating, but anthropology had no other calendar. Then came various new systems. The Douglas tree-ring calendar was highly useful for American archaeologists, but it reached back only about 200 years B.C. Then came radioactive-carbon tests and atomic-disintegration tests, which were found highly accurate for dating bones, even fossils, and almost any artifacts that might be found.

But the landmark discoveries were made before atomic calendars. Among the oldest skeletal evidence yet found was what has long been known as Java Man. Several skull portions, jaws, teeth, and other fossil bones were found near Trinil, Java, by a Dutch surgeon, Dr. Eugene Dubois, in 1899. Java Man was named *Pithecanthropus erectus* by the scientists. He was declared to be definitely human, not ape. He had a brain capacity somewhat below that of modern man, but well above that of any known ape. No tools or implements were found associated with Java Man's fragmented bones. He was dated at about half a million years old.

Just before World War I, the first skeletal remains of Peking Man were found near Chicken Bone Hill in northern China. Subsequently, parts of more than thirty-five examples of Peking Man were found in the same area, as well as chipped stone implements and evidence that Peking Man had used fire. Peking Man was given the scientific name *Sinanthropus Pekingensis*. It was believed to be about the same age as Java Man.

Peking Man and Java Man were believed to have had about equal intelligence, or brain capacity, and undoubtedly were of the same era. For some years they were the earliest specimens of very early man that came to light.

NOVEMBER 8

In 1924 Raymond Dart and Robert Broom, digging in South Africa, unearthed fossil bones of what appeared to be a remarkably manlike ape. It was more primitive than Java Man and Peking Man. But its particular significance was the fact that it was found in Africa. Until then it had been thought that man, or even pre-man, had originated in central Asia. Eventually Dr. Louis S. B. Leakey added another remarkable chapter to the story, also in Africa; but before we turn to this chapter, we must return to England and backtrack a few years.

In 1908 an amateur archaeologist named Charles Dawson announced that he had discovered parts of an ancient skull in a gravel pit near the village of Piltdown, England. What he had found and showed to A. Smith Woodward, of the British Museum, were a number of skull fragments and a slightly damaged jawbone. Woodward named the creature from which the bones presumably came *Eoanthropus dawsoni*, or Dawson's dawn man. He and others who should have known said that Piltdown Man was at least a million years old.

Anthropologists were astonished by the reconstructed skull. It had a brain case as big as that of modern man, and yet a primitive, apelike jaw. Java Man's bones had indicated that his body evolved faster than his brain. Piltdown Man's bones indicated just the opposite. A few scientists were skeptical, and challenged the validity of the discovery. Some even said the jaw and the skull did not belong together. But they were overruled by many of the top experts, who welcomed Piltdown Man as another link in the story of man. A baffling link, but still a link, they said.

Over the years, however, the questions multiplied. It was said that Piltdown Man had what seemed to be a middle-aged skull, a young jaw, and an old man's set of teeth. Finally, early in the 1950's, J. S. Weiner, a lecturer in Oxford's anatomy department, acted on his suspicions. He took a modern chimpanzee jaw from the anatomy collection, filed down the teeth so they resembled those of Piltdown Man, stained the jaw to make it resemble a fossil, and took it to Sir Wilfred Le Gros Clark, head of the department and a famed anatomist. Le Gros Clark at once saw the resemblance to the Piltdown Man's jaw. They examined the Piltdown jaw under a magnifying glass and could easily see that the teeth had been filed down. They even had the file marks on them.

Then, using a newly devised fluorine test, which made fossil dating far more accurate than ever before, these men proved that the Piltdown jaw was modern and that the skull fragments came from several modern skulls as well as from probably ancient skulls. The whole of Piltdown man was pronounced a fraud in 1953. It seemed likely that it was Dawson, the "discoverer," who had planted these bones, but this will never be proved. Dawson died in 1916, thirty-seven years before the fraud was revealed.

NOVEMBER 9

Flint implements tentatively dated at about the same age first given to Piltdown Man have been discovered elsewhere in England. There are evidences of human use of fire that seem to date from about the same time. But no skeletal remains have been found with these fragments of evidence.

The next authenticated remains in Europe, which seem to date from the pause between the third and fourth advances of the Pleistocene glaciers and may be about 250,000 years old, are represented by Heidelberg Man. His jawbone, but no other recognizable part, was found in glacial deposits near Heidelberg, Germany. Anthropologists relate Heidelberg Man to Neanderthal Man, discovered in 1856 in a cave in a gorge of the Neanderthal River near Düsseldorf, Germany.

It should be noted that a considerable assortment of stone implements believed to be about the same age as Heidelberg Man has been found in eastern England. They are credited to members of the Heidelberg group, who could easily have traveled back and forth between present England and the Continent because the North Sea had not yet been formed and England was a peninsula, not yet an island.

Neanderthal Man has become the prototype for a whole race that ranged over Europe, Africa, and Asia during early and middle Pleistocene times. Neanderthal Man had a low, sloping forehead, prominent eyebrow ridges, and a broad, flattened skull. His brain was slightly larger than that of the average modern European. He was short and stocky, and big-boned and powerful in build, and had strong jaws and a retreating chin.

Some anthropologists believe Neanderthal Man was the ancestor of later, more advanced races. Others believe the Neanderthals were conquered and displaced by an invasion of more intelligent, more vigorous people who originated in the plateau region of central Asia. The Neanderthals, however, clearly had evolved a rather full Stone Age culture. Their stone weapons and tools were the best yet made by man, and a wide assortment of them has been found in their camp sites. The Neanderthals opened quarries and worked them for the special types of stone they needed. They evidently had a rather complex and advanced social order. There is even evidence that they put flowers in the graves with at least some of their dead. For a long time Neanderthal Man was popularly conceived of as a primitive, oafish, dim-witted creature. This was wholly wrong.

If the Neanderthals were displaced by invaders from the rigorous environment of Asia, this was in the pattern of subsequent history. Outlanders, barbarians from a rigorous homeland, repeatedly overran and conquered native races that had grown relatively soft and content in a more hospitable land.

Whatever happened, three different types of primitive man were in Europe during the later stages of the Ice Ages of the Pleistocene, all of them of the modern human species and all with somewhat higher intelligence than the early Neanderthals. Best known of them, and probably most advanced, were the Cro-Magnons.

NOVEMBER 10

Cro-Magnon Man was named for a rock shelter called Cro-Magnon in Dordogne, France. Five fossil skeletons were discovered there in 1868. Subsequently, Cro-Magnon remains were found in many other places in Europe.

The Cro-Magnons were larger in stature than the average modern European, more than six feet tall, and had slightly larger brains. Their heads were shaped somewhat like those of the modern Eskimo, the skull narrow and the cheekbones wide, with a strong jaw and a well-developed chin, the forehead high. In point of time, the Cro-Magnons overlapped the late Neanderthals. Possibly they had a hand in eliminating the Neanderthals, perhaps by war, perhaps by absorption and cross-breeding. Neanderthal bones, cracked for their marrow, have been found in a Cro-Magnon cave in Yugoslavia. The inference is that someone of cannibalistic tastes helped eliminate the Neanderthals, and the finger seems to point at the Cro-Magnons.

Cannibalistic or not, the Cro-Magnons had a considerably higher type of culture than the Neanderthals. They it was who left the remarkable examples of prehistoric art that have been found in various caves in France and Spain. They made excellent tools and weapons from bone and stone. They knew how to use the drill and the chisel. Some anthropologists believe that traces of the original Cro-Magnon stock can still be found in ethnic pockets of southern France and Brittany, though it seems likely that the Cro-Magnons declined as a race and subsequently vanished. One theory is that Europe was overrun and repopulated by an unknown people from Asia or Africa, who became the basic stock for modern Europeans. These later people, whoever they were, established the Neolithic, or New Stone Age, culture, with ground and polished stone implements and some form of primitive agriculture.

There are traces of two other primitive races that seem to have influenced the types of certain modern Europeans and that lived in Europe and probably elsewhere too, at about the same time as the Cro-Magnons. One, the Chancelade—named for the site in western France where the first skeletal remains were found—was of short stature and much like the present-day Eskimo. The other, the Grimaldi, was a Negroid type and probably came from Africa. The Grimaldi skeletal remains were found in a Cro-Magnon cave in Italy.

NOVEMBER 11

It was spitting snow when I got up this morning, and by eight the grass in the pastures was grizzled. It was not a real snowstorm, though. The temperature was in the thirties, there was almost no wind, and the cloud cover was thin. By noon the snowfall had ended and the sun came out, and before dark you wouldn't have known we had a flake of snow. It all melted. Tonight is chilly but not icy, down to thirty at dusk, down only to twenty-eight by nine o'clock.

So we have had our warning. Snow. We could still have another spell of Indian summer, of course. We sometimes do in mid-November, and it comes as a bonus. But I don't expect much of November in the way of pleasant weather. After all, November is transition time, from fall to winter, when the weather systems are beginning to take on winter characteristics—cold, snowy, fast-moving. Most of the time for the next few weeks they will drop their snow in the mountains of the West and arrive here more boisterous than troublesome. But before the month is out, we probably will get a real snowfall. Now and then we get snow for Thanksgiving, though not as often as tradition says they got it a century or more ago. Remember the "Over the River and Through the Woods" song about Thanksgiving at Grandfather's? Remember those lines, "The horse knows the way/ to carry the sleigh/ through the white and drifted snow"?

This morning, watching those white flakes drift down, I tried to think like a Neanderthal man facing winter's first snowfall. It was difficult. One normally thinks within the framework of one's own life, one's environment, and I am *Homo sapiens,* a man of the twentieth century, a member of the species that now virtually dominates life on this earth.

My kind has the means to wipe out, perhaps destroy forever, almost any species including my own. I can somewhat reconstruct the past from bones and stones and layers of sand and rock, some with fossil footprints still in it. But, being the unpredictable creature I am, I can only half imagine what another thousand years will bring, what my kind will do to life, or what life will do to my own kind.

The best I could do this morning, consciously trying to think Neanderthal, was to say to myself, "I'd better haul a few more dead trees up close to the cave for firewood. And bring in some more meat, another deer if I can kill one nearby. It may snow a long time, for days. Snow is cold."

Which, I admit, is not exactly profound. That is the best I can do when I consciously try to slip back into another age. But sometimes, when I am not trying and when everything is just right, I find myself back there somewhere in the swirling mists of remote prehistory, a part of evolving life. I still am that, of course, but not even an anthropologist wakes up in the morning thinking that he is a step in the evolution of man from an African hominid to whatever he will be in another thousand years.

NOVEMBER 12

A little while back, I spoke of Dr. Louis Leakey and his discoveries in Africa. Now perhaps we can take a longer look at this man and his family, and what they have done. I will admit that since the first time I read about the Leakeys and their discoveries I have felt a little quiver run down my spine at the very mention of Olduvai Gorge. It touches something very primitive in me, something that reaches up into central Asia, then to Siberia, then across the Bering Strait to Alaska, and down the American continents. And at the same time out of central Asia into northern Europe, to the dark forests, and south into the French mountains, to the caves where those who came before me drew those magnificent pictures on the smoky walls. To the Aztecs, on the one hand; to the Cro-Magnons on the other. . . . But that is a very personal matter.

It was Mary Leakey who found the skull, not Louis, who was sick abed with a fever. It was embedded in the rock, by which it was dated as being at least 600,000 years old. More accurate dating later showed it to be 1,500,000 years old or more. That was in 1959. It was the beginning of a concentrated search that changed the whole picture of early man.

What they had found, of course, was evidence of the hominid stage, the "almost-man" stage, that carried the verifiable story back to five, maybe ten or even more millions of years ago. And they found chipped stone tools and proof of the use of fire by *Zinjanthropus,* the first discovery, as well as by *Homo habilis,* a later one.

Louis Leakey was born, of English parents, in Kenya in 1903. He spent much of his childhood and youth with native tribesmen and absorbed a great deal of knowledge of their traditions and cultural background. He was sent to England for his education and at Cambridge became interested in anthropology. Back in Africa he began unraveling the origins of the native people there. This led to Olduvai Gorge and to human fossils. His wife, Mary, was the great-great-granddaughter of John Frere, the first prehistorian to identify flaked-stone tools found in England as the work of early man. She has become a leading authority on early man's technology. Dr. Leakey died in December, 1973, but Mary Leakey continues the work in Olduvai Gorge. Her oldest son, Richard, has been digging and finding another rich lode of fossils at least as old as those in Olduvai Gorge in a new field on the eastern shore of Kenya's Lake Rudolf.

The Olduvai Gorge is a tremendous crack in the earth's surface running from East Africa all the way north into Israel. The sides of this vast canyon, as we would call it in our own Southwest, are like the pages in a book—layer after layer of geological history, the successive layers of the Pleistocene period, during which most of human evolution apparently occurred. The work the Leakeys have done there has shifted man's probable origin from Asia to Africa, pushed his recognizable ancestors back several million years, and shown that he was using stone tools several million years earlier than had been thought.

NOVEMBER 13

There were other African discoveries, but most of them were either incidental or wrongly timed. I have already mentioned Raymond Dart and Robert Broom, and their discovery of *Australopithecus prometheus.* It occurred in the 1920's, when nobody was looking for important archaeological discoveries in Africa. The Dart-Broom bones were dubbed "Fire Ape" because they were found along with proof that the creature had used fire and made crude stone weapons. The idea of dawn-man in

Africa just didn't catch the imagination until Louis Leakey came along and made the Olduvai Gorge spectacular. Leakey was a showman.

Reading Leakey—and Louis Leakey makes it all very vivid—I can see myself squatting beside a stream, picking up a fist-size stone, rapping it sharply against an even larger stone. By sheer chance, the angle is exactly right. A sharp-edged flake almost as big as my palm is fractured from the stone in my hand. I pick it up, awed. It is the first knife I ever saw. I have chipped the first tool. I pick up another stone, try to flake off another knife. It takes a dozen tries to get a flake of any size, and I never do, that day, get another knife like that first one. But I keep trying, and eventually I learn to cleave sharp-edged chips with which I can skin my deer, cut my meat, shape the hides I save to keep me warm.

This isn't science, of course. It is racial memory of very special intensity or it is plain, everyday imagination. But what other animal is there besides man that can imagine such a thing, put it into words, and tell someone else so that he, too, can imagine it?

It is now generally believed that man and the ape came from common stock far back, from that shrewlike arboreal early mammal, very likely. But that line branched, perhaps twenty or more million years ago, into apes on the one hand, pre-men on the other. The pre-man branch evolved into hominids and came down through the dwarfish "Fire Apes," which were not apes at all. And from them down through the Leakey discoveries to *Homo erectus,* the man who walked erect, of several million years ago, and from there to Java Man, Peking Man, Heidelberg Man, Neanderthal and Cro-Magnon.

NOVEMBER 14

This was a raw November day with a few spits of snow but not enough to whiten the grass. Temperature was in the forties, and the dampness of the air made it feel ten degrees lower. After lunch I went out to stretch my legs, up across the home pasture and into the woods on the lower hillside. I followed the brook, which was chattering from one small fall to the next, and I was soon at the edge of the upper meadow, a small clearing now largely overgrown by wild raspberry bushes. As I approached the raspberry tangle, a place I stay out of because the thorns are like flesh-hooks, two ruffed grouse took off just to my left, with a roar like the takeoff of a racing car. I saw them for only one long flash before they whirred around a big pine and were gone. Those birds can take off as quietly as an owl, if they choose to. I have seen them do it. But if they choose to startle someone who might have a gun, and thus get another second or two of safe escape time, they wait till the intruder is close by, then take wing with that roar which can startle most hunters.

I stood there and watched, when the grouse had flown, and I was back again in that remote time Dr. Leakey explored, a *Homo habilis*. I wore a breech clout and had a tanned wolf skin slung over one shoulder. I had two throwing-clubs, and a rabbit I had just killed with one of them. I looked for and found two fist-size stones, struck one against the other and flaked off a sharp-edged shard with which I slashed the rabbit's skin, then stripped it off the carcass in one piece. I slit the belly with that new knife, gutted it. Then I built a fire, not even thinking whether I yet knew how to strike a spark from a stone or had a smolder of a coal in some ingenious container. Somehow I built a fire, cooked my rabbit, ate. And sat there on the hillside, looking over the trees on the lower slope to the rocky ledges across the valley. And deliberately pulled my gaze back from Africa where *Homo habilis* lived perhaps three million years ago. Back to the valley of the Housatonic, to the cultivated home pasture, to the red-shingled farmhouse where my lunch was almost ready for me.

Then I came back down the path beside the brook, back across the pasture, back to now.

It snowed for a little while this afternoon, this time enough to cover the grass, enough to remind me that there was a time, when man was young, when the snow came and stayed, when the snow became ice, the ice became glaciers, the glaciers plowed down across the continents from the north and, with slight pauses and retreats, remained for thousands of years.

NOVEMBER 15

Most of our autumn hoarding is done. It was done, in fact, a month ago, before the hard frost got a chance to blight what we wanted to save, squashes and carrots and potatoes. All the apples we can use have been gathered and stowed or made into sauce or jelly. Pears have been canned. We got only a few ears of late sweet corn. The raccoons found it was prime before we did. I don't think they needed it, with all the field corn there was, but they took it.

Now when I look around I can't for the life of me feel guilty about this hoarding. Thrift is as natural a process as growth. The big sugar maples across the road from our house are as thrifty as I am, maybe even more so. Every tree in the woodland is, for that matter. They put on a lavish display of color a month ago in what seemed at the time an extravaganza. What use to anyone was all that color? And then they shed all those colorful leaves, just let them fall to the ground. Where is the thrift in that?

Well, color is a by-product in leaves, a chemical consequence of photosynthesis. Photosynthesis is the chemical process by which plants make sugars and starches out of air, water, and sunlight. In the autumn the trees seal off their leaves, withdraw the sap to the roots, and settle down for a few months of rest. The leaves have traces of acids, sugars, starches, and other substances still in them, and sunlight and cold weather help to change these chemicals to pigments. The green chlorophyll in them fades and the other colors are revealed. The colors, so far as we know, have no particular purpose. Most of the animals have no color vision. Man does have the ability to distinguish a wide range of colors, so the autumn display in the woodland is beautiful to him. But I lack the arrogance to believe the autumn color is there just to please the aesthetic sense I happen to have.

Those leaves, however, whether they are colorful or not, go back to the earth, to the soil. They become mulch and leaf mold to protect and nourish future growth. The trees don't rake leaves or burn them. They shed them and they, or other plants, use them in one form or another next year and the year after. Rob any woodland of its mulch and leaf mold for a few years and the trees begin to starve and die. The whole process of plant life is thrift. I may call it an untidy mess, but nature thrives on the litter that accompanies every autumn. Nature is a hoarder.

NOVEMBER 16

Animals and insects are classic hoarders. The squirrels, the field mice, the chipmunks, the beavers and all their kin, and the ants, the bees, even the beetles, are hoarders of the first water.

Most of the squirrel hoarding was done a month ago, but when I go into the woods even now I see them at their hyperthyroid industry in the oaks and the hickories. They even resent my presence, though they have already taken far more than I could find even if I were trying to stock up on nuts for the winter. The chipmunks are still out on sunny days, gathering small acorns and other seeds for their graneries, which are already stuffed. The instinct won't let them simply come out into the thinning sunlight and bask. They have to be busy. So do the ants and the bees. Even this diminished sunlight says to them, "Gather! Stow! Prepare for the cold that is coming!" So they gather and stow, the ants storing seeds in their underground bins, the bees making more honey in their combs, though where they get pollen and nectar with the late asters now frosted is a mystery to me.

Less provident insects, those whose short lives create no such winter need, do their hoarding in another way. They hoard life itself, in egg and pupa, to pass on to another generation. Even the woolly-bear caterpillars, which I still see from time to time on warm afternoons, hoard their precious spark of life in hibernation. They find a beam or a nook in a barn or garage, curl up and freeze solid. Next spring they will thaw and undergo the next stage of their life and become pink-tinged yellow moths that feed hungrily on the plantain I call a weed in my lawn.

I may wish that some insects, such as gypsy moths and tent caterpillars and bean beetles, were less successful at hoarding life in the egg; but they, too, have the instinct. And if they were anything more than concentrated reflexes and hungers, they might wish that I and all my kind were less proprietary of the trees they feed upon to sustain their lives.

NOVEMBER 17

With luck and normal weather—that is to say, the weather we have four years out of five—autumn continues all the way to Thanksgiving, and in specially favored years it continues till Christmas week.

Now that I have said this, I see that autumn as we know it here in our valley coincides quite closely with traditional almanac autumn. It runs about three months, and a part of it is very frosty, the kind of weather that would be called winter in a good many places. What I am thinking, I suppose, is that our autumns are a kind of leisurely summary of the year. The trees have summarized their annual growth, the pastures and meadows are summarized in our barns, the gardens are consolidated in our root cellars and pantries. Even the days and nights achieve a kind of recapitulation. Indian summer days come without the heat and humidity, and Squaw winter comes without burying us under snow. Man is invited to participate in all this, and if he lives on the land he can't very well do anything but participate. Autumn is all around him, wherever he looks or walks, urging him to slow down to the season's pace and accept the world on its own terms, not his, for a change.

Those terms are not really difficult to accept. Autumn, after all, is only another phase in the endless cycle of growth and time. There is an incorruptibility in it, in a sense, that not even man can distort, for autumn is both a consequence and a prolonged occasion beyond human management. It is an achievement and fulfillment, something so rare in the affairs of man that if we stop and consider it we cannot help being awed. It isn't completion, even though it is ripeness and maturity. Completion is a human concept. Nature is change and a constant going on; and autumn is inevitably a part of that change.

NOVEMBER 18

We had a light snowfall again today, not enough to clog roads but enough to whiten the pastures. And to make me aware of infinity, of the impossibility, even with all our sophistication, of counting a great many things. Snowflakes, of course, but also leaves, grass blades, flies, stars— the list could go on and on. There aren't numbers enough to count the snowflakes that fell on the porch roof outside my study window this morning, let alone those that fell in the home pasture just beyond the back yard. But the infinity of snowflakes is cold and inert. For all their crystalline perfection and complexity, snowflakes cannot grow or reproduce. They overwhelm me only with countless numbers.

Last spring the peepers yelped in the lowlands and the pussy willows cautiously opened their fuzzy male catkins. The peepers mated and laid their masses of minute, glutinous eggs in the chilly water. The inconspicuous female willow flowers reached their receptive stage and the silky male catkins ripened their yellow pollen and fertilized them, made seed from which other willow trees will grow. The batrachian eggs hatched into tiny, wriggling tadpoles. Neither were as countless as the snowflakes, but still were far beyond counting, life incredibly resurgent. And perhaps in the untold eons of springtime since frogs first mated in the primal swamplands and the somewhat fewer eons since trees began strewing pollen on the marshy margins, perhaps as countless as the snowflakes of all the winters I shall ever know.

Only now and then are we really aware of this amazing procreative force, but when we do see it, it is like a glimpse of the big, enduring secret. A few years ago we saw it on a warm spring evening.

The peepers had called, mated, laid their eggs. So had all the other frogs and toads that populate the riverbank just beyond our dooryard. Mild weather came and held. To me, it was only ideal weather for farm crops and winter-weary people. But the miracle was happening on my very doorstep.

Then came the mild evening when we walked up the road close beside the river to know again the smell of opening buds and leaf mold stirred by worms. It was early darkness and I had a flashlight in case a leisurely shadow turned out to be a skunk looking for a late supper. I have found that a flashlight beam will delay a startled skunk's reaction long enough for a watchful walker to retreat safely.

We walked a little way, and suddenly realized that the whole road was alive. Unseen creatures were moving all around us. I turned on the flashlight and we saw countless hordes of small frogs and toads, a seething carpet of them as far up the road as I could see. They were like a scourge of locusts on the march, but they were only moving from the riverbank across the road into the open pasture and beyond.

We stood there and they were all around us, underfoot and blindly leaping at our legs and over our feet. It seemed that the river, wide as it was, could not possibly have held so much amphibian life as was carpeting that country road. We watched for ten minutes, fifteen, and still they came. Then we turned and came back to the house, scuffling our feet to push the frogs out of our way.

I went out again an hour later, and while the mass migration had ended, there were still hundreds of small toads and frogs crossing the road from riverbank to pasture. But by the next morning there wasn't one in sight, and when I walked out into the pastures I didn't see a frog or a toad. Those untold thousands, perhaps millions, spawned in the river unknown to me, had migrated across my consciousness by sheer chance, there in the darkness, and vanished completely. Yet I doubt that what I saw was a phenomenon of fecundity. It undoubtedly happens every spring. I merely saw it for the first time.

NOVEMBER 19

Fecundity is one of nature's primary ways to keep the stream of life flowing. In everyday terms, all forms of life are experimental. Evolution and variation seem to be the basic rule, and forms of life that don't fit into the big pattern, whatever it is, are discarded. If a life form is disruptive, it is discontinued and soon wiped out. But there are all kinds of ways to control the overly fecund. They can be crowded out, or starved out, or simply eaten by some other form of life. One way or another, they eventually are checked before they completely upset the always precarious balance.

The extremes of fecundity undoubtedly are to be found in the microscopic forms of life, germs, microbes, bacteria, etc. Of visible life, the insects are at the top of the heap.

One July morning a few years ago the dew made every spiderweb in sight gleam like a pearly white handkerchief left lying on the grass. The webs were everywhere I looked, but there was a special concentration under a sick little flowering dogwood in the side yard. The tree was dying. I had to take it out a few weeks later. I still don't know whether this had anything to do with the number of spiders, but I counted thirty-nine webs, all of the common grass spider, *Agelena naevia,* in a twelve-foot circle around the tree.

I had read not long before, in a book by George Ordish, the British entomologist, that in Tudor England there were sometimes as many as two million spiders per acre in rural areas. I wasn't in the mood to argue, but I did wonder where Mr. Ordish got his data. So I got pencil and paper and did a bit of arithmetic. That twelve-foot circle was roughly 1/385th of an acre. Multiplying 39 by 385, I got only 15,015, the theoretical number of spiders per acre on my lawn. That was somewhat short of two million.

But that was merely the probable adult spider population of that area at that moment. Big spiders lay eggs that hatch into little spiders. Sometimes a spider lays only a few eggs per cocoon, but sometimes she lays several hundred; cocoons have been found with as many as 900 eggs. And even here in the lower Berkshires, spiders may make as many as nine cocoons of eggs in a season. Even being ultraconservative and saying each of those spiders that made my webs that morning laid eggs that produced 500 spiderlings a season—say five cocoons with 100 eggs each—that small area would have about 20,000 spiders. Carry that rate over an entire acre and the total would be something more than seven and a half million.

I grant that this was an unusual concentration of spiders, here under my sick dogwood. Suppose I over-calculated by half. It still meant there were more creepers and crawlers around here than I could handily count. No matter where I turned, I was going to be dealing with astronomical figures.

NOVEMBER 20

Take houseflies. Some biologist, or maybe a mathematician, once calculated that the offspring of one pair of houseflies, if all survived and reproduced normally, in six months would become 191 quintillion flies. A quintillion, in case you have forgotten, is denoted by a one followed by eighteen zeroes, thus: 1,000,000,000,000,000,000. I can't begin to comprehend such numbers, but this biologist, or mathematician, maybe, went on to estimate that 191 quintillion houseflies would cover the earth to a depth of forty-seven feet.

An equally anonymous entomologist, or mathematician, has estimated that if all the aphids produced in one season were to survive they would exterminate all life on earth simply by destroying all vegetation. This estimate made no mention of numbers, but I am sure the total number of aphids would also be in the quintillions. Aphids have an advantage over houseflies: they don't need two individuals to start having offspring. One can do it, all alone, since aphids usually reproduce by parthenogenesis, without mating.

Locusts and grasshoppers have long been notorious for devastating numbers. I don't recall ever seeing specific numbers for their swarms, which may be significant in itself, for they usually are recorded in square miles covered or in tons of insects. For example, one swarm in the Middle East covered 2,000 square miles, an area almost forty-five miles square. Another swarm, in Brazil, extended along a sixty-mile front and took four hours to pass a given point. I doubt that one could begin to estimate such swarms. I know that in one devastated area of Turkey the farmers collected 100 tons of grasshopper eggs and 1,200 tons of grasshoppers in three months. Twelve hundred tons, 2,400,000 pounds, 38,400,000 ounces. Figure what one grasshopper weighs, and proceed from there. Make your own calculation.

In the 1930's, when Japanese beetles had first got a foothold and were moving inland from New Jersey, the Department of Agriculture put on a special anti-beetle campaign in the Philadelphia area. Hundreds of beetle traps baited with geraniol were put out in the infested places and their catch was hauled to a central station not far from where I lived. Pickup trucks made the rounds several times a day and came in with huge cans of dead beetles that were dumped on a pile that was kept burning day and night. That pile was about ten feet in diameter and six to eight feet high, and it never seemed to diminish. The pyre was kept going three months, and still the Japanese beetles spread across the land. How many were trapped and burned, I wouldn't even guess, but billions seems a small number.

NOVEMBER 21

Although we live close beside the Housatonic River, we are relatively unbothered by mosquitoes, gnats, and midges, except in early spring, when what we call "sap flies" pester us for a time. But I know there are periodic hatches of midges and other small insects on the river all summer. We often sit in the evening and watch swallows and night hawks seining the air above the river, catching those flecks of insect life by the hundreds and the thousands. And late in the season, usually by the end of August or early in September we have evidence of a midge population that is almost incredible.

I go out one late August morning and find the floor of the big front porch virtually covered with dead insects. I go down to the riverbank and see them floating downstream, a band of them four to five feet wide along each shore. We have gone out in the boat and seen those dead insects still coming downstream five miles away. We have never found the end of them.

I first thought they were mosquitoes, male mosquitoes. But their bushy antennae, like microscopic bottle brushes, put them in the midge classification, probably *Chironomidae,* which somewhat resemble mosquitoes but don't bite. Male mosquitoes don't bite either, but their antennae are nowhere near as bushy as the antennae of these midges.

I once tried to calculate their numbers, giving each one of them a generous quarter-inch square of space. That meant sixteen to the square inch, 2,304 to the square foot. The concentrated band of midges on the water extends four or five feet from the bank. Take an average of four feet, and one mile of river would mean 21,120 square feet along each bank. With 2,304 dead midges to each square foot, that would mean 48,660,480 midges floating along each bank, close to 100 million along both banks per mile. The river at this point is sluggish, with a flow of maybe three miles an hour, but it sometimes takes the better part of a week for the slowly diminishing flow of dead midges to pass our house. Others can carry on the mathematics if they want to deal in big, big numbers.

NOVEMBER 22

Or take ants. Normally we have no trouble with ants, seldom see more than a few of them at a time, out in the dooryard. But a year ago last summer I saw a column of medium-sized black ants crossing the far corner of the yard, going from the old chicken house into the home pasture. It seemed to be quite a column, so I decided to do some counting. I counted the number of ants that passed a given point in a minute and sat down to time them. I watched for an hour and there still seemed to be no end to the column. I came indoors and went out every half-hour to check the ants. They continued to march almost five hours. My calculations set their numbers at roughly 25,000. They all came from a colony I had never even noticed. Then I made a tour of the dooryard and counted almost fifty colonies around the edges of the lawn. If each of those colonies had as many members as that one on the march, we had 1,250,000 ants in our dooryard.

Unless they invade the house, we are seldom aware of the number of ants in any suburban or rural area. But almost any colony has a big population. Derek W. Morley, a British entomologist, once reported a wood ant colony containing half a million members. In my boyhood in eastern Colorado I knew the big western harvester ants, *Pogonomyrmex occidentalis,* which build conical mounds eighteen inches high and as much as four feet across the base. Galleries beneath these cones may extend ten feet down and reach out fifteen feet or more from the center. I have never seen population figures for such a colony, but they must be well up in the thousands. In some parts of the Great Plains I have seen as many as forty such colonies on an acre, probably with several million ants in them. In August, when the winged males and virgin queens emerge for mating flights, they sometimes cloud the air.

NOVEMBER 23

From millions let's drop back to mere thousands and take in the wasps, of which the hornets or yellow jackets, the Vespula, give the greatest appearance of hordes because they live in colonies. The *Dolichovespula,* which build those big spherical paper nests in trees and bushes, may have as many as 5,000 workers in such a nest-city at one time, and there may be 10,000 or more egg cells in a nest's nursery. Here in the North-east such hornet nests seldom have more than 500 inhabitants at one time, but over the summer they may produce several thousand. Only the fertile queens live through the winter, and a new nest is built each year. A queen can lay as many as 25,000 fertile eggs from her one mating.

Last summer a colony of these hornets built a big paper nest on the window of our old chicken house, which I use as a carpenter shop to make minor repairs around here. They started on the window frame, but as the nest grew, it spread out across the glass until it almost covered the pane. From inside the shop I could see scores of those hornets working inside the nest and I watched them for several weeks. Needless to say, I came and went quietly and with due deliberation. The nest was egg-shaped, one of the biggest I ever saw, two feet wide and two and a half feet long. It withstood the winter rather well, and when I took it down this spring I was surprised at the toughness of its paper walls.

NOVEMBER 24

The numbers we have been dealing with in discussing insect fecundity seem fantastic, but even the quintillions mentioned are only a slight sampling. The U.S. Department of Agriculture says there are about 95,000 species of insects in North America (there are more than 900,000 in the world), and virtually all of them are incredibly reproductive. Nearly all of them, fortunately for us, have countless natural enemies—a part of that elaborately complex system of natural balances. Birds do more than any other agency to keep the insects in check. One flicker, for instance, may eat as many as 5,000 ants in a day.

The conditions of balance are unbelievably complicated. Insect eats insect. There are even minute wasps called fairy flies, only 1/100 of an inch long, that are parasites within the eggs of insects the size of flies. There are parasitic insects that live on parasites, and parasites that live on those in turn. And birds, even the seed-eaters, feed their nestlings on insect fare, which is necessary for their quick growth. Many animals, from skunks to anteaters to bears, include vast numbers of insects in their diets. Without insects, most of the birds and many of the animals would starve.

And yet every time I deal with these figures I pause at the quintillions of flies and aphids. I wonder if anyone ever ran the data through a modern computer to see how valid those figures are. I wonder if those

191 quintillion flies really *would* cover the earth to a depth of forty-seven feet. How much of it? All of it, or only the continents?

NOVEMBER 25

Man seems to be the only form of animal life that has in any way learned to control the consequences of extreme fecundity, and even there the results are not what I would call worth celebrating. Even with abortion, contraceptives, and antifecundity pills, the total human population of the earth continues to rise at a rate that means fatal overpopulation within a few more lifetimes. Right now there are places where human fecundity has so overpopulated the land that it has been robbed of its normal plant and animal production. This has put and kept the human population on the verge of starvation. India is a prime example of this. China was, until famine and war wiped out millions of people. Famine and war are not what are commonly termed enlightened control methods—unless they are happening in enemy countries, of course—but they can be effective in restoring balances.

Eventually there is a showdown. Usually, in the past, it has been so quiet that even if man had been there he probably wouldn't have known what was happening. But the balance was restored, and it will be again, when necessary. The dinosaurs didn't vanish overnight, but they are gone. You never had a dinosaur steak for dinner, did you? Neither did your grandfather. Neither did the Cro-Magnons, who drew pictures of all the animals they saw on the walls of those fabulous caves.

Who is next on the program after man?

NOVEMBER 26

We have come to that time when every morning is frosty. We have no snow storms yet, not enough snow to last more than a few hours, but that will come too. Today we had what we call "a snow sky," but we got no snow from it; only a raw wind that made it more comfortable indoors than out. But by midafternoon I was restless, had to get out. So I put on a heavy jacket, slung a muffler round my neck, and walked across the home pasture and up the mountain a little way, following Millstone Brook.

We call it Millstone Brook because I once found a millstone in it, a miniature stone, square hole, grooves and all, but only about fifteen inches in diameter. Nobody around here ever saw one like it. Today I found a stone pestle not fifty yards from where I found the millstone. Half a pestle, to be exact, the lower half; the upper half, the handle end, was missing. Like the millstone, it is made of native rock, a schist. It must be considerably older than the millstone. White settlers were the first to use millstones here. Before that, the native corn was ground in stone mortars with such pestles as that one I found today.

We find Indian artifacts from time to time. Last summer, while showing the vegetable garden to a visitor, I picked up a perfect quartz arrowhead in the middle of a row of green beans. It was one of the better examples of chipped stone work I have found here. One of my neighbors owns a field that once was the site of an Indian village where a stone-worker must have had his shop. At least two quarts of arrowheads and lanceheads have been found there, most of them unbroken. But few of them show better than mediocre workmanship. I have looked at several collections of stone arrowheads found in this area, and all of them contain few examples of really first-class work. I have rarely seen an arrowhead or spear point as good as most of the chipped stone points I found on the High Plains when I was a boy.

I am not going to try to compare Indian cultures or skills, area by area. But anyone who knows handcrafts knows that the midwestern and western tribes did some of the best flint work ever done in America, and that of the East Coastal tribes was generally second-rate. The cultures were totally different. But they all came from a common source, and it is that point that interests me, the Indians themselves, who they were, how and when they came here, and from where.

NOVEMBER 27

It snowed. We got about two inches in the night from a little storm that passed swiftly, left this light cargo, and was followed by this morning's clear, bright skies. The effect was like magic, a dazzling beauty that happened without evident cause. The only thing missing is the miracle of snowfall itself.

As a boy, I knew snowstorms intimately. On the rolling flatlands of the West there were few fences and fewer landmarks, and even a quiet snowstorm created a brand-new world. Even in the daytime it could be totally confusing. At night it could be both terrorizing and deceptively comfortable, especially if one had a lantern. It was a world only as wide as one could see, and that might be only ten or fifteen feet. In that small circle all was normal. Beyond it, in all directions, was an unknown hidden by that curtain of falling snow. Underfoot it was white. Overhead it was white. One was in a cocoonlike world that moved with one, unchanged, whichever way one turned. It had no markers. It was eternally the same. It was a world in which, if the temperature was low and one was weary, one could easily lie down and freeze to death. So one kept moving, in that little white world that never seemed to move or change, hoping to find a fence, a gully, a building, something of reality and substance, to provide shelter or guidance to shelter.

NOVEMBER 28

A chilly night, and the temperature was only ten degrees above zero this morning. There is a scum of ice along the river's edges and the small ponds are frozen over. Winter begins to proclaim itself.

We have had a strange bird flitting about the yard the past few days, avoiding the bird feeders but finding food, evidently, where the regular boarders haven't bothered to look. I finally got a good look at it today, and identified it as a mockingbird.

Mockers have been in this area from time to time for at least fifteen years, and I have heard of pairs nesting this far north at least five years. But I have yet to hear one singing. Every winter, during the Audubon Christmas Bird Count, a few mockers are seen.

Forbush's *Birds of Massachusetts* says that mockingbirds were resident on Nantucket Island as early as 1877, and on Martha's Vineyard about the same time. Also, that they nested in the Boston area and at Springfield and Northampton in 1909. It also says that lone mockers often show up in Massachusetts in June, July, and early August, only to disappear later. Now I see that the superhighway builders are taking credit for the northward spread of the mockingbirds. The roadbuilders often use multiflora roses in their plantings on the divider strips. The roses have many hips. The mockers eat and relish those rose hips. So, the mockers followed the superhighways north. Which is all very interesting. But the fact is that a good many mockingbirds, as Forbush shows, came north long before the superhighways did.

NOVEMBER 29

It now seems certain that nowhere in the Americas is there evidence of really ancient man. Nothing has been found comparable to Java Man or Peking Man, and there is no evidence of Neanderthal or Cro-Magnon. Whatever his biological origins, man appears not to have seen the Americas until well along in the Ice Ages. Then, perhaps 30,000 years ago, perhaps twice that, circumstances invited man to migrate from Asia to this twin-continental New World.

The massive glaciers of the Ice Ages locked up so much of the earth's water that the oceans were shrunken in their beds. Sea-level dropped at least a hundred feet in the Pacific, and this exposed a land bridge perhaps three hundred miles wide between what now are Siberia and Alaska. This bridge was in existence tens of thousands of years, its extent varying with the ebb and flow of the glaciers. At times it may have been almost as wide as Alaska. While it existed, this land bridge blocked cold Arctic water and allowed warm Pacific water and air to temper the climate. In consequence, the bridge was an area of luxuriant growth of grass and shrubs, pasturage for camels, ground sloths, big-horned bison, musk oxen, hairy mammoths and horses. They grazed their way from Asia to the American mainland.

Man had continued to evolve and, by the evidence, had become a skillful hunter. As these major game animals of the time crossed the land bridge to this land of new forage, the hunters inevitably followed them. Not as migrants, but simply as tribesmen who lived by the chase. As the Plains Indians of a much later time followed the vast herds of bison north and south, from present-day Texas to Canada and back, with the seasons.

They were not hominids. They were men, who had the use of fire, who made and used stone tools and weapons, who had a spoken language and the rudiments of a culture. They were not Africans, nor were they Asians as we think of races today. They were simply men, of some basic stock.

When they came cannot be pinpointed, but it was long ago. It is known that man reached the farthest tip of South America about eleven thousand years ago, and it must have taken a good many thousand years for the earliest arrivals in present-day Alaska to trickle down the length of the two continents, generation by generation.

But whatever the precise date—30,000 or 60,000 years ago, or more, or even less, perhaps—man came to America from Asia, not from

Africa or from Europe. And the original hunters who followed those herds across the land bridge were the ancestors of the Indians the Europeans found here when they arrived in the fifteenth century. Or in the eleventh century, if we accept the Norse sagas, which are most persuasive.

NOVEMBER 30

Many have speculated about the racial origins and cultural sources of the American Indians. Read them all, and you come out convinced that, though Asiatic in origin, they were not Mongolians and that their various cultures were essentially their own. They were not a stupid people or unimaginative, and they had ample time to evolve social, religious, and political systems before the Europeans arrived.

Racially, they were of an earlier strain than the Mongolians. It is possible they were more like the Cro-Magnons of Europe than any other of the ancients. The Cro-Magnons themselves are supposed to have reached Europe from the East, from Asia. So the American Indians may be direct descendants of that strain of man which the seekers have never verified in Europe.

Speculation about sources of cultural achievements follows familiar patterns: ancient Egypt, early India, ancient Indonesia, early Wales. How else, ask the speculators, explain the remarkable achievements of the Incas, the Mayas, the Aztecs? They forget that the Indians were clever enough to breed maize from native plants in some manner now wholly lost to plant breeders. They forget the calendars they developed, more accurate than those of ancient Rome or Greece. They ignore the fact that the Indians invented the hammock, the toboggan, the tobacco pipe, the hollow rubber ball, an intricate system of ventilating and cooling ceremonial halls, and many other things. Even in medicine, they were ahead of most Europeans and Asians: they invented the enema and they devised the surgical techniques of trepanning.

In what is now the southwestern United States, they developed a system of irrigation for their fields of maize and beans and pumpkins. They dammed rivers, dug ditches, some of them thirty feet wide, and carried water to fields as much as twenty-five miles away. They built stone apartment houses, some in the open, some in vast canyon cliff-caves, colonies with as many as 800 rooms. In the Midwest, they built incredible earthworks and established trade routes with connections as far away as Mexico. And they evolved and lived by elaborate political systems and ritualized religions.

Those who have studied the arts, the religions, the social systems of these Toltecs, Aztecs, Mayas, and Incas at the peak of their glory are constantly amazed, and they still wonder to what heights of achievement they might have risen had not the Spanish invaders looted their temples and murdered their leaders.

Can that be the way the Cro-Magnons went? Nobody knows.

DECEMBER

DECEMBER 1

We got about six inches of snow. Snow plows are out, and sander trucks.

I have been trying to remember when people stopped using tire chains and shifted to snow tires. It was quite a while back. I still have a set of tire chains in my garage, and I well remember the clank-clank of a broken cross-chain against a fender, one of those night sounds by which you could identify the car of a friend. A careless friend, let's say, who didn't carry repair-links and the special tool to put them in and close them. That sound was a poor substitute for the jingle of harness bells on horses hitched to a pung or cutter.

"Pung" comes from the same Algonquian Indian root word as "toboggan." It requires a bit of tongue-twisting, I find, but the source is there—the Indians used their word as the name for a kind of cargo sled made of animal skins. The origin of the word "cutter" for a rather swank one-horse sleigh is obscure, except that "cutter" was used in the sense of something sharp, ultra-fashionable, back in the nineteenth century.

There are no pungs or cutters out today.

DECEMBER 2

The whole span of human evolution is full of gaps and missing chapters, with peculiar mysteries along the way and traps even for the wary. Not too long ago it was believed that a race of human or pre-human giants lived in southeast Asia about a million years ago and either perished as misfits or were killed by medium-sized primates who considered them freakish rivals. Eventually the bones were identified as those of huge apes, rather than of either man or pre-man.

On the other hand, the first hominids found in Africa were pygmies, only about four feet tall, and their brains were less than half the size of modern man's brain. At first, they were described as rather advanced types of apes. But further search revealed that they used tools and possessed fire. They were pre-men, perhaps, but they did have enough intelligence to use tools and at least experiment with fire. They, too, vanished, and one theory suggests that primitive men we recognize as our own ancestors killed them off because they were potential rivals.

Those medium-sized early primates were not the kind of people we would welcome as neighbors, it seems. And yet, there still are members of the race who bitterly resent any who are different. We have no reason to be smug.

One wonders why and how man evolved at all. Not why in a spiritual sense, but in a physical and intellectual sense. One wonders about the factors that dictated lines and directions of evolution, and one looks at the time span and is even more puzzled. At the very most, man has been here in recognizable form no more than two million years, in humanoid form perhaps 10 or 15 million. That is but a small fraction of time on the grand scale. Life of some kind has been here on earth at least five hundred times that long. Were 1,250 million years spent preparing for the evolution of man? Arrogant as man is, that does seem somewhat too much to believe.

Over the long millennia there were countless upheavals of land, changes of climate, and alterations of living conditions. Is one to believe that the convulsion which lifted the Himalayas or some other mountain chain, perhaps, was the only event that created precisely the right conditions to compel one particular kind of animal to sharpen its wits, vary its diet, double its brain capacity, and become a two-legged creature that could learn to talk and tame fire?

It seems incredible.

DECEMBER 3

Down the long corridors of time at least half a dozen incredible events occurred, as we now read the evidence.

Life appeared. That was the first one, and we still have to take that on faith and the evidence of life around us today.

Then several single-celled bits of life came together and became a living unit of primitive complexity. That was the second incredible event.

From that first form of complex life evolved a fish. That was the third miracle.

A fish left the water and became an amphibian, and the amphibian became a land-dwelling reptile with lungs. That was the fourth one.

Somewhere along the way a larval form of sea life crept ashore, breathed air, and became an insect. That was the fifth miraculous happening.

And a reptile became a bird and another reptile became a mammal with a brain that had the latent power of thought and reason.

If I can accept these six incredible events—and I must, in the light of present knowledge—then I must accept the most incredible one of all, the rise of man, the existence of myself and all my own searching, sentient kind.

I can accept it, but the *whys* persist. And the evolutionists' theories and their facts can explain but they cannot answer. Each time one of these incredible changes occured, I am told, there was a waiting gap in the spectrum of life, a place for the new creation. But was the gap really there, or did the new type of life create the gap by its own vigorous pressure? Did man evolve because there was a place waiting for him, or did he create that place by his own cunning and his ruthlessness?

DECEMBER 4

Change, I am told, is the one certainty of life. Change and adaptation have been continuous.

I can accept that. But why, if change is inevitable, does the simplest form of life, the form that presumably was among the very earliest in existence on this earth, still persist? And if there is a ruthless weeding out of the unfit and the weaklings, why did the insignificant primitive mammals not perish through the 150 million years of big-lizard supremacy? Why did man, a physical weakling even among the mammals, survive long enough to perfect a big brain and his own dominant intelligence?

The persistent whys!

But, significantly, it is man himself, not the amoeba or the fish or the lizard or the bird, who asks the questions. And that, ultimately, is the mark of man—the search, the need to know, to understand.

DECEMBER 5

The snow that fell the other day is still here. The days have been cold. Not bitterly cold, but in the teens and the low twenties, which doesn't melt snow even at midday. And now there is a band of ice along the river's banks, five or six feet of it, that narrows the visible flow of water. With the snow for contrast, that water is almost charcoal black.

Old-timers tell me that in their youth the river always froze over early in December and stayed frozen till March. They say the ice seldom was less than five inches thick, often ten, and that it was cut and stowed in ice houses on all the farms. This farm had an ice house between the present house and the barn, but it was gone some years before we came here. It also had a tobacco barn, I am told, and tobacco was grown here at one time. It is still grown over in central and eastern Connecticut, but I doubt that it has been grown here in the past seventy-five years, maybe longer.

The climate has changed. No doubt about that, to my mind. Since we have lived here, almost twenty-five years, there hasn't been ice on the river more than five inches thick. Winters have shortened and eased even since we came here. Scientists say we are in the long interval between Ice Ages and that the next big ice sheet will be coming our way within another thousand years. I don't know how that agrees with these warm winters, but I do think the ice will return.

DECEMBER 6

I opened a fresh comb of honey this morning, and as I sliced into it I reflected that while any drafting student could draw more uniform hexagons, there wasn't a draftsman or chemist who could secrete the wax, build the comb, and fill it with honey of his own manufacture. That comb and every drop of honey in it were made by insects that have virtually no measurable intelligence, but only a complexity of instincts. To make this one-pound comb of honey the bees had to visit two million flowers and collect nectar from them.

Then I remembered the insect-rich fossil beds at Florissant, Colorado, which prove that bees much as those we know today were here and undoubtedly making honey and probably storing it in hexagonal combs during the Tertiary period, about 60 million years ago. Bees and nectar and honey are no new phenomena.

But bees and blossoms do raise questions.

If life had no more than an accidental beginning, mathematically probable though it may have been, and if it is no more than a chance, fortuitous combination of chemical elements in a special order, how did such different but now intimately related living things as a bee and a nectar-yielding blossom come into being? Why did the blossom, with no vital need for the plant's excess sugar, develop the means for secreting it as nectar to lure a bee that will assist in pollinating that particular flower? And how did the bee learn that this nectar could be made into concentrated, high-energy food, honey? How did the bee learn to gather nectar, convert it into honey, store it in just this way?

A host of other questions might be asked about this particular matter, but they all lead toward more fundamental ideas, toward the very basis of life, why it evolved and what is its meaning.

DECEMBER 7

Life has its own urgencies, even the mutual urgencies of the bee and the blossom. And we are told that change is a law of nature. I see evidence of this all around me, though I note that there are exceptions. There are holdovers from virtually every stage of evolution, of basic change.

But even if I grant that law of change, I must ask where that law originated. In nature, I am told, in the nature of "things as they are." Very well. But if change is a law of nature and inevitable, then the law of change itself must be some kind of exception. There can be no immutable laws unless something beyond nature, beyond the whole scope of our knowledge of changing nature, established and enforces those laws.

Science deals with facts, and the largest fact of which I am aware is the universe. Of that universe, the only portion I can even hope to know intimately is the earth. I am of that earth, a member of its vast community of living things. All around me are evidences of the earth and life upon it. Facts.

I keep wondering if facts are enough. I wonder if the facts really add up.

DECEMBER 8

When the first men arrived in America, it has been estimated, there were at least 40,000,000 large animals here, woolly mammoths, long-horned bison, camels, giant elk, musk-oxen, saber-toothed tigers, huge ground sloths, dire wolves, horses, and giant cave-bears. It was a hunter's paradise.

The Ice Age had created a wet, foggy climate, many streams and shallow lakes, and it had fostered lush vegetation. But that Ice Age ended in death, almost incredibly widespread death. Most of the large animals were wiped out. Forty million of those large animals were somehow dispatched within a very short time. Great heaps of their fossil bones are found in various places, and in the frozen muck of Alaska are the bones, even fragments of skin and flesh and sinew, of thousands of those animals, old and young.

What happened? There are several theories, each based on such facts as a particular group of theorists could muster.

One theory is that the human hunters, by then quite numerous and well organized, killed them with chipped stone spears and stone axes, and by driving the animals over precipices or into shallow water, or by surrounding them with fire.

Another thesis is that the quick ice melt changed the climate almost overnight and the animals, unable to survive the change, died of exposure or starvation or something like pneumonia.

Still another theory is that the melt-back was followed, or perhaps in part caused, by a series of violent volcanic eruptions that filled the air with poisonous gases, then with fine volcanic ash. The gases killed all those big animals, by this theory, but didn't greatly reduce the human population. And while the rain of volcanic ash covered all those animals and helped preserve them, it didn't preserve even one human skeleton, so far as the searchers have yet been able to discover.

Each of these theories has some basis in fact. Those prehistoric hunters were killers, not conservationists. Like the later Indians, they would drive a whole herd of bison over a cliff to get a dozen carcasses for food. And the melt-back definitely changed the climate, with consequences we can gauge fairly well. And there is evidence that violent volcanic activity at about that time did cause a rain of volcanic ash that is found today over heaps of bones of animals that could have been killed by volcanic gases.

But which set of facts adds up to what really happened?

DECEMBER 9

To go any further, I have to recapitulate.

To the best of my knowledge, bolstered by the knowledge of other questioners, life first appeared here on earth in the simplest single-cell form imaginable. From that form all the kinds of life I know have evolved. It required, according to the approximate timetable science now uses, about one and a half billion years to reach the multitude of complex life forms of today, with man the most complex of all. That is the way we think of it, though there still are processes in nature that we cannot explain. Often we can say how, or when, or where, but only occasionally why.

Life changed. It evolved, presumably upward, or at least toward the more complex. Those original single-celled flecks of life began congregating and specializing, and multicelled forms appeared. This presumably, was in response to that law of change. Change, of course, could have been downward instead of upward, and it probably was in many instances. Instead of combining, some of those flecks of life must have disintegrated, destroyed their own living entity, and turned back toward nonliving forms. But there was another factor at work, and this one we cannot explain. That was the persistence of the simple, the uncomplex. The single-celled form of life did not vanish in the urgency to combine and become increasingly complex. It continued, and it still persists, substantially as it must have been in the beginning. In other words, there was an exception to the law of change.

True, change did occur repeatedly and even magnificently. Multicelled creatures became fish with backbones. Multicelled plants became seaweed and rushes and horsetails. And, for some reason we ascribe to the climate, some of the fish left the water and some of the plants ventured onto dry land. Why did the first amphibians and the first land plants leave the water? Because, we say, life had evolved to the point where it could live in this new, open-air environment, and when land appeared above the waters it invited life. Nature, as we say, tends to populate the vacant environment.

But life seems to have been successful, even to the point of continued evolutionary change, in the old environment, the water. Why should this venture away from the water have been made at all? It was full of chance and danger, and from all the evidence we have it was made by both plants and animals that were not yet ready to make the change completely. They kept returning to the water, the animals to lay their eggs, the plants both to survive and to distribute their spores. And, again, some of the original water-dwelling examples of life persisted where they were.

Was change really essential? Particularly such violent change, such demanding change, as from water to land?

DECEMBER 10

This day we have only nine hours and nine minutes of daylight, according to the almanac. We are still twelve days short of the winter solstice, when theoretically we have the year's shortest span of daylight. Actually, though, that "shortest" span, give or take a few seconds, extends almost a week, from the 18th through the 25th, and it is only five minutes shorter than it is today.

With that little sunlight on this part of the earth, the cold can settle in. That's why our winters here in lower New England are traditionally long and cold. Today, as an instance, was a bright, beautiful, sunny day, but the temperature ranged from the mid-twenties to thirty degrees, and there was a razor-edged wind. Tonight is calm, clear, and crackling cold, well down in the teens.

DECEMBER 11

At about the time the first plants and animals were adventuring onto land, the first of the primitive insects appeared, insects and spiders and scorpions. One widely accepted theory is that they evolved from larval forms of sea life. How they evolved is a persistent mystery. Some believe they first ventured onto land to escape enemies in the water. But the forms of sea life from which they are supposed to have evolved remained in the water and persisted, despite those enemies. Yet here came the spiders and the insects, to achieve a perfection of form and a way of life that have continued with little change for perhaps 100 million years. Even if I grant the urgency of change at the beginning, at the time of their emergence, how shall I explain the relative lack of change after they had achieved their successful way of life in this new environment, the open air? What happened to that law of change?

DECEMBER 12

Life originally, as far as we know, reproduced by a simple process of self-division. That method is still in use among a vast number of simple life forms, essentially unchanged from the process that was in use a billion years ago. But along the way the spore-bearing plants evolved, and the spore-bearers became flowering plants, with seeds. And along the way the animals began to lay eggs, each egg a minute fraction of one parent. Those eggs required fertilization with sperm, minute fractions of the other parent. Sex entered the picture.

Was this, too, an example of the law of change in action? If that were so, why did the spore-bearers persist among the plants, and why do primitive animals survive and continue to lay primitive eggs? From the naked, water-borne egg to the fetal, mammal-born child is a long step, but no longer than from the spore of the fern to the multikerneled ear of Indian corn. The spore has an essential simplicity about it, wasteful as it may be as a reproductive means, and the kernel of corn on a maize plant is infinitely complex, the result of an involved and elaborate process. And the mammalian method of reproduction is a slow, involved process that produces immature offspring with a long and precarious childhood. Is complexity an end in itself, or is it merely a result of persistent and immutable change?

DECEMBER 13

As I understand it, the rule of change tends toward improvement, toward perfection. There are contrary examples, where reversions have occurred, but they seem to be relatively rare. Perfection implies a purpose, and I suppose one might state that purpose, in life terms, as the ideal adaptation to environment. And since the environment persists in changing, then the purpose itself, or at least the ideal of adaptation, must change with it.

But is environment the only governing factor?

There have been a number of major steps in this process of change, steps that were outstanding landmarks in the history of life. Some may have been dictated by changes in environment, but others seem to have preceded environmental changes. And for these major steps man has only the sketchiest of explanations.

The single cell grouped with its neighbors to become a complex organism, a single community of related cells.

The primitive fish became amphibian and learned to live part of its life on land.

The reptiles laid eggs that had been fertilized in the female and that had their own protective coverings and contained food for the hatching young.

The mammals hatched their eggs inside their own bodies and gave birth to live young.

Primitive nodes of cranial nerves, which served primarily to transmit instinctive orders, grew into brains of varying complexity and capacity.

Man appeared, a physically weak animal endowed with more brain power than any creature that preceded him. He learned to remember, to reason, to think, to talk.

Why did these epochal things happen? They were far beyond the probability of even persistent change and adaptive evolution, beyond even the probable response to changing environments. Yet they did happen, and in several instances they appear to have happened with almost explosive speed and impact on the life around them.

DECEMBER 14

Groping for answers to the doggedly persistent questions, we sometimes come up with mutations. There are variations within every species, we point out, a result of genes which for some reason rearrange themselves and create altered patterns. We do not know why mutations occur. We do know that some mutations die out, and that mutations better fitted to survive than offspring that closely follow the parental pattern survive and multiply. Thus, we say, the various species originated. And if we are baffled by the vast differences between the bee and the bear, the mole and the elephant, the spider and the mockingbird, we are reminded that life has been changing for many millions of years and that there must have been many mutations and a long process of evolution.

Why have we so little evidence of transition forms? Such forms in the process of change, we are reminded, must have been rare until the direction of change was well established. That is why our fossil evidence gives us only a cross section of relatively stable life forms.

It all sounds plausible. That is the way it could have happened. But *did* it happen that way? Were there no other forces at work?

The arrogance of man's "explanations" is matched only by the magnitude of his errors. Only a little over a century ago, many were saying, with self-assured certainty, that the earth was created about 4,000 B.C. Only a little over a century ago, the idea of evolution was a fugitive thought, counter to most conviction and belief. While Darwin and Wallace certainly did not propound their theories of evolution in a vacuum, scientific knowledge was so limited at the time that those theories inevitably created great intellectual turmoil.

Seventy-five years ago, it was believed that the atom was the ultimate particle of matter. Now we have found thirty or more elements of matter or energy in the atom, and describe it as a kind of submicroscopic universe. We have found that light, heat, energy, matter itself, are closely interrelated. We have propounded "laws" that govern the phenomena of matter and energy. But no one has yet found the source of those "laws," those patterns of form and action.

We have come a long way in piecing together our scraps of information and our fragmentary knowledge of life and time and matter. We may be on the trail of ultimate truth. On the other hand, we may be only rationalizing our knowledge to this point and blinding ourselves to something beyond. Our scientists may yet synthesize a chromosome or a gene, but will they even then have discovered the source and meaning of life?

DECEMBER 15

In following the trail of man and pre-man through the murk of the distant past, I have wondered from time to time about man's relationship to the animals around him, when he became a herdsman, when he domesticated the dog, tamed the horse and the cow. I even wondered if man was unique in taming and using other animals. Then I remembered the ants and the way they enslave captives and make them work, and how they often maintain "dairy herds" of aphids from which they "milk" the honeydew. I still can't think of any other examples of enslavement.

Man, of course, has a long list of domesticated animals—the dog, the cat, the horse, the goat, the sheep, the cow, the hog, the camel, even the elephant. But it has generally been conceded that early man was a hunter, not a herdsman. And it has seemed certain that those men who crossed the Bering land-bridge from Siberia to Alaska had no domesticated animals, not even dogs. From time to time estimates have been made of the dates when the various animals were tamed, but until recently nobody did any really accurate dating.

Late in 1971 the first credible answers to these questions were given by Dr. Rainer Berger, associate professor of anthropology, geophysics, and geography at the University of California, Los Angeles, and Reiner Protsch, a graduate student there. They examined bones found in nineteen sites in Europe and the Middle East and dated them by radiocarbon analysis. They found that dating by other methods had been in error by as much as 1,000 years. They re-dated the specimens using the new, far more accurate method. This is what they found:

Sheep and goats apparently were the earliest known domesticated animals, judging by bones found in west-central Iran. The date for them is about 10,000 years ago. The dog seems to have been tamed first in England, in Yorkshire, about 9,300 years ago. Another dating for sheep, from bones found in Thessaly, Greece, was 9,700 years ago. Bones of cattle and swine found in the same area were about 9,000 years old. The horse seems to have been tamed first on the steppes of the Ukraine less than 6,500 years ago. This is much later than had been believed, but apparently before that the horse was just so much meat and hairy hide to the men with the stone-tipped spears.

DECEMBER 16

We are approaching the holy season observed by the Christian world, Christmas, the Nativity, and the whole framework of legend and belief. Something of the kind, some equivalent, is a part of all religions—a leader, possessing phenomenal power, often of miraculous character, is born or somehow made manifest, and from his life and example lays down rules of conduct and establishes social systems and ethical codes that nearly always approximate the Ten Commandments of the Judeo-Christian creed.

Religion is one of the marks of *Homo sapiens*. It seems unlikely that any other species of life ever achieved the mental and emotional equipment to, first, wonder about the source of life and, second, create a system of belief that not only accounted for beginnings but established an all-wise, all-powerful deity, or system of deities, who directed the course of human life. Perhaps one can conceive of the ants having some tenuous instinct that could be compared to religion. Perhaps the queen of the colony, from whom all the other ants presumably descended, could be the supreme goddess. Or perhaps there could be a Great Goddess Ant from whom all queens receive their power. The religious core would be belief in a power beyond that of the individual or the community, a power that created the earth and laid down and enforced the rules of life. Perhaps one can believe in such a religion, for ants. I find it very difficult, primarily because any religious impulse of which I can conceive requires the kind of mind that can create imaginatively, that can believe implicitly in supreme power, and that can accept guidance from a source beyond personal contact.

The primitive human mind could create and believe and accept, but any creature whose life and actions are governed by reflexes and instincts almost certainly could not do any of these things. Therefore, religion seems surely to have been, from the beginning, a peculiarly human achievement. And let us not be stuffy about *which* religion or which kind of religious beliefs. At this time of the year we are thinking of the Christian religion and the legendary birth of Jesus, which at various times has been commemorated at various seasons. Currently, it is remembered and solemnized in late December. After all, in any religious observance, it is the event, not the precise date, that matters. The dating depends on the calendar used, and calendars, as I believe I mentioned early in this journal, have varied considerably in the past 1,900 or 2,000 years. By our current calendar and by current Christian practice, Jesus was born in Bethlehem, in Judea, on December 25. This is the date of the Christ Mass, now commonly called Christmas.

DECEMBER 17

Any religion starts with the need for a kind of super-parent, one with the power to punish or reward, one who represents Good—God and Good have the same linguistic root, by the way—one who can be held responsible for the major events of life. Opposed to this God, inevitably, is the representative of Evil, the Devil, or his equivalent. Thus religion establishes the fundamental conflict, the struggle between God and Evil.

Among the primitive American Indians there was a double form of religion, one relating to the individual, the other to the tribe or clan. Both were based on magic power. Both had certain ethical aspects, but ethics were primarily personal. The magic power was inherent in various natural objects, or aspects of nature, which were believed to be more powerful than the natural powers of man. There is no Indian term that expresses this completely. The English word "wonderful" comes close.

In contrast to beliefs of European and Asiatic religions, which think of the world we know as the creation or thought of a supreme god, the Indian religions generally accepted the world and went on from there with the creation of man and all the animals and the natural events, even including flood and fire in some instances. Animal tales are common in Indian accounts of creation and the subsequent events. Hence, the frequent belief in the necessity of seeking the friendship and help of certain animals and the propitiation of others. But all of them were believed to have magic powers, and that magic was central to the Indian religion. All man's actions were in some degree regulated by the desire to keep in the good graces of those animals friendly to him and to control those that were hostile. Among all Indians it was common custom to express friendship and goodwill toward all food animals. This, of course, was to insure success in the hunt. After the hunt, as well as before, there were certain required rituals of apology and thanks, of purification and of respect. The bear, among most tribes, was treated with reverence after it had been killed, and the first animals killed at the beginning of a new hunting season were treated with special care. Presumably, their spirits carried word back to the others of their kind.

DECEMBER 18

We have been out gathering greens, for Christmas decorations, and thus we have participated in ancient pagan as well as Christian traditions. The evergreens have been symbolic for a long, long time of life and hope in the midst of winter and darkness. Long before the first Christian missionaries reached the dark forests of northern Europe, the natives were observing the winter solstice with bonfires on the hilltops and evergreen boughs and even whole trees in their tribal halls. If the trees could maintain their green life through the long, cold nights of winter, surely the sun could turn in its course and climb the sky again and bring summer once more. The bonfires, the evergreens, the prayers and supplications always had worked in the past, and surely would work now. They did. The sun turned back from the abyss and climbed the sky toward summer.

Christmas was not observed in Rome until about 200 A.D., and not generally throughout Christendom until at least a century later. And when the Christian missionaries went into such pagan lands as northern Europe and found the solstice observed as it was, the Church soon adopted that date as the time of Christ's birth. The Christ Mass was celebrated, then, on approximately the same day as the pagan festival for the sun. This was typical of the early Church, which grafted its own holidays onto many pagan festival dates. In consequence, the Christian Christ Mass adopted the evergreens of the solstice festival as symbolic of enduring faith and everlasting life.

For a long time, Christmas was of secondary importance on the Church calendar, ranking below Easter, Pentecost, and Epiphany. Here in America, it was virtually ignored in New England until the nineteenth century.

So we are really reaching back to pagan days when we go up our mountainside and cut a pine for a Christmas tree and hemlock boughs for decorations. We are celebrating the winter solstice, though we shall leave the greens up for Christmas. I see no need to be selfish or narrow about this. I imagine those old Teutons who tended the hilltop bonfires in the name of the sun were just as devout, in their own way, as the priests who tended the altar in the name of the Father, the Son, and the Holy Ghost.

DECEMBER 19

This was one of those winter days that set no records but make one wonder why man ever left the tropics.

Overnight we got about six inches of snow topped by ice, for the temperature eased toward morning and the snow turned to sleety rain. Then that mild pocket of air passed and it dipped into the teens, freezing everything. It was barely ten degrees above zero when I got up, soon after six, and all day the temperature didn't get above twenty degrees. With a wind that rattled the ice-covered trees and shook the ice-covered utility wires. The sun burst through the thin clouds soon after it rose, and the shattered ice coating on trees and wires made a constant dazzle.

The house was hard to heat because of that wind. It isn't a particularly porous house, it has storm sash and storm doors, and in normal cold weather it is a comfortable place to be. But this wind drives the cold right through the walls. It seemed that the furnace was going most of the day, and we still had to wear extra sweaters and extra socks. I suppose this is because we, like virtually all modern mankind, are softened and made vulnerable to the cold by our way of living. We still want to act like semitropical people, and feel comfortable while we are about it. Far back, of course, it seems certain that early man was essentially tropical. . . .

This evening is one of those winter evenings that atone for the discomfort of the day. I could touch the stars from the top of Tom's Mountain, and the moon, which will be full in two more days, is incredibly beautiful.

DECEMBER 20

Rereading what I wrote about yesterday, I came to that last line and wondered if any other creature on earth except man has a concept of beauty. Dogs, wolves, coyotes, perhaps others of the canine family, respond to moonlight—they bay the moon, as we say—but I doubt that it is in response to any aesthetic reaction. What we know as aesthetics is subjective and understood, or at least recognized, only by man. Certainly colorful sunrises and sunsets, rainbows, brilliantly colored flowers, even the beauty of colorful birds and insects, can appeal only to those creatures with some means of sensing color.

Color, to be sure, does not encompass the whole range of aesthetics. Shape, rhythm, sound, words—they all are involved. But when I say the moonlight was incredibly beautiful, I am passing judgment wholly on aesthetic grounds. And now I wonder if Cro-Magnon man, who incised and colored those remarkably beautiful drawings in the French caves, was equally aware of the beauty of moonlight. He must have been. So must those wandering hunters, possibly of the same strain as the Cro-Magnons, who crossed the land bridge from Siberia to Alaska and spread out over the Americas. There must have been an emotional response in them. It is that response which links us, which makes me pick up a flint arrowhead in my garden and feel, in the back of my throat, the taste of charred venison.

DECEMBER 21

Life is an amazing thing, but we have allowed some phases of our scientific thinking to obscure the wonder of it, of life itself. The purpose of science is to know, but periodically man becomes so persistent in his search for documented knowledge that he mistakes the documentation for the knowledge itself. Repeatedly, man has so engulfed himself in facts that he has lost sight of their meaning. Facts are tools, not an end in themselves, tools for shaping our understanding. Perhaps the most remarkable fact about life is that man both participates in it and tries to explain it to himself, to understand it. He sometimes loses sight of the fact that he is a part of the life he is so assiduously investigating. And he does not always remember that life itself is a fact.

There must be a pattern to life. There is no other way to explain it satisfactorily. All the evidence we have points directly away from the chaos of pure chance and toward order of some kind. Man is the best evidence we have close at hand; and although man himself is the investigator, it seems undeniable that the pattern has dictated life as we know and experience it. Perhaps change is inevitable, but not random change. Random change leads to the wild, uncontrolled growth we call galls in plants and to the outlaw growth we know as cancer in ourselves. The whole order of life, from the single-celled form down to man, denies the possibility that random change is a part of the picture.

DECEMBER 22

If there is a law of change, then there must be some pattern to the change. I can accept the belief that certain external factors somewhat dicate the manner of that change. On the evidence at hand, I cannot deny this. But behind that law of change there must be a force of change, a life-force of some kind. Call it urgency, call it persistence, call it what you will, it must be there, somewhere.

Those who explain the origin of life as a chance combination of chemical elements which they admit could not happen under the conditions of today are falling back, perhaps unconsciously, on some force that brought about that chance combination. What was it? Those who believe that life appeared in the primordial seas from some remote place in outer space are admitting the existence of life somewhere else at that time. Where and how did *that* life come into being? Recently another group of researchers has announced that thunderstorms and the action of tides and waves in the very ancient oceans produced chemicals essential to the origin of life. Thus they account for amino acids in a world whose original atmosphere was a poisonous mixture of methane, ammonia, and water vapor. Still others have said for some time that the germ of life came from nucleic acid, but they admit they cannot say where either the genes or the nucleic acid received their power of life or the patterns they dictate. Wherein lies that power? Is the pattern inherent in the way those elusive elements combine? If so, why?

DECEMBER 23

The questions are persistent and most difficult. They are posed by everything around me—the bee in the hive, the clover blossom at the roadside, the honey on my breakfast toast, a man asking questions. Perhaps we shall never know the answers. Perhaps man, at his present stage, cannot accept an answer that does not conform to chemical formulas or mathematical equations. Or perhaps the formulas and equations will eventually lead to the simplicity of a pattern, a force, a rhythm that is really ultimate and we shall be forced to accept a fact, a documentation, without the ultimate meaning. If so, that force, that pattern or purpose, will persist despite the equation. And some will call it reason, and some will call it God, as man has done for thousands of years. The naming will not too much matter. The recognition will be of overwhelming importance.

DECEMBER 24

We have survived the winter solstice, which occurred three days ago. I have to trust the astronomers about the solstice, since it is a matter of celestial mechanics. I trust my own eyes and other senses about survival, though I still cannot see any change in the angle or duration of sunlight. It will take at least till the end of the year to see that, and even then I will have to measure shadows and the change will be only about the breadth of my thumb. But being a man, a member of *Homo sapiens,* with a memory, an imagination, and a capacity for anticipation, I can believe in an annual solstice and can accept the dates as given, as well as the fact that it is the earth, not the sun, that changes its position now. But I shall go right on saying that the sun rises and sets, that it moves south in winter, and that at this time each year it starts to move northward once more.

Now we are settling down into winter, which seems strange, in a way, for now the days will become longer, the sunlight will gradually strengthen, and we will be climbing that long, cold slope toward spring. But the earth has already cooled off and it will not warm up again—not where we live, in this northern hemisphere—until April. I wonder if the birds know this? I wonder if the foxes know, or the muskrats? Do the woodchucks know, comatose in their dens? Do any of them know, as I know, that winter will pass and summer will come again? Why should I know? To help me endure the cold and darkness of winter? To give me sustaining hope?

DECEMBER 25

In Genesis it says: "In the beginning, God created the heaven and the earth."

In Matthew it says: "Behold, a virgin shall be with child, and shall bring forth a son, and they shall call his name Emmanuel, which being interpreted is, God with us."

In Matthew it also says: "Now when Jesus was born in Bethlehem of Judea in the days of Herod the king, there came wise men from the East to Jerusalem, saying, Where is he that is born King of the Jews? for we have seen his star in the east, and are come to worship him. They saw the young child with Mary his mother, and fell down and worshipped him; and . . . they presented unto him gifts, gold and frankincense and myrrh."

In the ancient Egyptian *Hymn to the Sun* it is written: "Every lion cometh forth from his den. All serpents, they sting. Darkness broods. The world is in silence. He that made them resteth in his horizon."

In the voice of the wind today I hear the words: "Peace. It has all been said."

DECEMBER 26

We have come into a spell of clear, cold weather, with a bright sun and the midday temperature getting up to the low twenties, then dropping at night close to zero. Without wind, such weather is almost enjoyable. We have gone for a walk, up the road, not across the snow-covered pastures, almost every evening the past week. The moon has passed its full, now rises late, but the stars are magnificent. They seem to have the deep fireglow of eternity, and though I admire the mathematics, I almost resent being told that some of those stars I am seeing have been dead and without a glimmer of luminescence for a thousand or two thousand years. The light I see, I am told, and no doubt with ample reason, is simply light that was cast this way by those stars before they died.

Even so, to walk abroad now is to walk in the midst of infinity. There are no limits to either time or distance, except as man himself may make them. I have only to touch the wind to know these things, for the wind itself is full of starlight, even as the frozen earth underfoot, starlight and endless time and exalted wonder.

I look at the red-gold star we call Arcturus, and even as the ancients I strain for a closer look, through this peephole, this spark-burn in the blanket of night, hoping for the slightest glimpse of Beyond. I turn to the star called Betelgeuse, even redder than Arcturus, and I have to accept the factual truth of the astronomers, and yet wonder if that is all, the whole, the ultimate truth.

Time, and distance, and wonder—we walk up this valley in the midst of eternity.

DECEMBER 27

No matter where my thoughts may reach, here I am, and here are millions of other human beings, on a habitable earth that we now believe has been spinning around the sun for thousands of millions of years. Our astrophysicists, seeking facts and probabilities, tell us that it will continue to spin in such a habitable orbit, such a pattern, for perhaps another 5,000 million years. And to the best of our knowledge, man as a species has been here at most two or three million years.

Here I am, in one small valley on this earth, with the necessities of life and human comfort available to me, endowed with the means of reason and thought. By my own judgment, I am among the most fortunate of the earth's creatures.

Around me are not only the works of man, good and bad, but the vastly more enduring creations of nature. I have not the simplicity of the newt or the fiercely efficient society of the ants and the bees, and I have not the quiet patience of the maple tree or the age-old economy of the algae that live and proliferate in the stagnant water of the bogland just down the road. I am a complex organism, subject to pain and worry and hurt and disappointment and disease, but also capable of joy and love and satisfaction.

I am an entity, a fraction of life privileged to be aware of my surroundings, to know, to love, to cherish a mate and a family, to be a part of the living community of sentient beings.

DECEMBER 28

The questions remain and persist, simply because I am of that strange form of life endowed with imagination and the power to wonder.

Who am I?

I am the latest, but probably not the last—barring incredible folly and self-destruction by madmen in the seats of power—in a long, unbelievably long, line of changing life. I know that far more simple forms of life have persisted much longer than my own kind. I know that there are forms of life that are, in terms of efficiency in living, far more successful than mankind has yet proved itself to be. But I have no knowledge of any other living thing that can live as variously and can think and feel and create as successfully as I can.

I have tried to trace my beginnings, and most of the findings are speculative. My kind left very few clues. It is almost as though those ancient ancestors were trying to hide their own heritage, hide from the future as completely as they hid from the enemies they knew in their own present. I can trace the newt more easily. I can follow the beginnings of the bear and the camel more easily than I can even find the trail of pre-man and early man himself.

But here I am, perhaps a successful mutant that should have perished under slightly changed conditions, perhaps still doomed to erasure as a curse and a blight on my environment. Or perhaps a strange agent of change, and nothing more.

DECEMBER 29

The second question: Where am I?

I am in one small valley on one relatively insignificant mass of land on a minor planet in the solar system. The solar system, I am told, is one of a multitude of such systems of planets circling a parent sun.

My planet circling about the sun receives light and warmth from the sun that makes possible the kind of life I know. My solar system is one of many in a universe of which I am aware, for the most part, only on cloudless nights, a universe vastly larger than I can readily comprehend. Perhaps I cannot comprehend simply because, being a human being, I am unwilling to comprehend anything so much beyond the scope of my own environment. In any case, this planet, this solar system, this universe as far as I can know it, is a part of a pattern that remains complex beyond my understanding, even in the face of all the knowledge my own kind have amassed.

But this planet itself is proof, to me, of such a pattern, such a system of order and meaning.

DECEMBER 30

The third question: What time is it?

I can discover no absolutes in time. Time is all relative, whether I speak of a year or a microsecond, of a million years or of today. Time, for me, is comprehensible in terms of my own lifetime and its relationship to this earth.

Time, in one sense, is experience. In another sense it is duration.

Science gives me approximate timetables for the earth, the solar system, the evolution of life, the disintegration of the atom. But to man, the sentient, questioning creature, time has simpler dimensions. It is only with difficulty that I can look back beyond yesterday or last year into the one or two or three million years we now are told man has been here as man. And when I am asked to envision five *billion* more years on a habitable earth, I stand in awe at the incomprehensible.

Both these assumptions in terms of time have vast importance, I am sure; but they still remain somewhere out in that haze of intangible time to a creature tied to a twenty-four-hour day and a year of slightly more than 365 days.

What time is it? It is now, today. It is that stage of man's development and man's self-education in living with his own kind and all other kinds of life on this earth. In that sense, it is not much after dawn. For man, at least. On that I can rest, believing that life does have meaning, pattern, is worth whatever span of time is mine to participate in this amazing thing, life.

DECEMBER 31

This is a cold morning, and there is a spit of snow in the air again. The forecast is not encouraging, if one wants mild temperatures and clear skies.

Year-end, now. And year's-beginnings, and an old custom to face realities when the totting-up has been done.

The headlines in the morning's news are not encouraging. Man still cannot be trusted to save himself from his own folly. The greatness and the glory seems all to be in the past. Perhaps it was always thus—greatness and glory are hard to recognize in the glare of today, any today. And yet there is that about which to dream as well as the lure of visions. And forever there is change, the one constant. Change.

Here we are, in the homeland. It is winter, and it will be spring again. We have known other winters, and survived them.

We have known this year, intimately. We have set down the questions and sought the answers and set them down. And here we are now, at year's end, watching the weather, accepting it, knowing all things change, knowing spring follows winter.

I can report now that grass grows, flowers bloom, birds sing. I can report that the sun rises and sets, the moon keeps its own schedule, the stars follow patterns they have followed since man first saw them in the night sky. I know these truths. Lesser truths will take more learning, but I can live with what I now know.

A NOTE ABOUT THE AUTHOR

Hal Borland, one of our foremost contemporary nature writers, is the author of thirty books, including the classic novel *When the Legends Die*. Born in Nebraska, he grew up in Colorado and has lived in New England since 1945. He is a contributing editor of *Audubon* magazine. Since 1942 he has written the "nature editorials" so familiar to *New York Times* readers. Among his many honors is the John Burroughs Medal, awarded for *Hill Country Harvest* in 1968. He and his wife, author Barbara Dodge Borland, live on their Connecticut farm beside the Housatonic River in the lower Berkshires.

A NOTE ON THE TYPE

The text of this book was set on the Linotype in FAIRFIELD, a type face designed by the distinguished American artist and engraver Rudolph Ruzicka. This type displays the sober and sane qualities of a master craftsman whose talent has long been dedicated to clarity. Rudolph Ruzicka was born in Bohemia in 1883 and came to America in 1894. He has designed and illustrated many books and has created a considerable list of individual prints in a variety of techniques.

The book was composed, printed and bound at American Book–Stratford Press, Saddle Brook, New Jersey.

The typography and binding design are by Christine Aulicino.